Autonomy, Consent and the Law

Autonomy is often said to be the dominant ethical principle in modern bioethics, and it is also important in law. Respect for autonomy is said to underpin the law of consent, which is theoretically designed to protect the right of patients to make decisions based on their own values and for their own reasons. The notion that consent underpins beneficent and lawful medical intervention is deeply rooted in the jurisprudence of countries throughout the world. However, *Autonomy, Consent and the Law* challenges the relationship between consent rules and autonomy, arguing that the very nature of the legal process inhibits its ability to respect autonomy, specifically in cases where patients argue that their ability to act autonomously has been reduced or denied as a result of the withholding of information which they would have wanted to receive.

Sheila McLean further argues that the bioethical debate about the true nature of autonomy – while rich and challenging – has had little if any impact on the law. Using the alleged distinction between the individualistic and the relational models of autonomy as a template, the author proposes that, while it might be assumed that the version ostensibly preferred by law – roughly equivalent to the individualistic model – would be transparently and consistently applied, in fact courts have vacillated between the two to achieve policy-based objectives. This is highlighted by examination of four specific areas of the law, which most readily lend themselves to consideration of the application of the autonomy principle: namely, refusal of life-sustaining treatment and assisted dying, maternal/foetal issues, genetics and transplantation.

This book will be of great interest to scholars of medical law and bioethics.

Sheila A. M. McLean is International Bar Association Professor of Law Ethics in Medicine, Director of the Institute of Law Ethics in Medicine and of the Centre for Applied Ethics and Legal Philosophy at the University of Glasgow.

Biomedical Law and Ethics Library

Series Editor: Sheila A.M. McLean

Scientific and clinical advances, social and political developments and the impact of healthcare on our lives raise profound ethical and legal questions. Medical law and ethics have become central to our understanding of these problems, and are important tools for the analysis and resolution of problems – real or imagined.

In this series, scholars at the forefront of biomedical law and ethics contribute to the debates in this area, with accessible, thought-provoking, and sometimes controversial ideas. Each book in the series develops an independent hypothesis and argues cogently for a particular position. One of the major contributions of this series is the extent to which both law and ethics are utilised in the content of the books, and the shape of the series itself.

The books in this series are analytical, with a key target audience of lawyers, doctors, nurses and the inquiring lay public.

Available titles:

Human Fertilisation and Embryology (2006)
Reproducing Regulation
Kirsty Horsey and Hazel Biggs

Intention and Causation in Medical Non-Killing (2006)
The Impact of Criminal Law Concepts on Euthanasia and Assisted Suicide
Glenys Williams

Impairment and Disability (2007)
Law and Ethics at the Beginning and End of Life
Sheila A. M. McLean and Laura Williamson

Bioethics and the Humanities (2007)
Attitudes and Perceptions
Robin Downie and Jane Macnaughton

Defending the Genetic Supermarket (2007)
The Law and Ethics of Selecting the Next Generation
Colin Gavaghan

The Harm Paradox (2007)
Tort Law and the Unwanted Child in an Era of Choice
Nicolette Priaulx

Assisted Dying (2007)
Reflections on the Need for Law Reform
Sheila A. M. McLean

Medicine, Malpractice and Misapprehensions (2007)
Vivienne Harpwood

Euthanasia, Ethics and the Law (2007)
From Conflict to Compromise
Richard Huxtable

Best Interests of the Child in Healthcare (2007)
Sarah Elliston

Values in Medicine (2008)
The Realities of Clinical Practice
Donald Evans

Autonomy, Consent and the Law (2010)
Sheila A. M. McLean

Forthcoming titles include:

Medicine, Law and the Public Interest
Communitarian Perspectives on Medical Law
J. Kenyon Mason and Graeme Laurie

Healthcare Research Ethics and Law
Regulation, Review and Responsibility
Hazel Biggs

About the Series Editor

Professor Sheila McLean is International Bar Association Professor of Law and Ethics in Medicine, Director of the Institute of Law Ethics in Medicine and of the Centre for Applied Ehtics and Legal Philosophy at the University of Glasgow.

Autonomy, Consent and the Law

Sheila A. M. McLean

Routledge
Taylor & Francis Group

LONDON AND NEW YORK

First published 2010
by Routledge
2 Park Square, Milton Park, Abingdon, Oxon, OX14 4RN

Simultaneously published in the USA and Canada
by Routledge
711 Third Avenue, New York, NY 10017

Routledge *is an imprint of the Taylor & Francis Group, an informa*
business

© 2010 Sheila A. M. McLean

Typeset in Garamond by
Taylor & Francis Books

British Library Cataloguing in Publication Data
A catalogue record for this book is available from the British Library

Library of Congress Cataloging in Publication Data
A Catalogue record for this book has been requested

ISBN10: 0-415-47339-X (hbk)
ISBN13: 978-0-415-47339-2 (hbk)

ISBN10: 0-415-47340-3 (pbk)
ISBN13: 978-0-415-47340-8 (pbk)

ISBN10: 0-203-87319-X (ebk)
ISBN13: 978-0-203-87319-9 (ebk)

Contents

Introduction

In the modern world, we are increasingly accustomed to a culture which is based on liberty; the freedom of individuals to act as they choose, albeit within certain limits that usually concern the avoidance of harm to others. Thus, for example, the right to free speech is constrained by laws on defamation which limit what we can say when our freedom to say it would cause harm to others. However, given the emphasis on liberty and freedom, we generally anticipate a relatively 'hands off' approach from the state (or other organisations), thereby facilitating our ability to determine the shape of our own lives; to make our own decisions – to be autonomous. Atkins says:

> It is the particularity of our points of view that we respect when we respect autonomy. Autonomy, in the liberal tradition, is generally understood as self-determination: the freedom to pursue one's conception of the good life, just as long as it does not impinge upon another's identical freedom.[1]

Laws, therefore, that constrain the exercise of individual choice are generally framed carefully to ensure that they can nonetheless maximise individual freedom. This serves two purposes. First, it acknowledges the respect due to autonomy, and second it allows for the development of the concept of privacy, within which individuals are free from state scrutiny and control. Before moving to a more in-depth consideration of autonomy and the making of autonomous decisions, it is worth touching on the privacy issue briefly. As early as 1965, the US Supreme Court declared a Connecticut statute that prohibited 'any person to use any drug or article to prevent conception' unconstitutional. The Court concluded that, although the US Constitution does not expressly recognise a privacy right, it can be inferred from other Constitutional rights, such as those contained in the First, Third, Fourth and

---

[1] Atkins, K., 'Autonomy and the Subjective Character of Experience', *Journal of Applied Philosophy*, 17(1), 2000: 71–79, at p 74.

Ninth Amendments.[2] This approach was later endorsed in landmark cases such as *Roe v Wade*[3] which declared abortion in the first trimester to be essentially a private matter.

In the United Kingdom and other states which have incorporated the European Convention on Human Rights into their jurisprudence,[4] Article 8 guarantees the right to private and family life, subject only to derogations that broadly equate to the 'harm principle'. For example, in perhaps the most famous UK case to explore the limits of individual freedom, *R v Brown*,[5] it was held that – even although carried out in private – the participation of the accused in (consensual) sado-masochistic homosexual behaviour, resulting in considerable personal injury, was not protected by Article 8 of the European Convention on Human Rights. The harm caused by their behaviour and associated videotapes was sufficient to engage Article 8(2) which permits intervention in the exercise of the Article 8 right when, amongst other things, it is necessary for the protection of public health.

The categorisation of behaviour as private is important as it limits the legitimacy of the state in constraining choice (providing the harm exemption does not apply). Despite what can sometimes seem to be a trend of states to be increasingly interventionist, the separation of private activities from state control remains an important aspiration. Laurie characterises the modern (Western) state as being 'typified by a glut of legislation stemming from paternalistic attitudes of the state towards its citizens.'[6] Yet individuals reasonably anticipate that their private interests will be both respected and protected by that same state. The device most commonly prayed in aid of this is the distinction generally drawn between public and private behaviour and concerns. Private issues are those which should be essentially free from state control; public ones attract legitimate state interest. The right to have autonomous decisions respected, supported by the developing sphere of privacy, is the mark of a mature society, and serves to maximise the potential for human liberty.

Despite the importance of this distinction, however, Williams argues that '. ... the public-private distinction, as traditionally used, does not mark the boundary between collective coercion and individual autonomy.'[7] That being

---

[2] *Griswold v Connecticut* 381 US 479 (1965). See particularly, the Court's argument at pp 481–86.

[3] 410 US 113 (1973).

[4] In the United Kingdom, this was achieved by passing the Human Rights Act 1998.

[5] [1993] 2 All ER 75. The decision in this case was subsequently upheld in the European Court of Human Rights in the case of *Laskey, Jaggard and Brown* (1997) 24 Eur HR Rep 39. The judgement was also reported with favour in the case of *ADT v UK* (2001) 31 EHRR 803, although in this case the outcome was different.

[6] Laurie, G, *Genetic Privacy: A Challenge to Medico-Legal Norms*, Cambridge University Press, 2002, at p 9.

[7] Williams, S H, 'Comment: Autonomy and the Public-Private Distinction in Bioethics and Law', available at http://muse.jhu.edu/journals/indiana_journal_of_global_legal_studies/v012/12.2williams_s. pdf (accessed on 19/10/2007).

the case, Williams proposes that we also need to focus 'on whether the distribution of power at issue promotes the value of autonomy or whether it frustrates autonomy in the interest of other values.'[8] This argument can, of course, be accepted without negating the importance of the public/private distinction; on the contrary, it acknowledges its significance, while at the same time helpfully highlighting the extent to which autonomy can be frustrated by power imbalance, particularly where this is unidentified or deeply entrenched. In any case, 'there are also public interests in privacy protection.'[9] This has particular significance for the relationship between professionals and 'clients', where the power imbalance is clear, and the route to empowerment of the client can be opaque.

There are, therefore, clear parallels between the notion of privacy and that of autonomy. Each presumes that there are certain behaviours that are within the prerogative of the individual; the ability and the right to make self-regarding decisions is protected by each concept albeit in slightly different ways. Nonetheless, even where people are legally presumed to be autonomous, the conundrum of how to facilitate their exercise of that autonomy from a traditional position of relative weakness has become pressing and is arguably particularly urgent in modern healthcare. As medicine's capacities expand, and become ever more esoteric, the gap in the knowledge between doctor and patient becomes ever greater, even given the massive expansion in the availability of information, for example from the internet. In order to facilitate or protect the capacity of an autonomous person to make an autonomous choice – one that reflects his or her own values – it is necessary to develop standards that can ensure meaningful patient participation in healthcare decisions. As we will see later, this is generally said to be the function of the legal doctrine of consent.

It is the concept of autonomy and its relationship to the concept of consent in law that lie at the root of what follows. As will become obvious, this apparently simple relationship is deceptively nuanced and complex. In addition, the fact that someone is legally considered to be autonomous does not necessarily imply that their decisions are in fact truly autonomous. The extent to which they can properly be called autonomous will hinge on a number of factors, such as information, understanding and opportunity. For example, Saks and Jeste note that:

> An incompetently made choice is, in an important sense, not an autonomous choice. That choice may well not reflect the chooser's goals or values. If these goals or values represent the core of the person, then a

---

[8] Williams, S H, 'Comment: Autonomy and the Public-Private Distinction in Bioethics and Law', available at http://muse.jhu.edu/journals/indiana_journal_of_global_legal_studies/v.2williams_s.pdf (accessed on 19/10/2007).

[9] Laurie, G, *Genetic Privacy: A Challenge to Medico-Legal Norms*, Cambridge University Press, 2002, at p 8.

choice that fails to serve them is, in a sense, not the chooser's choice, and is therefore not reflective of the core of the person. It is not his or her choice.[10]

Deciding on who counts as an autonomous person is relatively easy; more problematic is the analysis of what amounts to an autonomous decision – that is, what characterises autonomy in decision-making. Is it merely making a decision, or is it more subtle than this? One main strand of this discussion concerns how the law approaches autonomy and in particular how suited the law is to reflecting its subtleties. In conclusion, it will critique how close are the concepts of autonomy and consent and the extent to which consent law facilitates or protects the individual's desire to make autonomous decisions.

In this narrative, following a general attempt to clarify what is meant by autonomy, and how it is translated from an ethical doctrine into a legal reality, a series of specific situations will be explored in order to identify the extent to which autonomous decisions are *in reality* respected in law. Two issues will be focused on; first, questions will be raised about the role played by consent law in describing, facilitating or enhancing autonomy and, second, an analysis will be made of what model of autonomy the law actually applies. Following from this, and from the presumption that consistency in law is an important value, the last strand of the argument will consider whether or not consent law as interpreted by courts in particular shows evidence of adherence to a particular definition of autonomy. This critique is important, I would argue, because it may be too simplistic to assume that the individual's autonomy is in fact protected by the rules of consent (or refusal). The law has imperatives of its own and often encapsulates policy and other considerations in deciding on the quality and standing of individual decisions. Concepts such as respect for precedent and societal well-being, for example, can, and do, have an effect on how judges (and legislators) approach problem solving and these are important factors that may not encourage or permit the full searchlight of the law to be focused on one concept – autonomy – when other important values are in play. Therefore, no matter what conventional wisdom says, there may be a dissonance between the aims of respect for autonomy on the one hand and the law of consent on the other.

If individuals believe that they can expect the law to support their self-determining decisions and that the rules of law will insist that they are enabled to make them, yet the law pays no more than lip service to this, there are potentially grave consequences for liberty and for the interest that people have in maintaining the privacy rights which protect their decisions from authoritarian or over-intrusive law and state. In healthcare, it is particularly important that this kind of examination takes place, as decisions

---

[10] Saks, E R, Jeste, D V, 'Capacity to Consent to or Refuse treatment and/or Research: Theoretical Considerations', *Behav Sci Law*, 24, 2006: 411–29, at p 412.

about accepting or rejecting medical treatment are immensely significant to individuals. In a world in which human rights are highly valued, the right to be self-determining in health is increasingly prized. If consent law is found lacking in protecting this right, the consequences for the autonomy of patients can be serious, and may call consent law itself into question – if it is not there to reflect respect for autonomous decisions, what is it for?

Before exploring the law of consent, I begin with a discussion of how autonomy has come to the position of authority in healthcare that it currently occupies. This is followed by a more in-depth evaluation of two specific models of autonomy – individualistic and relational – which have been selected because they are commonly appealed to in biomedical ethics and law and are often said to be polar opposites. From there, the discussion will proceed to an analysis of what principles courts apply when disputes arise about whether or not patients have been provided with enough information to make an autonomous decision. Thereafter, four discrete areas have been selected for consideration. In each of them the roles of consent and autonomy are scrutinised both to see what kind of autonomy is applied in law and to explore the extent to which there is any consistency in this. These situations raise starkly the importance given to self-determination in particularly sensitive matters. Finally, I will evaluate the extent to which consent and autonomy relate to each other in any real sense, and will conclude on the extent to which coherent and consistent principles emerge from this discussion.

Chapter 1

From Hippocrates to paternalism to autonomy: the new hegemony

The art of medicine has been practised for centuries. Over that time, some of its ethical foundations have been modified, reflecting the social, political and other changes that have occurred. Medical ethics have ultimately transcended the 'closed shop' ideology of Hippocrates, largely eschewed the dominance of paternalism and now flourish (or not) in the spotlight of autonomy. In the time since the Hippocratic Oath was first promulgated, the practice of medicine has changed dramatically and this is reflected in the way doctors now engage with patients and public alike. The rudimentary techniques available to the early physicians have been replaced by a discipline firmly grounded in science, although, of course, an element of 'art' remains in everyday practice. In addition, since probably around the mid-19th century, medicine has become thoroughly professionalised with the concomitant responsibilities – legal and ethical – that flow from this. Moreover, medicine, its practitioners and its patients now live in a world where the dominant language is that of human rights. The traditional, relatively simple, reliance on the physician has shifted towards recognition that those whom they serve also have legitimate interests and viewpoints, and a right to be engaged in treatment decisions.

Patients' medical interests are no longer seen as separable from their personal ones, and the assumption that the best medical advice determines the optimal outcome of the doctor/patient encounter no longer holds. Acceptance that '[h]ealth care choices involve profound questions that are not finally referable to professional expertise … '[1] has had significant consequences for the doctor/patient relationship. The assertion that patients have rights in making healthcare decisions is reflected in the general recognition that autonomy is the transcending principle of modern bioethics, and its influence pervades – at least in theory – every clinical encounter and every medical act. Personal choices about healthcare are taken, by and large, to be definitive,

[1] Schultz, M M, 'From Informed Consent to Patient Choice: A New Protected Interest', *The Yale Law Journal*, 95(2), December 1985: 219–99, at p 222.

albeit that they will often be rooted in clinical advice and recommendations. Reinforcing this notion of 'patient power', Schultz says that in most situations where healthcare decisions have personal consequences and cause little or no harm to others, then 'the case for respecting patient autonomy in decisions about health and bodily fate is very strong'.[2]

The emergence of autonomy as the guiding concept in biomedical ethics has occurred relatively recently and co-exists with the growth in the importance of the language of human rights. Autonomy rules, then, but as we will see, its precise meaning is far from agreed and some commentary seems unclear about whether the mere existence of (legal) decision-making capacity – which is a pre-existing condition of autonomy – is sufficient to demand respect for decisions made by the competent person. The way in which patients' decisions are dealt with in both law and medicine is shaped in part by the history of medical practice itself, so before analysing autonomy, autonomous decisions and the law of consent in more depth it is important to explain how the physician/patient relationship has developed throughout the main stages of its history. The earliest of these stages is the Hippocratic era.

The Hippocratic tradition

Despite the fact that doctors still cling to some of the commitments of the classical Hippocratic Oath, many of its terms are 'honoured' as much in the breach as in the observance. For example, although the obligation of confidentiality is still taken seriously,[3] there is no longer a commitment to providing free education to the offspring of your teacher or giving your teacher money in the event of hardship.[4] And while doctors still (in some countries at least) forebear from assisting a patient to die, not all of them do, and many of them will participate in the termination of pregnancy.[5] The standing of the Oath, therefore, has changed over the years. Miles says that:

---

[2] Ibid., at p 220.

[3] 'What I may see or hear in the course of the treatment or even outside of the treatment in regard to the life of men, which on no account one must spread abroad, I will keep to myself, holding such things shameful to be spoken about', available at http://www.pbs.org/wgbh/nova/doctors/oath_classical.html (accessed on 5/5/2008).

[4] 'To hold him who has taught me this art as equal to my parents and to live my life in partnership with him, and if he is in need of money to give him a share of mine, and to regard his offspring as equal to my brothers in male lineage and to teach them this art – if they desire to learn it – without fee and covenant; to give a share of precepts and oral instruction and all the other learning to my sons and to the sons of him who has instructed me and to pupils who have signed the covenant and have taken an oath according to the medical law, but no one else.'

[5] 'I will neither give a deadly drug to anybody who asked for it, nor will I make a suggestion to this effect. Similarly I will not give to a woman an abortive remedy. In purity and holiness I will guard my life and my art.'

The possibility that Greek medical ethics was simply about clinical ethics and bedside etiquette must be kept in mind as the *Oath* is examined for evidence that it spoke of the civic responsibilities of physician or of norms to address professional conflicts with the social order. Today we tend to describe societal ethics using words like human rights, fairness, and justice.[6]

Currently, updated and/or substitute versions of the Hippocratic Oath abound,[7] many of which incorporate values which can be described as more modern, such as knowing when to admit ignorance, and not 'playing God'. They also remind doctors of their role as members of a society; not simply as experts in medicine.[8] Interestingly, modern oaths have ditched some of the main planks of the Hippocratic Oath – even those that were traditionally seen as the most fundamental. Thus, in a study in 1993,[9] for example, it was found that 'only 14 percent of modern oaths prohibit euthanasia, 11 percent hold covenant with a deity, 8 percent foreswear abortion, and a mere 3 percent forbid sexual contact with patients.'[10]

In a brief article published in 2000, Graham actually doubts the value of oaths (classical or modern) themselves and proposes that the medical profession needs to engage with this issue, presumably since medicine is an inherently social enterprise which needs to be socially relevant and morally nuanced.[11] Indeed, in their seminal writing, Beauchamp and Childress note that there is concern about 'whether the codes specific to areas of science, medicine, and health care are comprehensive, coherent, and plausible.'[12] They also observe that the codes promulgated by and on behalf of doctors have seldom been open to the critique of patients (and others) and 'have rarely appealed to more general ethical standards or to a source of moral authority beyond the traditions and judgments of physicians.'[13] The classic Hippocratic tradition, and the codes associated with it, can be said to describe what is seen (at any given time) as professionally appropriate behaviour, but fail to offer a morally relevant rationale for according it societal authority. in large part this is because, as Pellegrino and Thomasma say, '[a]ll codes to date have been

[6] Miles, S, *The Hippocratic Oath and the Ethics of Medicine*, Oxford University Press, 2004, at p 56.

[7] A Google search for Hippocratic Oath brings up a large number of examples.

[8] Available at http://www.pbs.org/wgbh/nova/doctors/oath_modern.html (accessed on 6/5/2008).

[9] Orr, R D, Pang, N, Pellegrino, E D, Siegler, M, 'Use of the Hippocratic Oath: A Review of Twentieth Century Practice and a Content Analysis of Oaths Administered in Medical Schools in the U.S. and Canada in 1993', *The Journal of Clinical Ethics*, 8 (Winter), 1997: 377–88.

[10] See report, available at http://www.pbs.org/wgbh/nova/doctors/oath_today.html (accessed on 6/5/2008).

[11] Graham, D., 'Revisiting Hippocrates: Does an Oath Really Matter?', *JAMA*, 284(22), 13 December 2000: 2841–42.

[12] Beauchamp, T L, Childress, J F, *Principles of Biomedical Ethics* (6th edn), Oxford University Press, 2009, at p 7.

[13] Ibid., at p 8.

devised by the profession, for the profession, and without the participation of patients or society.'[14] In addition, in their view, 'the principles guiding physician behaviour have rarely been justified on philosophical grounds';[15] something which they firmly believe must be changed. The limitations of codes, which it should be noted still have some currency in modern medicine,[16] therefore serve to cast doubt on their authority.

The need for moral (and perhaps legal) authority, the limitations of the Hippocratic Oath and those that followed it, coupled with the increased professionalisation of medicine, demanded a different conceptualisation of the role of the clinician. No longer members of an inward looking profession, doctors instead became the source of a 'good' medical act, which has both personal and societal significance. While the commitments of medical practitioners moved beyond the professionally self-serving text of the classical Oath, and became more alert to and constrained by the well-being of patients, they nonetheless did not directly confront the question of what should be the balance of authority between physician and patient in a way that would satisfy the modern patient. If anything, having moved from the classical Hippocratic position, medicine was for many decades, if not centuries, firmly lodged in the tradition of what some call beneficence, but which all too often was more akin to paternalism. While beneficence is generally a characteristic of a 'good' medical act (and, I would argue can include respect for autonomous decisions), paternalism seldom is and we must be careful to distinguish the two.

From Hippocrates to paternalism

The tradition of paternalism has a long and remarkably robust history in medicine. Post-Hippocrates, with its emphasis on medical fraternity, the welfare of the patient (or beneficence) began to emerge as a priority. It was, however, often assumed that the welfare or best interests of the patient was primarily to be identified by what doctors believed to be the correct choice or treatment, rather than by what patients themselves might want. The intimate link between health improvement and beneficence commended itself to clinicians but, in practice, beneficence became a central justification for the notion of paternalism. Perhaps because of the admitted expertise of the clinician and its likely lack in the average patient, the assumption that 'doctor knows best' was all too easily absorbed into medical practice.[17]

---

[14] Pellegrino, E D, Thomasma, D C, *A Philosophical Basis of Medical Practice*, Oxford University Press, 1981, at p 193.

[15] Ibid.

[16] See, for example, the codes issued by the World Medical Association which still carry considerable weight. These can be found at http://www.wma.net/e (accessed on 22/12/2008).

[17] For a full discussion of beneficence, see Beauchamp, T L, Childress, J F, *Principles of Biomedical Ethics* (6th edn), Oxford University Press, 2009, at Chapter 6.

Indeed, it has been said that paternalism was ' ... the dominant, and indeed the accepted, model of the clinical relationship for most of medicine's history.'[18] Teff also notes that, until relatively recently, it seemed to have been accepted that patients were essentially 'passive recipients of medical care.'[19] The developing traditions of medicine encapsulated the assumption of authority by doctors over patients – also known as paternalism. This, it was argued, served the interests of patients because the doctor was uniquely qualified to decide on what was in the patient's best interests, having regard specifically to his or her clinical condition. Nonetheless, however well-intentioned paternalistic practice may be – in at least some of its forms – it seems *prima facie* antipathetic to the idea of autonomy.

According to O'Neill, the need to move from the fully paternalistic model was one of the earliest agreed aims of modern medical ethics; she suggests that this model was recognised as being 'defective' and antagonistic to providing 'an adequate context for reasonable trust',[20] trust being an essential component of the ideal relationship between patient and doctor. It follows, therefore that '[a] more adequate basis for trust required patients who were on a more equal footing with professionals, and this meant that they would have to be better informed and less dependent.'[21] In other words, replacing the paternalistic model with one based in trust means the sharing of information as well as the provision of advice, thereby facilitating the patient's ability to act autonomously. Arguably, this model of the patient/doctor relationship represents the best clinical enterprise – on the one hand, physicians share their knowledge and advice with patients and on the other patients are able to act in an autonomous manner based, but not solely dependent, on that information.

However, the move away from paternalism was sometimes resisted by those who had previously wielded the real power in the doctor/patient relationship – clinicians themselves. Clinical expertise and superior knowledge (in the medical sense) had been the foundational justifications for both professionalism and paternalism, and indeed some continue to claim that paternalism is not entirely without merit. For example, Kelley suggests that:

> What was wrong with the old paternalistic ideology in medicine was not so much that physicians did not really know what was best for patients – at least in a clinical sense they often *do* know what is best and that expertise carries with it greater responsibility – the mistake was to

---

[18] Pellegrino, E D, Thomasma, D C, 'The Conflict Between Autonomy and Beneficence in Medical Ethics: Proposal for a Resolution', *Journal of Contemporary Health Law and Policy*, 3(23), 1987: 23–46, at p 25.

[19] Teff, H, *Reasonable Care: Legal Perspectives on the Doctor-Patient Relationship*, Oxford, Clarendon Press, 1996, at p xxiii.

[20] O'Neill, O, *Autonomy and Trust in Bioethics*, Cambridge University Press, 2002, at p 18.

[21] Ibid.

confuse greater responsibility with the notion of greater authority over a patient's choices and preferences about life and death.[22]

Pellegrino and Thomasma would go further, and do not simply link the modern hostility to paternalistic practices to a perceived over-emphasis on the implications of clinical expertise. Rather they say, ' ... the revulsion many competent adults feel about medical paternalism may more properly derive from anger about physicians' pretensions as a superior class than from any inherent property of professionalism itself.'[23] What makes us prefer the concept of autonomy to that of paternalism is, Atkins suggests, the need to 'accede to our fundamental fallibility and an epistemological humility.'[24] On this account, while self-evidently we consult doctors precisely *because* they have expertise in health matters, neither their knowledge nor their recommendations define our 'best interests'. These will, or may, be identified from more than clinical diagnosis and prognosis and will also be derived from our hopes, fears, aspirations and even simple convenience. Although it seems obvious that the possession of expertise is relevant to the motivation for patients to engage with doctors, the dependence that may result from this can be disabling – even counter-productive where the relationship is constrained by paternalism rather than respect for autonomy. Illich, for example, says:

> Man's consciously lived fragility, individuality, and relatedness make the experience of pain, of sickness, and of death an integral part of his life. The ability to cope with this trio in autonomy is fundamental to his health. To the degree to which he becomes dependent on the management of his intimacy he renounces his autonomy and his health *must* decline.[25]

Thus, paternalism – and the dependence which flows from this (in part encapsulated in Parsons' conceptualisation of the 'sick role')[26] – has, for Illich, both ethical and practical consequences. Paternalism debases its 'victims' by infantilising them, diminishes or deflects the respect to which they

---

[22] Kelley, M, 'Limits on Patient responsibility', *Journal of Medicine and Philosophy*, 30, 2005: 189–206, at p 197.

[23] Pellegrino, E D, Thomasma, D C, 'The Conflict Between Autonomy and Beneficence in Medical Ethics: Proposal for a Resolution', *Journal of Contemporary Health Law and Policy*, 3(23), 1987: 23–46, at p 26.

[24] Atkins, K, 'Autonomy and the Subjective Character of Experience', *Journal of Applied Philosophy*, 17(1), 2000: 71–79, at p 75.

[25] Illich, I, 'Medical Nemesis', *J Epidemiol Community Health*, 57, 2003: 919–22 (reprinted from an article in *The Lancet*, I, 1974: 918–21 to mark the death of the author in December 2002), at p 922.

[26] Parsons, T, *The Social System*, London, Routledge & Kegan Paul, 1951. Parsons' work has been extensively critiqued; for one example, see, for example, Williams, S J, 'Parsons revisited: from the sick role to ... ?', *Health (London)*, 9, 2005: 123–44.

would otherwise be entitled and inhibits their ability to act with due regard for their own values. Ultimately, it has been argued that '[p]erhaps the biggest failure of medical paternalism is its assumption that medical values or medical good is the highest good, and that it has an absolute quality which overrides other values.'[27] Separating the clinical from the personal or private, or perhaps ideally rendering them complementary, is a necessary goal of the anti-paternalism rhetoric that now permeates bioethics and the law. While it may be intelligible that paternalism had such a firm hold in medical practice, it is 'beginning to lose ground in part because of growing sympathy for the view that patients are entitled to decide what is done to them.'[28]

Paternalism was often justified as being based in concern for patient welfare; a noble goal of medicine. While we both expect and need the beneficent and compassionate concern which is said to be central to the good practice of medicine, patients still claim the right to make decisions that are appropriate *for them*. However, even if autonomy is of critical importance for patients, for those caring for them it will be 'only one of a number of moral principles governing the caring relationship among which it finds beneficence a more resonant expression of medicine's fundamental ethos.'[29] While this is intelligible, it seems to assume that beneficence and autonomy can be clearly distinguished, whereas they are in my view distinct and separate only when the former crosses the line into paternalism. Harris suggests that '[c]oncern for welfare, and the paternalistic control it is so often used to justify, ceases to be legitimate at the point at which ... it operates to frustrate the individual's own attempts to create her own life for herself.'[30] Therefore, even if there are some situations in which paternalism (or more appropriately beneficence) can be justified, they disappear when paternalism collides with respect for autonomy.

Additionally, while it may be true that the doctor/patient relationship has developed into one in which paternalism is increasingly eschewed, the paternalistic tradition is by no means finally dead and care must be taken to avoid opportunities for it to resurface where it interferes with autonomy. Giesen, for example, cautions that '[t]he potential for medical paternalism is increased by the growing informational imbalance that exists between doctor and patient, extending the power of the former and the dependency and vulnerability of the latter.'[31] Williams, on the other hand, has postulated

---

[27] Pellegrino, E D, Thomasma, D C, 'The Conflict Between Autonomy and Beneficence in Medical Ethics: Proposal for a Resolution', *Journal of Contemporary Health Law and Policy*, 3(23), 1987: 23–46, at p 36.

[28] Teff, H, *Reasonable Care: Legal Perspectives on the Doctor-Patient Relationship*, Oxford, Clarendon Press, 1996, at p 131.

[29] Tauber, A I, 'Sick Autonomy', *Perspectives in Biology and Medicine*, 46(4) (autumn) 2003: 484–95, at p 486.

[30] Harris, J, 'Euthanasia and the Value of Life', in Keown, J (ed), *Euthanasia Examined: ethical, clinical and legal perspectives*, Cambridge University Press, 1995 (reprinted 1999), 6–22, at p 11.

[31] Giesen, D, 'From Paternalism to Self-Determination to Shared Decision-Making in the Field of Medical Law and Ethics', in Westerhall, L, Phillips, C (eds), *Patient's Rights – Informed Consent, Access and Inequality*, Stockholm, Nerenius & Santerus Publishers, 1994, 19–38, at p 20.

that the contemporary availability of information outside of the doctor/ patient consultation may serve to decrease that vulnerability, resulting in patients shopping around for healthcare services.[32] These are both critical contentions for our later consideration of the issue of consent to treatment and the provision of information in a form that is intelligible to, and potentially empowering of, patients.

Meantime, the direction of this narrative moves inexorably towards consideration of autonomy itself. While professional codes may set some worthy benchmarks, and beneficence/paternalism may be rooted in good intentions, the power of the language of human rights which has come to dominate people's perceptions of the ideal relationship between authorities and citizens (or doctors and patients in this case) has resulted in a clear focus not on the skills or the intentions of healthcare providers but rather on the interests and rights of recipients. In tandem with this, although medical ethics (narrowly defined) once dominated the clinical literature, the more modern discipline of bioethics is now widely regarded as the foundational ethical basis for medical practice. In bioethics, as in rights language, the dominant concept is said to be autonomy, which Rothman says shows the often underestimated role of the law in bioethics.[33] He notes, for example, that the idea of consent (or informed consent) 'was born in a court, owes practically nothing to traditional medical ethics, and to this day, seems to be a less than adequate formulation of the doctor-patient relationship to many physicians.'[34] To a large extent, then, it is legal support for human rights that has changed the face of the clinical encounter and introduced a new agenda into healthcare. Annas says that '[t]he disciplines of bioethics, health law, and human rights are ... all members of the broad human rights community ... '.[35] If so, then any exploration of the fundamentals of the doctor/patient relationship will owe a great deal to the underpinning principles of human rights, and in particular the right to respect for autonomy.

From paternalism to autonomy

Attention to patient autonomy requires bearing in mind that '[i]f the basic rule of medicine is "First, do no harm", then the harm done to patient autonomy by paternalistic medical environments and overcontrolling caregivers must be scrupulously avoided.'[36] The change of emphasis from paternalism

[32] Williams, S J, 'Parsons revisited: from the sick role to ... ?', *Health (London)*, 9, 2005: 123–44.

[33] Rothman, D J, 'The Origins and Consequences of Patient Autonomy: A 25-Year Retrospective', *Health Care Analysis*, 9, 2001: 255–64.

[34] Ibid., at pp 256–57.

[35] Annas, G J, 'American Bioethics and Human Rights: The End of All Our Exploring', *Journal of Law, Medicine & Ethics*, Winter 2004: 658–63, at p 658.

[36] Waller, B N, 'The Psychological Structure of Patient Autonomy', *Cambridge Q of Healthcare Ethics*, 11, 2002: 257–65, at p 263.

to autonomy, however, 'posed a serious challenge to the historical authority of physicians'[37] and caused concern in some quarters about its likely impact on patient care. Autonomy, like paternalism, has its own critics. While conceding that 'medical paternalism can fail to distinguish contexts and their role in medical and ethical decision-making ... ',[38] so too, it is said, can the autonomy model, which can be argued, as we will see below, to disassociate or decontextualise the individual from his or her social (including clinical) situation. Critics of the modern dominance of autonomy are not only concerned that it might affect patient care by potentially reducing the influence of medical knowledge or advice on patients' decisions, but also suggest that it makes the relationship between healthcare professional and patient sterile. Thus, Pellegrino and Thomasma argue that:

> ... autonomy should not be viewed as an absolute model for the doctor-patient relationship itself because it is insufficient to claim, as the move to patient autonomy often does, that medical paternalism is a direct outgrowth of professionalisation ... Modern medicine incorporates moments of patient choice as well as moments of necessary, beneficial paternalism.[39]

However, if patient control over healthcare decisions is the ultimate goal, the place of paternalism in modern healthcare is moot. While there may be a role for beneficence, as I have already suggested this is not the same as a justification for paternalism.

It is incontrovertible that – arguments about beneficence and paternalism aside – many (if not most) patients want to be treated as an interested participant in healthcare decisions; this is hardly surprising. For them, the importance of control over their lives is that it permits them to make decisions that reflect their own values and encapsulate their own interests. In other words, autonomous people want their autonomous decisions to be taken as definitive. This, however, begs the question as to what constitutes an autonomous decision. There are many accounts of autonomy and they rest on a variety of ethical and philosophical traditions. As a lawyer rather than a philosopher I cannot attempt to do them all justice. However, it would be impossible to discuss autonomy without reference to the work of Immanuel Kant, most particularly his *Fundamental Principles of the Metaphysics of Morals*

---

[37] Bulger, R E, Bobby, E M, Fineberg, H V (eds), *Society's Choices: Social and Ethical Decision Making in Biomedicine*, Committee on the Social and Ethical Impacts of Developments in Biomedicine, Division of Health Sciences Policy, Institute of Medicine, National Academy Press, Washington, DC, 1995, at p 34.

[38] Pellegrino, E D, Thomasma, D C, 'The Conflict Between Autonomy and Beneficence in Medical Ethics: Proposal for a Resolution', *Journal of Contemporary Health Law and Policy*, 3(23), 1987: 23–46, at p 36.

[39] Ibid., at p 27.

(1785).[40] Kant's philosophy has been highly influential, and has spawned endless commentary and critique, in-depth discussion of which lies beyond the scope of this narrative. However, he is perhaps most remembered for his casting of the 'Categorical Imperative' – in *Fundamental Principles of Metaphysics and Morals*, he says: 'There is therefore but one categorical imperative, namely, this: Act only on that maxim whereby thou canst at the same time will that it should become a universal law.'[41] Or, to put it another way, ' ... I am never to act otherwise than so that I would also will that my maxim should become a universal law.'[42] O'Neill notes that Kant's philosophy is not based in individual autonomy, however; rather it is concerned with description 'of the *autonomy of reason*, of *the autonomy of ethics*, of the *autonomy of principles* and of the *autonomy of willing*.' (original emphasis).[43] She says:

> Kantian autonomy is manifested in a life in which duties are met, in which there is respect for others and their rights, rather than in a life liberated from all bonds. For Kant autonomy is *not relational, not graduated, not a form of self-expression*; it is a matter of acting on certain sorts of principles, and specifically on principles of obligation. (original emphasis)[44]

This conceptualisation of autonomy is, as we will see, often at odds with the way in which the language is currently used, at least in law. While autonomy nowadays has come to mean, as much as anything else, the satisfaction of individual wishes or desires, for Kant '[t]o be autonomous ... is emphatically not to be able to do or have whatever one desires, but rather it is to have the capacity for rational self-governance.'[45] Oshana, however claims that the Kantian approach is essentially unhelpful, because '[a] theory of personal autonomy premised on a strict adherence to impartial and abstract principles, or a conception that discounts the roles that emotion and partiality play in our moral development and moral choices, is implausible and unnecessary.'[46]

John Stuart Mill,[47] on the other hand, posited a different conceptualisation of autonomy, while, as O'Neill notes,[48] scarcely using the term itself. He nonetheless developed a position that is arguably easier to equate to the

---

[40] *Fundamental Principles of the Metaphysics of Morals* (1785), translated by Thomas Kingsmill Abbott; available at http://philosophy.eserver.org/kant/metaphys-of-morals.txt (accessed on 1/5/2008).

[41] Ibid., transcript at p 20.

[42] Ibid., transcript, p 9.

[43] O'Neill, O, *Autonomy and Trust in Bioethics*, Cambridge University Press, 2002, at p 83.

[44] Ibid., at pp 83–84.

[45] Downie, R S, Macnaughton, J, *Bioethics and the Humanities: Attitudes and Perceptions*, Abingdon, Routledge-Cavendish, 2007, at p 42.

[46] Oshana, Marina A L, 'The Autonomy Bogeyman', *The Journal of Value Inquiry* 35, 2001: 209–26, at p 212.

[47] See, in particular, *On Liberty* (1869), transcript available at http://www.bartleby.com/130/4.html (accessed on 1/5/2008).

[48] O'Neill, O, *Autonomy and Trust in Bioethics*, Cambridge University Press, 2002, at p 30.

modern understanding of autonomy as the right to be self-governing than is Kant's argument. For Mill, the legitimacy of the state in interfering with the personal (private) decisions of others is constrained by the concept of freedom or liberty, save when harm to others might follow a failure to intervene. He says, for example:

> As soon as any part of a person's conduct affects prejudicially the inter-ests of others, society has jurisdiction over it, and the question whether the general welfare will or will not be promoted by interfering with it, becomes open to discussion. But there is no room for entertaining any such question when a person's conduct affects the interests of no persons besides himself, or needs not affect them unless they like (all the persons concerned being of full age, and the ordinary amount of understanding). In all such cases there should be perfect freedom, legal and social, to do the action and stand the consequences.[49]

This is not to say that either liberty or freedom is equivalent to 'selfish indifference';[50] indeed it entails that 'there is need of a great increase of disinterested exertion to promote the good of others.'[51] Mill's account emphasises 'self-respect or self-development ... ', and he concludes that 'for none of these is any one accountable to his fellow creatures, because for none of them is it for the good of mankind that he be held accountable to them.'[52] One important constituent of Mill's position is the importance he attributes to the division between public and private, which was briefly touched on in the introduction to this book. For Mill, private behaviour that has no negative consequences for others should lie beyond the reach of state intervention. In perhaps his most famous comment he says:

> ... the sole end for which mankind are warranted, individually or col-lectively, in interfering with the liberty of action of any of their number, is self-protection. That the only purpose for which power can be right-fully exercised over any member of a civilized community, against his will, is to prevent harm to others. His own good, either physical or moral, is not a sufficient warrant. He cannot rightfully be compelled to do or forbear because it will be better for him to do so, because it will make him happier, because, in the opinions of others, to do so would be wise, or even right. These are good reasons for remonstrating with him,

---

[49] *Fundamental Principles of the Metaphysics of Morals* (1785), translated by Thomas Kingsmill Abbott; available at http://philosophy.eserver.org/kant/metaphys-of-morals.txt (accessed on 1/5/2008), tran-script, at p 1.

[50] Ibid., transcript, at p 1.

[51] Ibid.

[52] Ibid., transcript, at p 3.

or reasoning with him, or persuading him, or entreating him, but not for compelling him, or visiting him with any evil in case he do otherwise. To justify that, the conduct from which it is desired to deter him, must be calculated to produce evil to some one else. The only part of the conduct of any one, for which he is amenable to society, is that which concerns others. In the part which merely concerns himself, his independence is, of right, absolute. Over himself, over his own body and mind, the individual is sovereign.[53]

Although this may sound highly individualistic, in fact as we have seen Mill positions the liberty of the individual clearly in the context of the rest of society, holding that harm to third parties – the so-called 'harm principle' – can justify interference with individual liberty, even when the decisions made might otherwise have been categorised as being 'private'.

This has obviously been a philosophically inadequate account of the theories of these two great philosophers, but as I have said my primary concern lies with the modern practice of medicine and the expectations of contemporary patients. For this reason, and for the effect they have on healthcare practice and legal pronouncements, I have selected for primary discussion two accounts of autonomy that are commonly discussed in contemporary literature and whose relevance to the healthcare setting is clear. Moreover, each is, one way or the other, of interest from the perspective of human rights which, it can be confidently argued, is the most powerful language of the 20th and 21st centuries and has also permeated the doctor/patient relationship. I will, therefore, focus on a highly individual account of autonomy and on one which concerns itself more with the person as part of a community; in other words, an individualistic and a relational account of autonomy.

The perceived need to shed the paternalistic past of medicine has resulted in a dominant focus on the individual *qua* individual. Rather than reflecting in depth on the metaphysical source of what it is to be autonomous, what has become central in modern legal debate concerns first the identification of competence and, second, flowing from that, consideration of the weight to be given to the decisions of the competent person, which will be considered in the following chapter. The question of competence might seem to be a rather arid, legalistic account of what it is to be an autonomous person, but it is the common starting point, the *sine qua non* of autonomy, and therefore requires consideration at this stage.

In legal terms, the primary indicator of the status of the individual and his or her subsequent decisions is that the person is competent. Competence is generally assumed in adults although this assumption can be rebutted by

[53] John Stuart Mill, *On Liberty* (1869), available at http://www.bartleby.com/130/1.html (accessed on 21/11/2007), transcript at p 9.

appropriate evidence to the contrary.[54] While legislation sometimes defines competence (or its absence),[55] in daily healthcare practice decisions about competence are by and large made by medical professionals rather than lawyers. In fact, unless there is an obvious reason to query the person's ability to make decisions – for example because of the patient's age – it is unlikely that the question of competence will ever be raised. So, although competence plays an important role 'by distinguishing persons whose decisions should be solicited or accepted from persons whose decisions need not or should not be solicited or accepted … ',[56] it is more often assumed to exist than not (at least when patients agree with clinical recommendations).

Competence implies decision-making authority which is sufficient to raise the expectation that the choices of a competent person will straightforwardly be respected. However, some commentators would argue that competence should be understood as more subtle than this account would suggest.

Kluge, for example, suggests that competence can be 'broken down into three distinct rubrics. They are, respectively, cognitive, emotional, and valuational competence.'[57] Cognitive competence relates to 'what, loosely speaking, may be called the rational capacities of the individual.'[58] This is probably the element of Kluge's account that relates most closely to its common legal understanding as it focuses on decision-making ability; the kind of test that is now enshrined in statue in England and Wales by the terms of the Mental Capacity Act 2005. This Act starts from the presumption that competence is to be assumed in adults,[59] and describes incompetence as follows:

s.2 (1) For the purposes of this Act, a person lacks capacity in relation to a matter if at the material time he is unable to make a decision for himself in relation to the matter because of an impairment of, or a disturbance in the functioning of, the mind or brain.
   (2) It does not matter whether the impairment or disturbance is permanent or temporary.
   (3) A lack of capacity cannot be established merely by reference to—
       (a) a person's age or appearance, or
       (b) a condition of his, or an aspect of his behaviour, which might lead others to make unjustified assumptions about his capacity.

---

[54] *Ms B v NHS Hospital Trust* (2002) 65 BMLR 149.
[55] In the United Kingdom, see, for example, the Mental Capacity Act 2005 (England and Wales), and the Adults with Incapacity (Scotland) Act 2000.
[56] Beauchamp, T L, Childress, J F, *Principles of Biomedical Ethics* (5th edn), Oxford University Press, 2001, at p 69.
[57] Kluge, E-H W, 'Competence, Capacity and Informed Consent: Beyond the Cognitive-Competence Model', *Canadian Journal on Aging*, 24(3), 2005: 295–304, at p 297.
[58] Ibid.
[59] s 1 (2).

(4) In proceedings under this Act or any other enactment, any question whether a person lacks capacity within the meaning of this Act must be decided on the balance of probabilities.

The second of Kluge's elements is said to acknowledge 'the fact that human beings are not automata but living beings who are embedded in psychosocial contexts and interact with other persons on more than merely cognitive terms.'[60] This introduces a contextual analysis, which will be discussed in more depth *infra*. Finally, Kluge refers to 'valuational' competence, which allows values to be taken into account when assessing competence, and makes the individual's decision 'ethically competent'.[61] While recognising that introducing this element runs certain risks, Kluge argues that this is not inevitable since it 'does not require valuational consonance between assessor and patient.'[62] While this may be true in theory, in practice the dangers are clear. As Elliston points out the rejection by patients of clinical recommendations can sometimes be seen as raising doubts about competence,[63] suggesting that the values of the 'assessor' are indeed sometimes relevant and may challenge the default position that assumes competence to be present. In fact, it could be argued that Kluge confuses the status of competence with making competent decisions. Competence in law is generally a status question, whereas making a competent decision is often an evaluative one.

Other commentators offer different accounts of competence. Morreim, for example, prefers the term 'rational competence' which 'concerns our ability to function as rational beings, to make judgments and choices in rational ways.'[64] This entails both the availability of relevant information and understanding (which are discussed in more detail in the following chapter), the weighing of relevant matters to make choices and 'where appropriate, to bring oneself to act in accordance with one's decisions.'[65] As with Kluge's first rubric, and the terms of the Mental Capacity Act, this account seems to focus on cognitive capacities.

What is interesting about the legal view of competence as a fundamental requirement for being autonomous is the extent to which it rests on the ability (or perhaps the right) to take decisions. Irrespective of those philosophical approaches which seek to make autonomy a richer concept, it is the decision-making aspect of autonomy that dominates in law; (legally defined) decision-making ability predicts the status of competence and thereby the right to act autonomously. The individual is supreme, and once judged competent

---

[60] Kluge, E-H.W, 'Competence, Capacity and Informed Consent: Beyond the Cognitive-Competence Model', *Canadian Journal on Aging*, 24(3), 2005: 295–304.

[61] Ibid.

[62] Ibid., at p 299.

[63] Elliston, S, *The Best Interests of the Child in Healthcare*, London, Routledge-Cavendish, 2007.

[64] Morreim, H, 'Three Concepts of Patient Competence', *Theoretical Medicine*, 4, 1983: 231–51, at p 234.

[65] Ibid.

is entitled to make decisions on the basis of his or her own concerns and interests, subject only to the caveat that they do not harm third parties. This individualistic model of autonomy is largely unconcerned with what the decision is; rather, it is interested in the right to make it.

Perhaps because of the centrality of individualism in this version of autonomy, some commentators view with alarm the apparent stranglehold that it has in modern bioethical discourse. In particular, the version of autonomy that sees the individual as a person distinct from his or her community has come to be seen (in some ethical discussion at least) as inappropriate and unhelpful. However, there are still many who defend this account, arguing that ' ... autonomy itself is part of our concept of the person because it is autonomy that enables the individual to "make her life her own". Choices are self defining but also they are self creating.'[66] Indeed, Hoffmaster claims that individualism is to be valued in that it permits the avoidance of vulnerability and 'requires self-sufficiency ... '.[67] In essence, then, '[a]utonomy is good for you. A strong sense of competent self-control and effective choice-making promotes both physical and psychological well-being.'[68]

Despite some support for the individualistic model of autonomy, an important question remains; namely, whether or not it is *in fact* an appropriate model for life generally, or for healthcare specifically. While the vision of the individual as supreme authority over his or her life is seductive, it has been subjected to some powerful challenges. Most commonly – but not exclusively – these have come from communitarian and feminist theorists. This is a huge literature, and what follows is not intended as a fully comprehensive account of the debate. Rather, it is designed to highlight that there are different modern views of autonomy, and to serve as the basis for a subsequent analysis of the law's approach to the question of consent as well as to a series of scenarios involving questions of patient decision-making where there is the potential for conflict between the individual and the community.

Autonomy re-conceptualised

The individualistic account of autonomy outlined above has, as I have said, come under challenge from a range of critiques, which have fundamentally attacked its apparent over-emphasis on the individual *qua* individual, rather than conceptualising him or her as part of a wider community. Dodds, for example, argues that the abstract, individualistic model of autonomy is often

[66] Harris, J, 'Consent and End of Life Decisions', *J Med Ethics*, 29, 2003: 10–15, at p 10.
[67] Hoffmaster, B, 'What Does Vulnerability Mean?', *Hastings Center Report*, March–April 2006: 38–45, at p 42.
[68] Waller, B N, 'Responsibility and Health', *Cambridge Q of Healthcare Ethics*, 14, 2005: 177–88, at p 177.

inapplicable or inappropriate in the medical encounter because, '[m]any of the important, but by no means unusual, health-care decisions that individuals, friends, and families make are far removed from the cool, reflective, clear-headed decision making that is the paradigm of this view of autonomy'.[69] Two contemporary critiques of individualistic autonomy will be considered here; namely, the broadly communitarian and the feminist positions.[70]

One powerful argument against the individualistic model of autonomy is that it 'makes autonomy inconsistent with other important values'.[71] Thus, the individualistic model has been accused of 'disregarding duties and obligations as well as relationships and the interests of the community ... '.[72] This critique has resulted in attention has being turned to the notion of autonomy as a relational concept. Christman describes relational autonomy as being concerned to 'underscore the social embeddedness of selves while not forsaking the basic value commitments of (for the most part, liberal) justice.[73]

Williams expands on this definition, saying:

> In this model, the person is fundamentally embedded in social relations ...
> Relational models also reject the transparency of the liberal self. Once the social sources of our identities are recognized, it becomes apparent that someone else who shares my culture might be able to understand me better than I understand myself. Indeed, self-knowledge, in a relational model, is a difficult and important achievement, and self-ignorance is one of the greatest obstacles to autonomy.[74]

Thus, mere ability to make decisions is not what counts; rather, the autonomous person is one who recognises his or her inter-relationship with the society of which s/he is a part and is able to acknowledge that his or her choices are socially constructed and have consequences for the community. As I have said, the value of relational autonomy has been embraced both by communitarian and feminist commentators. While their reasons probably differ – for feminists, for example, it is one way to seize the initiative in

[69] Dodds, S, 'Choice and Control in Feminist Bioethics', in Mackenzie, C, Stoljar, N (eds), *Relational Autonomy: Feminist Perspectives on Autonomy, Agency, and the Social Self*, Oxford University Press, New York, 2000, 213–35, at p 217.

[70] It is accepted that feminist accounts vary, but they all have at their core rejection of a perceived state-supported, male-centred society.

[71] Dworkin, G, *The Theory and Practice of Autonomy*, Cambridge Studies in Philosophy, Cambridge University Press, 1988, at p 23.

[72] Gauthier, C C, 'The Virtue of Moral Responsibility in Healthcare Decisionmaking', *Cambridge Q of Healthcare Ethics*, 11, 2002: 273–81, at p 275.

[73] Christman, J, 'Relational Autonomy, Liberal Individualism, and the Social Constitution of Selves', *Philosophical Studies*, 117, 2004: 143–64, at p 143.

[74] Williams, S H, 'Comment: Autonomy and the Public-Private Distinction in Bioethics and Law', available at http://muse.jhu.edu/journals/indiana_journal_of_global_legal_studies/v012/12.2williams_s.pdf (accessed on 19/10/2007), at p 490.

combating the power imbalance between men and women – their conclusions are relatively similar. However, if the individualistic model of autonomy can be criticised, there are also problems associated with the relational version, which needs to be able to 'demonstrate that respect for autonomy need not be understood as a purely individualistic concept based on the self as unencumbered, without the influence of family, community, shared history and traditions, and without regard to shared values or the interests of the community'.[75]

A critical distinction between individualistic and relational autonomy is that 'relational theory opposes what it designates as the liberal conception of the subject.'[76] The liberal or individualistic model, is said to be 'predicated on self-sufficient individuals independently pursuing their respective life plans ... In juridical language, the liberal self is an autonomous, rational agent that chooses its relationships and obligations through the instruments of private property and contract.'[77] On the other hand, '[r]elational theorists characteristically contrast the liberal idea of obligation, which is voluntarily undertaken, with their notion of relational responsibility, which may be involuntary.'[78] Thus, it is concluded, '[a]utonomy becomes possible in social interactions through relationships, such as those with parents, teachers, friends, and agents of the state.'[79]

The development of, and support for, the concept of relational autonomy arise from much more than simply a gut or knee-jerk reaction to the perceived implications and consequences of individualistic autonomy. There are ethical, as well as practical, reasons used to question the individualistic model. Pellegrino and Thomasma, for example, note that what they call the 'retreat to private morality' has profound consequences, since it:

> ... leads to a kind of moral atomism in which each individual's moral beliefs and actions – unless they disturb the peaceable community – are unassailable. Moral debate is not only frustrating but futile, since each person is his own arbiter of the right and the good. The traditional notion of ethics as reasoned public discourse in search of the common good is discarded. The sense of community identity that derives from some consensus on things that *ought* to be done, and what *ought never* to be done is lost.[80]

---

[75] Gauthier, C C, 'Moral Responsibility and Respect for Autonomy: Meeting the Communitarian Challenge', *Kennedy Institute of Ethics Journal*, 10(4), 2000: 337–52, at p 338.

[76] Leckey, R, 'Contracting Claims and Family Law Feuds', *University of Toronto Law Journal*, 57, 2007: 1–41, at p 7.

[77] Ibid.

[78] Ibid.

[79] Ibid., at p 8.

[80] Pellegrino, E D, Thomasma, D C, 'The Conflict Between Autonomy and Beneficence in Medical Ethics: Proposal for a Resolution', *Journal of Contemporary Health Law and Policy*, 3(23), 1987: 23–46, at p 34.

Having taken this on board, however, relational autonomy does not seek to deny the importance of decisional freedom that is so dear to the heart of individualistic autonomy. Rather, socially and politically it seeks to accommodate what are seen as reasonable (and ethically justifiable) constraints on the excessive selfishness that individualistic autonomy would, opponents say, have few, if any, means of preventing. To that extent, it might be said that the implications of relational autonomy mimic the harm exception, which would perhaps paradoxically be endorsed in Mill's liberal philosophy. If so, then the purported difference between the two accounts might be less significant than is sometimes claimed. On the other hand, it is argued, the relational version, rather than the individualistic one, allows for the concept of autonomy to 'readily be coordinated with other moral principles governing the self acting within a social context. This generally takes the form of recognizing that autonomous choices must be made in response to obligations, duties, and responsibilities.'[81]

The importance attributed to the concept of responsibility or duty (the latter being more like a Kantian approach) seems to make for a critical distinction between the two models, as it seems to require more of the autonomous individual than the mere ability to exercise choice. Endorsing the relational account means accepting that just being *able* to make a decision is sufficient in and of itself neither to establish that one is behaving autonomously nor to validate the decision. On this account, the person making a choice needs to be aware that individuals are more complex than merely decision-making machines, isolated from others and without conscience, obligations or responsibility. As Jackson proposes, ' ... a model of moral reasoning which privileges the rational, self-directed individual relies on a partial and inaccurate understanding of what it is to be human.'[82] In contrast the relational account requires the individual to be seen as a rounded, socially situated person whose preferences are both shaped by, and of consequence to, society.

In an ideal world, 'free choice and responsibility are seen as complementary to each other and thus mutually interdependent.'[83] Indeed, Berg *et al* postulate that ' ... reconceptualising autonomy – to take account of how people are interrelated and how individuals' interests are rarely purely self-interested and often reflect social values – may actually bring theory in line with practice.'[84] This is an important point which will be of interest when considering how decisions to accept or reject medical interventions are dealt with in law.

[81] Tauber, A I, 'Sick Autonomy', *Perspectives in Biology and Medicine*, 46(4) (autumn), 2003: 484–95, at p 489.
[82] Jackson, E, *Medical Law: Text, Cases and Materials*, Oxford University Press 2006, at p 22.
[83] Ibid., at p 490.
[84] Berg, J W, Appelbaum, P S, Lidz, C W, Parker, L S, *Informed Consent: Legal Theory and Clinical Practice* (2nd edn), Oxford University Press, 2001, at p 33.

A strong challenge, therefore, has been mounted against a theory of autonomy which does not import ' ... the guidance of an internalized sense of moral responsibility', the absence of which has been said to have led to 'many of the individual and social problems that have motivated the communitarian critique.'[85] It is argued, rather, that we must deploy ' ... a richer conception of autonomy or self-determination that strikes a balance between the individual and community, between rights and obligations.'[86] Gauthier proposes that moral responsibility is 'an overarching virtue, covering all of our choices and actions that have a moral dimension.'[87]

This notion of 'moral responsibility' situates individuals in a community (whether narrowly or broadly defined) and informs choices which are ' ... based on their traditions, histories, and a variety of communal influences as well as their own consideration of all these factors ... '.[88] The individual remains respected as an individual, but is also expected to take account of his or her social situation which both does, and should, inform his or her decisions; indeed, it is this that makes them fully autonomous. This, it is said, 'is necessary for the assignment of moral responsibility to individuals by other members of the community.'[89] This account may serve to ' ... guide the determination of how to act in a way that promotes human goods in terms of human flourishing as well as the flourishing of families and communities.'[90]

The feminist position on individualistic autonomy, as I have said, is based at root in the need to critique and re-evaluate socially engineered – and endorsed – power imbalances between men and women. While the non-feminist account of relational autonomy does not necessarily imply such imbalances, the feminist critique depends on them. The endorsement of the relational model by many feminist commentators derives from the perceived need to 'right wrongs', which can in part be achieved by accepting that we are situated within a community where power imbalance is endemic. Thus, there are differences – albeit sometimes subtle ones – underpinning the rationale for valuing the relational model for the communitarian and the feminist. However, at first sight, Donchin's account of, and reasons for rejecting, individualistic autonomy seem on all fours with those of the communitarian approach. She says:

> Western philosophy, ever since the Cartesian turn, has been captivated by a paradigm of personal agency that incorporates two dubious

---

[85] Gauthier, C C, 'Moral Responsibility and Respect for Autonomy: Meeting the Communitarian Challenge', *Kennedy Institute of Ethics Journal*, 10(4), 2000: 337–52, at p 342.

[86] Gauthier, C C, 'The Virtue of Moral Responsibility in Healthcare Decisionmaking', *Cambridge Q of Healthcare Ethics*, 11, 2002: 273–81, at p 276.

[87] Ibid., at p 276.

[88] Ibid., at p 344.

[89] Ibid., at p 348.

[90] Ibid., at p 277.

assumptions: that individuals are isolated ahistorical monads and that the choices available to them are extracted from a fixed and immutable state of options.[91]

So, she concludes, since these assumptions are erroneous, '[a]ny conception of autonomy that fails to incorporate socially situated interpersonal relations rests on illusion.'[92] Ignoring community, Gross says, has consequences that are particularly profound for 'ethnic, racial, and religious communities, as liberalism draws a firm distinction between the private and the public spheres.'[93] In theoretical and legal terms, however, the shift from individualistic to relational autonomy could have important consequences, since, as we have seen, what is categorised as 'private' (individual) is subject in the liberal tradition to fewer restrictions than the 'public', which could be more closely equated with 'socially engaged' or relational decisions. In liberal Western democracies, the private – such as the decision to use contraception in a relationship[94] – is generally regarded as not being of legitimate interest to the state. Categorising behaviour as falling within the public sphere, or private decisions as appropriately tested against their relational values, may support greater societal authority and may constrain choice.

While feminism has at its heart the recognition of the inequality of power between men and women, and the struggle to rectify it, it also respects the idea of human rights. Indeed, arguably it has to if it is to have a basis from which to argue for equal respect. The fact that something can be categorised as 'public' or socially situated even in feminist terms does not offer a general justification for increased state intervention, save where that is necessary to right the wrongs perpetuated by a male dominated society. Prioritising individual rights, therefore, is not inevitably inimical to recognising our inter-relatedness nor to striving to upset power imbalances and the ideologies which underpin them.

From the feminist perspective, the modern concept of autonomy is, as we have seen, unacceptably individualistic, thereby resulting in a world in which individuals are seen as separate – even distant – from their community. The value, it is said, that is prioritised in the individualistic model is most closely linked to what might be called 'male' interests or behaviour; isolated, aggressive, confrontational and competitive. Women, on the other hand, are seen as more likely to be contextually aware and socially engaged. However accurate this analysis it has nonetheless posed some obvious theoretical

---

[91] Donchin, A, 'Autonomy, Interdependence, and Assisted Suicide: Respecting Boundaries/Crossing Lines', *Bioethics*, 14(3), 2000: 187–204, at pp 187–88.

[92] Ibid., at p 189.

[93] Gross, M L, 'Speaking in One Voice or Many? The Language of Community', *Cambridge Q of Healthcare Ethics*, 13, 2004: 28–33, at p 29.

[94] *Griswold v Connecticut* 381 US 479 (1965).

problems. For example, if autonomy *is* a masculine concept, then this might suggest that the best way for feminism to rectify the problems associated with it would be to ditch the concept itself. However, as Kalbian points out, 'rejecting autonomy altogether is not a viable option for feminists who are motivated by the goal of liberation … '.[95] Thus, while 'autonomy is better understood when one views the person as a social being, whose identity relies on the context of her relationships with others',[96] that person also has, and will lay claim to, rights. The primary right might be that of equality rather than autonomy, but these are neither contradictory nor mutually exclusive.

In fact, as Donchin acknowledges, rights language can be a useful device in the struggle for equality since '[a]ppeals to autonomy *rights* have an emancipatory aim that has often been one of the few defenses available to women, particularly marginalized women, to resist pressures to override their own decision making authority' (original emphasis).[97] In support of this, it has been argued that, in fact, '[r]enouncing autonomy would defeat feminist efforts to achieve justice and foster social change.'[98] For feminists, however, the concept requires to be unpicked and recast to provide a more 'feminist' or 'feminised' account of the individual as a member of a given society, but at the same time abandoning the concept itself would merely open the door to other harms. As Jackson among others argues, the autonomous person should not be seen in a 'sort of social and cultural vacuum, with needs and interests that emerge and can be satisfied without reference to the needs and interests of others … '.[99] She continues, ' … we should perhaps think about how we might reconfigure autonomy in a way that is not predicated upon the isolation of the self-directed and self-sufficient subject.'[100] Although feminist arguments are scarcely homogeneous, I would venture to suggest that the broad feminist position can be summed up by the following statement:

> If autonomy is to be a valuable human ideal, it cannot require that human agents and choosers act and choose in an eerie vacuum, in the world as it would be if no other human agents and choosers had ever existed. The self that is self-governing in any workable and attractive model of autonomy has to be a self that acknowledges and even celebrates its social formation. Of course I should try to influence you, as you should try to influence me. To suggest otherwise is to deny the

---

95 Kalbian, A H, 'Narrative *ARTi*fice and Women's Agency', *Bioethics*, 19(2), 2005: 93–111, at p 94.

96 Ibid.

97 Ibid., at p 189.

98 Donchin, A, 'Autonomy, Interdependence, and Assisted Suicide: Respecting Boundaries/Crossing Lines', *Bioethics*, 14(3), 2000: 187–204, at p 189.

99 Jackson, E, *Regulating Reproduction: Law, Technology and Autonomy*, Oxford, Hart Publishing, 2001, at p 3.

100 Ibid.

fabric of human interaction within which we are all, inevitably and fortunately, situated.[101]

However, Jackson concedes that feminist accounts can be flawed, saying '[t]he problem with the conventional feminist critique of autonomy is that it sets up a binary opposition between interdependence and autonomy, as if the two were mutually exclusive.'[102] Yet, as Oshana points out, the liberal account is not necessarily 'at odds with the goods and values provided within the community. A concern for the rights, liberties and autonomy of individuals need not be associated with detachment and a deficiency of intimacy.'[103] Indeed, even within the human rights agenda, some account is taken of societal interests. For example, even in the European Convention on Human Rights,[104] few rights are absolute; most contain permissible derogations in, for example, the interests of public health or public morals. Despite what Gross implies, it is possible both to maintain the public/private distinction for the benefits it brings for the respect due to individual choice while still acknowledging the interrelatedness of individuals with their community. Recognition that some matters are 'private' and that therefore decisions about them are essentially inviolate does not atomise people; merely, it takes account of the fact that, as in Mill's philosophy, what does not affect (or harm) others is rightly the domain of the individual. Even feminist arguments must surely accept this, since the idea that some behaviours are private – that people have an entitlement to make independent decisions – is not inimical to supporting the goals of recasting society in a non-discriminatory form.

In sum, therefore, it can tentatively be concluded that both the individualistic and the relational models of autonomy share an interest in the appropriate application of the norms of human rights. In many ways, I would argue, they are not as distinct from each other as some would suggest. While relational autonomy appears more appealing, the presumption that respect for its individualistic counterpart would result in inattention to the interests of society seems erroneous, not least because we cannot by and large help absorbing lessons from our upbringing, our faith and our experiences that make total isolation, and total indifference to others, implausible.

So why then is the individualistic account seen as problematic? While it is sometimes seen as enchained – even tainted – by its emphasis on difference rather than relatedness, arguably this is something of an overstatement and, as we will see in what follows, the individualistic approach may provide protection

---

[101] Mills, C, 'The Ethics of Reproductive Control', *The Philosophical Forum*, XXX(1), March 1998: 43–57, at p 44.

[102] Jackson, E, *Regulating Reproduction: Law, Technology and Autonomy*, Oxford, Hart Publishing, 2001, at p 4.

[103] Oshana, Marina A L, 'The Autonomy Bogeyman', *The Journal of Value Inquiry*, 35, 2001: 209–26, at p 230.

[104] Which was incorporated into UK law by the Human Rights Act 1998.

for important goals – goals which are of interest to societies as well as individuals. The lessons that the individualistic account can learn from the relational one are that the moral worth of decisions is predicted not by the mere *exercise* of choice but potentially also by the *impact* of that choice on others. For Manson and O'Neill the real problem with the individualistic account is that:

> If individual autonomy is seen as fundamental to ethics, but merely as a matter of choice, then the only permissible restrictions on choice will be those required to protect others' individual autonomy. All choices that leave others' autonomy intact – however bizarre, however self-destructive, however offensive, however degrading – will be permissible, and restrictions on them will be unacceptable. Nothing will be prohibited or unacceptable between consenting adults.[105]

Isaiah Berlin agrees that this cannot be allowed to stand. While freedom of choice and action are central to what it is to be autonomous, nonetheless '[t]he extent of a man's, or a people's, liberty to choose to live as they desire must be weighed against the claims of many other values, of which equality, or justice, or happiness, or security, or public order are perhaps the most obvious examples. For this reason, it cannot be unlimited.'[106] On this view, it is not merely the harm principle that can legitimately limit individual choice – more abstract considerations, such as justice, should also have a place in the evaluation of the quality of the decision.

Pellegrino and Thomasma further critique the 'absolutization of autonomy', claiming that it limits 'the idea of democracy itself.'[107] In this vein, they continue:

> Democracy is reduced to a procedure for settling otherwise irreconcilable differences among citizens, but without commitment to any common set of values except freedom of private judgment. Certainly one measure of a democratic society is the degree of freedom it affords for divergent and contrary opinion. But those freedoms must serve some common community purpose as well.[108]

One obvious attraction of the relational model, therefore, is the sense of unity that it brings to the human enterprise. Freedom arguably becomes

---

[105] Manson, N C, O'Neill, O, *Rethinking Informed Consent in Bioethics*, Cambridge University Press, 2007, at p 20.

[106] Berlin, I, 'Two Concepts of Liberty', in Berlin, I, *Four Essays on Liberty*, Oxford, Clarendon Press, 1961, at p 170.

[107] Pellegrino, E D, Thomasma, D C, 'The Conflict Between Autonomy and Beneficence in Medical Ethics: Proposal for a Resolution', *Journal of Contemporary Health Law and Policy*, 3(23), 1987: 23–46, at p 35.

[108] Ibid.

more meaningful when it accounts for, or at least considers, the interests of others. Proponents of this model reject the idea that testing decisions from this perspective would amount to a curb on the freedom to be a personal decision-maker. Rather, choices which take account of others are not only 'better' choices, they are essential if the individual is to be accountable for him or her self, accepting 'moral responsibility' for his or her behaviour and maximising social utility or happiness (a main goal of communitarians). Attending to the valid interests of third parties may also offer one way of establishing balance in society, by destroying the 'justification' for binding to a social system that values one group over another (a primary concern of feminism).

Although I may be out on a bit of a limb in arguing that the two accounts are not entirely distinct or fundamentally incompatible, one thing can surely be said to unite them; each accepts that autonomy is a value and each requires that autonomous decisions are to be respected, even if their sense of its underpinning values differ in some ways. Dworkin says that '[a]utonomy functions as a moral, political, and social ideal. In all three cases there is value attached to how things are viewed through the reasons, values, and desires of the individual and how those elements are shaped and formed'.[109] This seems to harmonise the two accounts and offers a rounded description of autonomy that seems both logical and functional. This is important since there are problems with the relational account that make it difficult to apply in practice. For example, if the value to be given to decisions depends on its relational qualities, it is difficult to see how this could realistically be measured. That being so, how are we in reality to measure the extent to which its constituent elements have been met? On the other hand, even 'irrational' or apparently selfish decisions may follow mature reflection and may in fact be authentic, contextually nuanced and reflective of the individual's values. In any case, there are some robust defences of the individual's right to make independent, self-regarding decisions. Although, as we have seen, he rejects the atomisation of individuals, Berlin gives a powerful account of the value of self-determination, saying:

> I wish my life and decisions to depend on myself, not on external forces of whatever kind. I wish to be the instrument of my own, not of other men's acts of will. I wish to be a subject, not an object; to be moved by reasons, by conscious purposes, which are my own, not by causes which affect me, as it were, from outside. I wish to be somebody, not anybody; a doer-deciding, not being decided for, self-directed and not acted upon by external nature or other men ... I wish, above all, to be conscious of myself as a thinking, willing, active being, bearing responsibility for

---

[109] Dworkin, G, *The Theory and Practice of Autonomy*, Cambridge Studies in Philosophy, Cambridge University Press, 1988, at p 10.

my choices and able to explain them by reference to my own ideas and purposes.[110]

This classic statement of the desire to be free from external control, and free to choose one's own life, exposes very clearly what underpins the value placed on autonomy in contemporary (bio)ethics. It is the right, the freedom and the ability to be accepted as a self-determining person, with the capacity to make self-(and other-) regarding decisions, that protects and fosters the worth of the individual both to him/her self and to others. At its simplest, it could be said that autonomy equates to freedom from external control. For Beauchamp and Childress, it is 'at a minimum, self-rule that is free from both controlling interference by others and from limitations, such as inadequate understanding, that prevent meaningful choice. The autonomous individual acts freely in accordance with a self-chosen plan … '.[111] More subtly, perhaps, it is what 'enables us to be held to account for what we do, and what enables us to take, for example, credit for or pride in our actions.'[112] Further, Gauthier refers to the need for 'the capacity for rational agency', which is what allows people 'to make choices and act according to their beliefs and values … '.[113] To be truly autonomous it is imperative that people are able to reason, to evaluate their decisions, to hold them as their own, to act on them and to accept their consequences. Importantly, there is nothing to suggest that the individualistic account of autonomy necessarily ignores or rejects the values of others, nor does it necessarily preclude the taking of responsibility for decisions made. In other words, it too may be described as socially contextualised, even if it is more obviously supports self-regarding decisions.

Autonomy, the patient and the doctor

In bioethics, autonomy is generally described as the equivalent to 'self-government.'[114] Describing autonomy in this way, however, does not offer more than a pretty basic account of its content and meaning, and it certainly seems inadequate in the healthcare setting where subtle (and not so subtle) pressures can be brought to bear and may affect the ability to act in a self-governing manner. As we will see, for example, some would argue that the

---

[110] Berlin, I, 'Two Concepts of Liberty', in Berlin, I, *Four Essays on Liberty*, Oxford, Clarendon Press, 1961, at p 131.

[111] Beauchamp, T L, Childress, J F, *Principles of Biomedical Ethics* (6th edn), Oxford University Press, 2009, at p 58.

[112] Coggon, J, 'Varied and Principled Understandings of Autonomy in English Law: Justifiable Inconsistency or Blinkered Moralism?', *Health Care Anal*, 15, 2007: 235–55, at p 243.

[113] Gauthier, C C, 'Moral Responsibility and Respect for Autonomy: Meeting the Communitarian Challenge', *Kennedy Institute of Ethics Journal*, 10(4), 2000: 337–52, at p 339.

[114] Varelius, J, 'The value of autonomy in medical ethics', *Medicine, Health Care and Philosophy*, 9, 2006: 377–88, at p 377.

nature of the patient/doctor relationship, coupled as it generally is with patients' anxieties about their health, makes the notion of true self-governance aspirational at best and implausible at worst. For the moment, however, it is worth noting that the concept of self-governance or self-determination plays an important role in the contemporary doctor/patient relationship. Indeed, The (UK) House of Lords Select Committee on Medical Ethics made just this point in the mid-1990s, noting that '[m]ost individuals wish to take more responsibility for the course of their lives, and this applies equally to decisions about medical treatment.'[115] This has not changed – indeed, it may have become more common that patients expect that their input in decisions that affect them will be definitive of the outcome of clinical interactions.

The dye is now cast: the rhetoric, if not the reality, of the relationship between physician and patient has been irrevocably changed by contemporary recognition of the importance of patient self-determination. Not only do patients increasingly view healthcare decisions as a matter of individual choice, medicine has had to respond to the changing climate. It is anticipated, then, that patients will be the primary decision-makers in the healthcare context, and there is considerably less significance attached to the importance of the physician as decision maker. This change is, according to some, a direct result of the failure of trust between patient and doctor. Perhaps because of the historical inattention to their rights and an accompanying diminution of trust, many patients now demand that doctors respect them and their decisions. Tauber proposes that the modern commitment to autonomy or self-determination 'filled an ethical lacuna left by the abandonment of trust, and patient autonomy became the sacrosanct principle governing medical ethics in most dire need of protection'.[116]

The issue of trust in healthcare clearly has both historical and contemporary importance. It is probably fair to suggest that the doctor/patient relationship has become more adversarial, or at least less acquiescent, over time. As I have suggested, one reason for this is probably the growth of the language of human rights throughout the 20th and into the 21st century, which acts to discourage passivity and seeks to redress power imbalances. Recognising the importance of individual rights prompts challenge and encourages emphasis on self-determining behaviour. Indeed, the rights that are central to every human rights declaration or treaty are essentially equivalent to respect for autonomy. The international community, in commending member states to the facilitation and endorsement of the norms of human rights, specifically requires that attention is paid to the extent to which the individual's autonomy is maximised in political, social (or professional) relationships. The very idea of autonomy, then, is inseparable in the modern

---

[115] *Report of the Select Committee on Medical Ethics*, HL Paper 21–1, 1994, at p 7, para 4.

[116] Tauber, A I, 'Sick Autonomy', *Perspectives in Biology and Medicine*, 46(4), (autumn), 2003: 484–95, at p 485.

world from ' ... the dignity of human persons and the claim they have on each other to privacy, self-direction, the establishment of their own values and life-plans based on information and reasoning, and the freedom to act on the results of their cogitations.'[117]

Self-determination arguably becomes of increased importance the more significant the enterprise, and there are few interactions of more personal importance than those between patients and healthcare professionals. Doctors are seen as an elite, with – sometimes – the power of life and death over their patients. Even in less extreme cases, doctors also stand as gatekeepers to the availability of clinical services; services which may have a profound impact on the well-being of individuals. While benign paternalism may have brought some benefits with it, and was for a long time accepted as the appropriate model, modern patients by and large want more. The backlash against paternalism when it came was – as is often the case – radical. The modern rights-based approach to medical relationships seems to be one important and powerful way of putting the patient in the driving seat; of reducing the imbalance between healthcare professional and patient, in much the way that feminists seek to achieve this outcome in the wider society.

However, the patient's rights model is not without its critics. Teff, for example, says that 'it tends to suggest the existence of an absolute entitle-ment regardless of surrounding circumstances',[118] and seems particularly akin to a highly individualistic model of autonomy. Couching the patient/doctor relationship in terms of rights rather than reciprocity is sometimes said to debase the relationship – indeed, it might even be seen as positively harmful, not least for the patient. However, as I have tried to suggest, it is not necessary that human rights arguments either depend on or entail self-ishness. Human rights are both individualistic and relational; human rights treaties depend not only (or always) on the rights of individuals against others, but rather are also concerned with the rights of groups and commu-nities. They demand equality and justice; not preferential treatment and discrimination. Teff's criticism can, therefore, be disputed. Any sense of 'entitlement' derived from the patients' rights model is no more than the legitimate demand for respect. It does not, and cannot, mandate an absolute entitlement, for example, to scarce medical resources. Rights give the patient (and the non-patient) the language that allows them to make (legitimate) claims but do not support inappropriate demands.[119]

---

[117] Pellegrino, E D, Thomasma, D C, 'The Conflict Between Autonomy and Beneficence in Medical Ethics: Proposal for a Resolution', *Journal of Contemporary Health Law and Policy*, 3(23), 1987: 23–46, at p 24.

[118] Teff, H, *Reasonable Care: Legal Perspectives on the Doctor-Patient Relationship*, Oxford, Clarendon Press, 1994, at p 95.

[119] For further discussion of the relationship between human rights and bioethics, see McLean, S.A.M, 'Human Rights and Bioethics', available at http://portal.unesco.org/shs/en/files/12528/12270930731Bioethis_and_Human_Rights – McLean.pdf/Bioethis%2Band%2BHuman%2BRights%2B-%2BMcLean.pdf (accessed on 25/11/2008).

As we will see, much of the contemporary discussion of autonomy and medicine has focused on the insistence that doctors facilitate and patients decide, but for some this is an unhelpful – perhaps inadequate – description of a 'good' patient/doctor relationship. Pellegrino and Thomasma, for example, propose that it is important that the inter-connectedness of patient and doctor is recognised because, they argue, decision-making is an 'inter-personal transaction'.[120] Therefore, wholehearted endorsement of what I have called the individualistic concept of autonomy would, they say, 'downgrade the bilaterality of the patient-physician relationship.'[121] This, they argue, is inappropriate because, '[d]octor and patient are existentially bound to each other in a way that makes moral atomism and absolute decisional autonomy unrealistic and undesirable goals for both parties.'[122] On their argument, the consequences of adopting a non-relational approach are harmful rather than beneficial; what is needed is what Teff has called a 'therapeutic alliance',[123] which will suit and serve both patient and professional. Stirrat and Gill regard the relationship as 'covenantal rather than contractual', implying that 'there is a mutual, unspoken agreement between the parties that recognises the duties and obligations of each to the other.'[124] While this may indeed be the best way to conceptualise the relationship, it does not necessarily mean that rights language is inappropriate. Recognition of the rights of each party is complementary to respect for autonomy not inimical to a good doctor/ patient relationship. In the ideal doctor/patient relationship, while power and responsibility are shared, someone has to be the decision-maker, and for the reasons already outlined this should be the patient. Nonetheless, Ackerman argues that, '[a]utonomous personal growth in illness depends for its fullest expression upon conditions in which physicians and patients interact as compatriots, not strangers, in the therapeutic endeavor.'[125] Therefore, it has been proposed that 'medical ethics should be set in the context of relationships and community ... ', which would entail 'a principled version of patient autonomy that involves the provision of sufficient and understandable information and space for patients, who has (sic) the capacity to make a settled choice about medical interventions on themselves, to do so responsibly in a manner considerate to others.'[126] But does this mean the end of the more individualistic model of autonomy?

---

[120] Pellegrino, E D, Thomasma, D C, 'The Conflict Between Autonomy and Beneficence in Medical Ethics: Proposal for a Resolution', *Journal of Contemporary Health Law and Policy*, 3(23), 1987: 23–46, at p 27.

[121] Ibid.

[122] Ibid.

[123] Teff, H, 'Consent to medical procedures: paternalism, self-determination or therapeutic alliance?', *Law Q Rev*, 101, July 1985: 432–53; see also, Teff, H, *Reasonable Care*, Oxford, Clarendon Press, 1994.

[124] Stirrat, G M, Gill, R, 'Autonomy in medical ethics after O'Neill', *J Med Ethics*, 31, 2005: 127–30, at p 128.

[125] Ackerman, T F, 'Medical Ethics and the Two Dogmas of Liberalism', *Theoretical Medicine*, 5, 1984: 69–81, at pp 79–80.

[126] Stirrat, G M, Gill, R, 'Autonomy in medical ethics after O'Neill', *J Med Ethics*, 31, 2005: 127–30, at p 130.

Emphasis on individual interests need not mean abandonment of community. It is unproven, and probably unproveable, that the patient who sees him or her self as a fully independent person with the right to make personally acceptable choices is anything like as selfish or indifferent as s/he is often portrayed as being. Making clearly self-regarding decisions need not negate or ignore the interests of others (or the community as a whole) and in any case the harm principle serves as an effective challenge to decisions which are inimical to those interests; indeed it is central to the liberal tradition. It is equally impossible to show that the person whose decisions are apparently grounded in the community is fully self-determining, or indeed that their choices are 'better', more authentic or more worthy of respect. If there is a value in autonomy – and it seems most of us believe that there is – it is in the recognition that those who can (the competent) should be free to decide for themselves. Where these decisions would result in harm to third parties, then even the most liberal account would feel free – indeed compelled – to challenge them. It is disingenuous to characterise the language of human rights or individual autonomy as a threat to good medical interactions. Too simplistic an attack on individualistic autonomy is every bit as unhelpful as too ready an acceptance that the community has, or should have, a dominant role in shaping our decisions. Most importantly, those who seek to pit one against the other, and to deny – inadvertently or not – the benefits associated with the language of human rights, do us all a disservice.

The inherent value of autonomy lies precisely in its ability to situate the individual in a decisional pole position as a possessor and exerciser of rights. This does not, however, necessarily mean that decisions taken by individuals *for themselves* are inherently selfish or de-contextualised. While there are intelligible reasons why some groups would want to categorise them as such, very often this is designed to achieve a political or ideological end. A more nuanced approach is surely needed in healthcare, tailored to the fact that what is at stake is not an ideology but a relationship. Trust is important in medical encounters, and this is generated not just by the 'trustworthiness' of the participants, but also by respect being appropriately allocated. For too long it was assumed that respect was needed only from patient to doctor. Respect for patient autonomy, on the other hand, requires that doctors also trust patients to make their own decisions and respect them once taken.

Two main issues emerge from this discussion. The first is that there are obviously different ways of conceptualising autonomy and different approaches when it comes to assessing autonomous decisions. At the extremes, on the one hand, is the commitment to little more than respect for the individual and his or her choices. On the other, is the argument that it is both inappropriate and unhelpful to focus on the individual as entirely separate from others. The rights and responsibilities of the individual include not merely freedom of choice, but concern for the impact of their decisions on others and responsibility for these decisions. To some extent, I have sympathy with this latter approach. Indeed, I have argued elsewhere that:

> The cult of individualism is one which will be familiar as a political tool. It is as much to be resisted, arguably, in health care as it is in politics ... the consequences of the exercise of autonomy must also be considered as part of the quality of the enterprise. It is not enough merely to evaluate the amount of information provided, the way in which it is provided and whether or not the patient can make some sense of it, equally the individual's exercise of autonomy should not be made in a vacuum since the person of integrity is one who will also take into account other considerations beyond the mere exercise of autonomy.[127]

This, however, does not entail abandonment of respect for individual autonomy nor does it require a wholesale endorsement of the relational account. Rather, while prioritising the rights of the individual it depends on the assumption (which I suggest is reasonable) that individual choices are seldom – if ever – made in the kind of vacuum abhorred by proponents of relational autonomy. Respect for individual(istic) autonomy also, as we have seen, does not and need not deny the legitimacy of other interests.

The British Medical Association (BMA) argues that autonomy is in and of itself only one of the guiding principles of good medical practice. Thus, while autonomy is 'an important principle', says the BMA it 'must be balanced in proportion with other moral precepts, such as the doctor's duty to avoid harm in its widest sense.'[128] Thomasma further suggests that '[t]he preoccupation with autonomy and self-determination in Western bioethics' is 'indicative of the extent to which cultural values influence our orientation to biomedical morality.'[129] This is probably true, but it does not mean that there is something wrong with this 'preoccupation'. In the absence of compelling reasons to the contrary, respect for autonomy trumps other duties or interests in the absence of harm to others and the brake placed on paternalism by respect for patients' rights is important.

The second issue relates to the function of the law, and its role in balancing the various interests that are at stake. Wicks, for example, says that the law's

---

[127] McLean, S A M, 'Talking to patients – Information Disclosure as "Good" Medical Practice', in Westerhall, L, Phillips, C (eds), *Patient's Rights – Informed Consent, Access and Inequality*, Stockholm, Nerenius & Santerus Publishers, 1994, 171–89, at p 182.

[128] Euthanasia and physician assisted suicide: do the moral arguments differ?, Discussion paper from the BMA's Ethics Committee April 1998, available at http://www.bma.org.uk/ap.nsf/Conetn/Euthanasia-physicianassistedsuicide (accessed on 14/4/2005).

[129] Thomasma, D C, 'Proposing a New Agenda: Bioethics and International Human Rights', *Cambridge Q of Healthcare Ethics*, 10, 2001: 299–310, at p 302.

role is 'crucial' in 'seeking a reconciliation between the ethical principles of autonomy and paternalism … '.[130] Depending on how autonomy is defined, and what it is taken to mean, this task may prove extremely complex and challenging. For example, Dworkin's contention that the notion of autonomy 'is not merely an evaluative or reflective notion, but includes as well some ability both to alter one's preferences and to make them effective in one's actions and, indeed, to make them effective because one has reflected upon them and adopted them as one's own … ',[131] may prove too challenging for a 'one size fits all' legal rule. Equally, O'Neill's preference for what she calls 'principled autonomy' may be difficult to incorporate in law. For her, 'principled autonomy is expressed in action whose principle could be adopted *by all others*. Any conception of autonomy that sees it as expressing individuality – let alone eccentricity – or as carving our some particularly independent or distinctive trajectory in this world is a form of individual rather than of principled autonomy.'[132] This account seems, as I have suggested, at odds however with what many patients would regard as the goals of respect for autonomy, which for them rests less on abstract principles and more on respect for their choices.

We may be seduced by the alternatives to individualistic autonomy in theory, perhaps because our preferred account 'shifts our focus from the internal deliberations of an individual to the network of relationships and institutions that provide the context for that deliberation … ',[133] or perhaps because it 'does not assume that simply being left alone is all that is required to allow for autonomy.'[134] However, the real question for this discussion is less about the moral superiority of one over the other(s) and more about what kind of autonomy the law recognises and what version of it (if any) legal rules can accommodate. Irrespective of one's preferred model of autonomy, and we have only scraped the surface of this debate to focus primarily on two approaches because of their contemporary relevance to both healthcare and law, the purpose of this discussion is to identify the role that autonomy actually plays in the law of consent to treatment; not to opt conclusively for a preferred or preferable account.

---

[130] Wicks, E, *Human Rights and Healthcare*, Oxford, Hart Publishing, 2007, at p 61.

[131] Dworkin, G, *The Theory and Practice of Autonomy*, Cambridge Studies in Philosophy, Cambridge University Press, 1988, at p 17.

[132] O'Neill, O, *Autonomy and Trust in Bioethics*, Cambridge University Press, 2002; Pellegrino, E D, Thomasma, D C, 'The Conflict Between Autonomy and Beneficence in Medical Ethics: Proposal for a Resolution', *Journal of Contemporary Health Law and Policy*, 3(23), 1987: 23–46, at p 27.

[133] Williams, S H, 'Comment: Autonomy and the Public-Private Distinction in Bioethics and Law', available at http://muse.jhu.edu/journals/indiana_journal_of_global_legal_studies/v.2williams_s.pdf (accessed on 19/10/2007), at p 491.

[134] Ibid., at p 492.

Conclusion

What the foregoing shows is that, while virtually every school of ethical, social and political thought places considerable emphasis on the value of what it is to be autonomous, there is less agreement as to what autonomy actually means or consists in than might have been anticipated given the current dominance of the principle itself. Theories range from the individualistic, to the deontological to the relational. Some require merely the (legal) capacity to make a choice, while others require the exercise of rational decision-making. Still others demand that account is taken of third parties and their interests before a decision is truly worthy of respect as being autonomous, and emphasise responsibilities as much as rights. Some way of identifying truly autonomous decisions would seem, however, to be necessary if the authority of an apparently autonomous choice is to be accepted. After all, Safranek argues, '[i]f both the virtuous and the vicious can act autonomously, then the mere possession of autonomy neither specifies an agent's moral character nor justifies his acts.'[135] It remains to be seen whether an inquiry into the 'virtue' of the decision-maker is feasible in law.

Having said that, within the field of healthcare an understanding of what actually is an autonomous choice is extremely important because on this evaluation may hinge whether or not it is accepted as legally valid. Patients seeking to make decisions that are given legal weight must be able to trust that their autonomous choice is respected; that they are, as Hoffmaster puts it, 'self-sufficient'.[136] This requires that in some way their decision-making must be seen as free, even though there may be reason for concern that the real or anticipated presence of ill health may affect a person's ability to act autonomously.[137] Before concentrating on consent, this issue needs to be addressed briefly here.

Of course illness can be debilitating and the patient is almost always in a relatively weak position in respect of the clinician, if for no other reason than the imbalance of knowledge and authority that accompanies being a patient. But *all* decisions are dependent on context, and many are taken in situations where a third party holds more overt power. When we talk with our lawyer, our accountant or other adviser we are inevitably in a relationship where we know less than the third party. That this is true the doctor/patient situation does not necessarily distinguish it from these other relationships and its impact may even be exaggerated. Nonetheless it is this inequality of power that the move from paternalism to autonomy was designed to counter-balance.

---

[135] Safranek, J P, 'Autonomy and Assisted Suicide: The Execution of Freedom', *Hastings Center Report*, 28 (4), 1998: 32–36, at p 32.

[136] Hoffmaster, B, 'What Does Vulnerability Mean?', *Hastings Center Report*, March – April 2006: 38–45, at p 42.

[137] Kalbian, A H, 'Narrative *ART*ifice and Women's Agency', *Bioethics*, 19(2), 2005: 93–111.

Whether it does so or not will ultimately depend on how the law accommodates autonomy and this is dependent on the law of consent.

Consent is said to lie at the centre of patients' rights as it – theoretically at least – protects their right to decide what can and cannot be done with or to them. Since the law of consent is generally said to be the vehicle by which respect for autonomy is translated into law, the next chapter will consider how and whether this is achieved. If autonomy were merely about the making of a choice, and consent is intimately linked to autonomy, then consent law would be easy to evaluate. One would only need to ensure that decision-makers meet the general requirements for competence and little more would be required beyond the provision of relevant information. If, on the other hand, an autonomous decision involves more than this, a 'morally acceptable theory of informed choice' will have to take account of the fact that '[p]eople are multiply disciplined by various social institutions, such as race, sex, class, religion, all of which affect the decisions they make about health care and other matters.'[138] Irrespective of the debate about how we should best describe autonomy, however, no one seriously doubts that it should be respected. Pellegrino and Thomasma say that:

> The autonomy 'model' of clinical decision-making is firmly grounded in the dignity of human persons and the claim they have on each other to privacy, self-direction, the establishment of their own values and life-plans based on information and reasoning, and the freedom to act on the results of their cogitations.[139]

Thus, although there may be important arguments about the kind of autonomy we should prefer, and the way(s) in which an autonomous decision can be recognised, there is no doubt that – at a minimum – it is expected to protect individual choice, even if we agree that there is an 'equal need for society to engage in the pursuit of some common moral grounds beyond autonomy.'[140] One of these 'moral grounds' can be found in the concept of trust, which was raised briefly at the beginning of this chapter. It is generally said that trust is the cornerstone of the doctor/patient relationship, and Rhodes claims that it 'dictates the model for medical practice.'[141]

This also entails the need to be trustworthy – to deserve trust – which 'provides an order and rationale for considering the virtues that good doctors

---

[138] Ells, C, 'Foucault, Feminism, and Informed Choice', *Journal of Medical Humanities*, 24(3/4), Winter 2003: 213–28, at p 222.

[139] Pellegrino, E D, Thomasma, D C, 'The Conflict Between Autonomy and Beneficence in Medical Ethics: Proposal for a Resolution', *Journal of Contemporary Health Law and Policy*, 3(23), 1987: 23–46, at p 24.

[140] Ibid., at p 34.

[141] Rhodes, R, 'Understanding the Trusted Doctor and Constructing a Theory of Bioethics', *Theoretical Medicine*, 22, 2001: 493–504, at p 496.

must embody.'[142] According to Rhodes, being trust*worthy*, thereby enabling patients to trust doctors, requires both professional competence and attention to patients' values. The consequences are to situate the doctor and patient within a relationship that recognises a role for each of them, with professional expertise and attention to patient interests and preferences combining to reinforce the value of the relationship, while at the same time respecting the patient. In a relationship of this sort, the patient is enabled to trust the doctor and take value from his or her expertise.

O'Neill believes that the trust relationship can be differentiated from the autonomy model, saying that '[t]rust belongs with relationships and (mutual) obligations; individual autonomy with rights and adversarial claims.'[143] However, again I would argue that the two are by no means so incompatible as she seems to propose. Each can co-exist with the other; it seems counter-intuitive to suggest that even a firmly individualistic form of autonomy *necessarily* ignores the link between those participating in a caring interaction based in trust – that is, the patient and the healthcare provider. A good interaction would result in the negotiation of a relationship that is more equal, but which would include respect for the individual's right to make his or her own decisions in a self-rather then other-regarding manner. Certainly, an adversarial model, even if inadvertent, seems unlikely to achieve this, but this is not necessarily the result of attention to the individualistic model, because this model – like the others discussed – is situated within a particular relationship. It cannot be divorced from this context, and to that extent at least it depends on relationships. If trust exists in the doctor/patient relationship it is not removed by the fact that the patient has the ultimate authority.

Whatever the ethically preferable or preferred approach to autonomy it must be accommodated by, and enforceable in, law if it is to have practical value. Arguably, it should also be consistently applied so that patients can predict with some certainty the extent to which their decisions will be respected. It is, of course, potentially difficult for a set of general rules to address or even reflect the nuanced ethical debate on autonomy. Nonetheless, law is the vehicle that has the task of translating values like respect for autonomy into personal and societal reality. Before considering what the law actually does, it is worth reflecting on the way in which, if at all, the concept of consent co-exists with or supports autonomous choice, and on what basis. This will be undertaken in the next chapter.

---

[142] Ibid.
[143] O'Neill, O, *Autonomy and Trust in Bioethics*, Cambridge University Press, 2002, at p 25.

Chapter 2

From autonomy to consent

The major consequence of being respected as autonomous is that it implies the capacity or liberty to make decisions, free from external control and in the expectation that they will be accepted as valid and binding on others. It also means that nobody has the authority to interfere with our bodies and minds without our agreement or consent (save in very limited circumstances where seeking consent is not feasible). As we will see in what follows, the drive to enhance patient engagement in, and authority over, their own healthcare decisions led to the development of requirements that consent be not just assumed, but real. However, as I will argue, the law on consent may do little to ensure that autonomous people are able to make autonomous decisions, and to that extent it arguably plays a limited role in actually protecting autonomy despite its perceived importance in modern biomedical ethics and law. What the law presumably intends is that a truly autonomous decision will be respected, but it is not clear how, if at all, it can recognise such a decision, nor is it obvious that it imposes an obligation on physicians to ensure that making one is feasible.

I start with a disclaimer. I will not use the language of 'informed' consent unless that terminology appears in other authors' writing. The reasons for this have been explained more fully elsewhere,[1] but are broadly concerned with the fact that 'informed' consent is a doctrine developed in US jurisprudence and was, according to Robertson,[2] specifically designed to expand the liability of doctors. Although, as we will see, some judges and commentators in the United Kingdom use this language, arguably they mean something different by it and UK courts do not have exactly the same understanding of the terminology as their US counterparts. It is, however, impossible entirely to avoid the language since it is either used with jurisprudential exactitude (as in US cases and commentaries) or as a loose descriptor (as is usually the case in the United Kingdom). Whatever the

---

[1] McLean, S A M, *A Patient's Right to Know: Information Disclosure, the Doctor and the Law*, Aldershot, Dartmouth, 1989.

[2] Robertson, G, 'Informed Consent to Medical Treatment' (1981) *LQR* 102–26, at p 112.

language used, however, the concern of the law on consent is to ensure that people have made knowledgeable choices about healthcare and to ensure that these are respected.

Having considered rules that apply to the law in respect of consent, I will then explore the extent to which (if at all) there is an identifiable relationship between consent and autonomy, however the latter is understood. This is an important question, since as Faden and Beauchamp say:

> It is always an open question whether an autonomous person with the capacity to give an informed consent actually has, in any specific instance, given an informed consent, in the sense of making an autonomous choice to authorize or refuse an intervention.[3]

Making a legally valid decision

There are several preconditions to what will be considered a legally valid decision. The doctrine of consent requires that a decision must be made following the provision of information (unless this is rejected), by a competent, non-coerced individual and may even expect to see some evidence that the person has understood the information they have been given.

Competence revisited

The issue of competence has already been touched on, but for completeness it will be briefly reconsidered here, as it is central to the *legal* evaluation of patients' decisions. Put simply, if a person is not competent then even an apparently free and uncoerced choice will not be legally respected. Although it is sometimes suggested that different levels of competence are needed to make different kinds of medical decisions – particularly in the case of children[4] – the presumption of competence in adults mandates that (assuming the additional considerations discussed below are met) irrespective of the actual decision made, it will *prima facie* be legally valid. The legal assessment of competence, therefore, stands alone from the nature of the choice that is actually made. This is not to say that there are no tests that the law requires to be met before accepting a decision as valid, and these will be discussed in the next chapter. However, the assessment of competence *prima facie* provides validation for an otherwise lawful decision.

---

[3] Faden, R R, Beauchamp, T L, *A History and Theory of Informed Consent*, Oxford University Press, 1986, at p 237.

[4] See, for discussion, Elliston, S, *The Best Interests of the Child in Healthcare*, London, Routledge-Cavendish, 2007.

Information

One way, it seems obvious, that we can facilitate the making of a valid choice, is by ensuring that the patient is provided with the wherewithal to make a decision in the first place. In other words, the patient needs information on which to base his or her choice. The 'informed', or more accurately informational, aspect of consent is the element that focuses on the patient's right to receive relevant and sufficient information in order to enable him or her to make a decision. It is generally assumed, then, that – in the absence of a competent refusal to receive any information that might be offered – a valid consent (or refusal) depends on the sharing of information with the patient. The doctor is, therefore, under an obligation to share information with his or her patient. This, of course, makes perfect sense, and underpins the shift, described earlier, from paternalism to respect for autonomy.

When paternalism was the dominant characteristic of the medical encounter, the physician's possession of knowledge and expertise was sometimes used to justify little more than minimal disclosure. After all, the patient consults the physician precisely because s/he lacks the doctor's expertise. Why then, it might be asked, should this expertise not be definitive of treatment decisions without the need for the time-wasting process of providing information? The answer seems self-evident. Although patients need access to clinical information and expertise to undertake a calculation of which decision is right for them, their choices can, and often will, be based upon and measured by more than just the anticipated clinical outcome. The information and recommendations provided by physicians flow into the total pool of information available to patients, who – if they are to be self-directing – need to be free to choose the course of action (or inaction) that best suits their wider, and not merely their clinical, needs. Lowey says that '[o]nly patients can pick their own goals and ends according to their own values.'[5]

Recognition of this has been a major factor in the downgrading of the value of paternalism. Clinical matters may form only one of the considerations that patients want to use in reaching healthcare decisions – albeit that they may be of considerable, even sometimes paramount, importance. To use a simple example – I may at one level want surgery to relieve existing pain, but at another, I may not be prepared to accept the scarring or the risks that may result from it. In order to decide what to do, I can legitimately claim a need to know about any alternative treatments which will not result in scarring, or which do not share the risks, even if they equally do not promise the best clinical outcome. My ultimate decision may not be for the clinically optimal treatment – it may indeed be to reject any and all treatment options – but it is my decision to take. Or I may need treatment, which will likely cause me to be nauseous. Although there are clinical benefits

---

[5] Lowey, E H, 'In Defense of Paternalism', *Theoretical Medicine and Bioethics*, 26, 2005: 445–68, at p 447.

associated with beginning the treatment as quickly as possible, on the other hand I may have an important family wedding coming up which I do not want to miss. I might therefore accept the risks associated with delaying treatment in order to attend to personal matters of great importance to me, however medically irrational this may seem to be. Nothing in the doctor's expert knowledge necessarily enables him or her either to know about, or be able to evaluate, the factors that will influence patients' decisions; arguably not even in the situation where the doctor has been treating the patient and perhaps his or her family for some time, since the knowledge obtained in the clinical context is by definition incomplete. While doctors are committed to being guided by the best interests of their patients, the competent patient is, and needs to be, the ultimate arbiter of what these interests actually are, and this will often be informed by a variety of non-medical matters.

The physician's role, then, is to make it possible for the patient to make a choice that is appropriate for them, by providing relevant information to the competent individual. At this stage, the doctor becomes facilitator rather than director of the encounter. Once the patient has reached a decision about a particular course of action, the doctor's role is 'to inform the patient whether that goal is attainable and, if not, to help him choose another and then to determine and discuss the means required to hopefully reach such a goal.'[6] This, of course, hinges on dialogue between doctor and patient (and *vice versa*). Katz has long lamented the fact that doctors have seemed reluctant to talk to their patients,[7] and it has also been pointed out that:

> The trust which doctors and patients expect to share, and from which they are said to receive such mutual benefits, is critically dependent on the disclosure and sharing of the information which goes towards the decision whether or not to enter into the proposed course of treatment/ investigation.[8]

While informing patients about risks, benefits and alternatives may make the decision 'informed' (in a non-technical sense) the mere provision of information may not be sufficient to fulfil the aim of the consent doctrine in its purported role of autonomy-protector. Nonetheless, it is a vital element since without information the patient is often in no position even to contemplate making a treatment decision, far less one that might reflect their personal circumstances and values. However, even accepting that information

---

[6] Ibid., at p 447.

[7] Katz, J, *The Silent World of Doctor and Patient*, New York, The Free Press, 1984. See specifically at p xxi ' ... physicians and patients must learn to converse with one another. Meaningful conversation, however, requires that both are also prepared to trust each other.'

[8] McLean, S A M, 'Talking to patients – Information Disclosure as "Good" Medical Practice', in Westerhall, L and Phillips, C (eds), *Patient's Rights – Informed Consent, Access and Equality*, Stockholm, Nerenius & Santerus Publishers, 1994, 171–89, at p 171.

needs to be provided to patients leaves one difficult question remaining; namely, what information needs to be offered?

It is probably unsurprising, for practical reasons at least, that there is an ongoing debate about just how much, and what kind of, information needs to be disclosed and no easy way of answering this question emerges from the literature. While it could be argued that only full and complete disclosure would allow for an autonomous decision to be made, in practice this would likely prove impossible and, some would argue, may even be counter-productive. It is increasingly recognised that demanding full disclosure of every piece of information within the healthcare professional's knowledge would be unreasonable and even potentially unhelpful. Waller, for example, argues that '[o]verwhelming a patient with information that she cannot assimilate is not a means of empowering the patient.'[9] Manson and O'Neill suggest that 'the best that we can hope for is a mutually agreed level of specificity in the disclosure for a particular transaction.'[10] Because we are all different and will have diverse interests and preferences, it is not possible to set absolute standards for disclosure and 'explicitness and specificity cannot be general requirements on all consent.'[11] Indeed, Buehler suggests that concentration on the 'information component' of consent means that the process is 'often reduced to a consent form alone ... ', and argues that this has 'serious ethical consequences.'[12] For Manson and O'Neill, as for many other commentators, what is important is not the mere provision of information but rather the need to recognise that:

> ... the habit of seeing information merely as content to be transferred and conveyed detaches that content from the full demands of successful communicative transactions, and downplays the complex social and normative framework that must be in place and must be respected for effective communication.[13]

Further, Coggon makes the point that a call for 'full knowledge' as a prerequisite of an autonomous choice is in fact 'really just a means of limiting action; sometimes an underhand means. No one has perfect knowledge and a demand for it permits those with power to close in when a person is trying to make an unusual decision.'[14] On the other hand, too much selectivity is

[9] Waller, B N, 'The Psychological Structure of Patient Autonomy', *Cambridge Quarterly of Healthcare Ethics*, 11, 2002: 257–65, at p 262.

[10] Manson, N C, O'Neill, O, *Rethinking Informed Consent in Bioethics*, Cambridge University Press, 2007, at p 16.

[11] Ibid.

[12] Buehler, D A, 'Informed Consent – Wishful Thinking?', *Journal of Bioethics*, 1983: 43–57, at p 48.

[13] Manson, N C, O'Neill, O, *Rethinking Informed Consent in Bioethics*, Cambridge University Press, 2007, at p 49.

[14] Coggon, J, 'Varied and Principled Understandings of Autonomy in English Law: Justifiable Inconsistency or Blinkered Moralism?', *Health Care Anal*, 15, 2007: 235–55, at p 245.

unlikely to furnish the patient with sufficient opportunity to act autonomously. Onora O'Neill concludes that:

> At best we may hope that consent given by patients in the maturity of their faculties, although not based on full information, will be based on reasonably honest and not radically or materially incomplete accounts of intended treatment, and that patients understand these accounts and their more central implications and consequences to a reasonable degree.[15]

The point is that the patient/doctor relationship requires trust and respect. Emphasis on the mutuality of the doctor/patient relationship is increasingly the subject of both academic and legal commentary. While paternalism denied the value of information sharing, and the half-hearted commitment to patient's rights required mere provision of information, the backlash has become more reflective and subtle as to the actual goals of information provision. However, even if there is a debate about the quantity of information that needs to be disclosed, offering some information is necessary, 'not just because without it a patient's autonomy may be compromised … but also because … a patient who makes a choice based upon insufficient information may be regarded as incompetent to choose.'[16] It matters, therefore, that patients are put in a position that allows them to exercise self-determination.

However, we must also address the question as to what is the function of information disclosure; a question which engages with the *quality* and not just the *quantity* of what is disclosed. Clearly, it cannot be to bring patients to the same level as doctors who will have trained for many years to reach their current stage of expertise and knowledge. For Brody, 'disclosure is adequate when the physician's basic thinking has been rendered transparent to the patient.'[17] This might seem rather too low a standard, and most people would probably agree that some rules can be formulated about what should be the content (broadly speaking) of the information which must be disclosed. The Mental Capacity Act 2005, which was briefly discussed in Chapter 1, is arguably somewhat vague on this matter, merely stating that:

> The information relevant to a decision includes information about the reasonably foreseeable consequences of—

(a) deciding one way or another, or
(b) failing to make the decision.[18]

[15] O'Neill, O, *Autonomy and Trust in Bioethics*, Cambridge University Press, 2002, at p 44.

[16] Wicks, E, *Human Rights and Healthcare*, Oxford, Hart Publishing, 2007, at p 79.

[17] Brody, H, 'Transparency: Informed Consent in Primary care', *The Hastings Center Report*, 19(5) (Sep-Oct), 1989: 5–9, at p 7.

[18] s 3(4).

Interestingly, while the law, and ethics, struggle to define precisely what information must be disclosed, medical professional organisations have arguably had more success, and set high standards for disclosure which often go further than is strictly required by law.[19] In doing so, they recognise that 'a substantial infringement of autonomy may result ... from inadequate information being given ... '.[20] Of course, it must be conceded that the possibility of making an autonomous decision is unlikely to be guaranteed simply by demanding that information is provided or by the mere fact of its provision. If the patient does not understand the information, however comprehensive, it can be argued that his or her ability to make an autonomous decision is significantly, if not fatally, impaired. Waller argues that while information is important to achieve 'autonomous control', the patient must have the 'confidence and competence to understand it', otherwise it 'provokes stress rather than providing comfort.'[21]

There are, of course, those who would argue that the provision of information does not in fact serve any real purpose at all. This, they would argue, is first because 'informed consent is actually deleterious to patients' health.'[22] Further, since 'patients do not understand or use the information they are given', it is a 'wasteful use of scarce resources' to require doctors to spend time on providing it.[23] On the other hand, however, some research suggests that patients can indeed benefit from information provided. For example, in their study Faden and Beauchamp found that '[f]ollowing disclosure, most patients indicated that they felt more confident about their decisions ... '.[24] Nonetheless, although over 93% of their sample said that 'they had personally benefited from the information provided ... ', their decisions were based on factors external to the information in 88% of cases.[25] This is scarcely surprising since ' ... in trying to determine what is the most appropriate medical approach in a given case there may be personal values, circumstances, or priorities which need to be explored.'[26] This does not minimise the importance of the disclosed information, especially in light of Faden and Beauchamp's findings, but it does reinforce the notion that the clinically optimal decision may not be the personally optimal one. Indeed, if patients

---

[19] See, for example, *Good Medical Practice*, London, General Medical Council, 2006 and associated guidelines.

[20] Beasley, A D, Graber, G C, 'The Range of Autonomy: Informed Consent in Medicine', *Theoretical Medicine* 5 (1984) 31–41, at p 33.

[21] Waller, Bruce, N, 'The Psychological Structure of Patient Autonomy', *Cambridge Quarterly of Healthcare Ethics*, 11, 2002: 257–65, at p 262.

[22] Berg, J W, Appelbaum, P S, Lidz, C W, Parker, L S, *Informed Consent: Legal Theory and Clinical Practice* (2nd edn), Oxford University Press, 2001 at p 154.

[23] Ibid.

[24] Faden, R R, Beauchamp, T L, 'Decision-Making and Informed Consent: A Study of the Impact of Disclosed Information', *Social Indicators Research*, 7, 1980: 313–36, at p 326.

[25] Ibid.

[26] Teff, H, *Reasonable Care: Legal Perspectives on the Doctor–Patient Relationship*, Oxford, Clarendon Press, 1994, at p 123.

report that even the process of being given information raises their level of confidence, it may well be that the decision that follows is truly authentic even if it is clinically sub-optimal.

In addition to ensuring competence and engaging in information sharing, it is generally agreed that the information that is disclosed should be provided in a manner that facilitates patient understanding. Nonetheless, Faden and Beauchamp sound an important note of caution. They argue that the 'consent component of "informed consent"' is 'especially vague in legal opinions'.[27] Thus, while courts concentrate on the adequacy of disclosure, they are apparently less interested in 'the equally compelling question, "What constitutes a valid consent (on the patient's part)?".'[28] To a probably large extent, this depends on the patient's ability to receive and understand the information disclosed.

Understanding

Beste argues that '[i]n order to deliberate rationally, a patient must be able to comprehend the relevant facts and circumstances of her situation. After considering her options for medical treatment, she needs to discern which option best coheres with her life plan.'[29] The Mental Capacity Act (which it should be remembered does not apply to Scotland) states that a person is not competent to make decisions for him- or herself if unable:

(a) to understand the information relevant to the decision,
(b) to retain that information,
(c) to use or weigh that information as part of the process of making the decision, or
(d) to communicate his decision (whether by talking, using sign language or any other means).[30]

Understanding, therefore, forms an important element in the definition of competence, which in turn is directly relevant to the *prima facie* ability to make autonomous healthcare decisions. It seems self-evident that information which is poorly or mis-understood is unlikely to help a person to make a reasoned or real choice. Faden and Beauchamp have said that understanding is 'of special importance for a theory of informed consent.'[31] Of course, it

---

[27] Faden, R R, Beauchamp, T L, 'Decision-Making and Informed Consent: A Study of the Impact of Disclosed Information', *Social Indicators Research*, 7, 1980: 313–36, at p 313.

[28] Ibid.

[29] Beste, Jennifer, 'Instilling Hope and Respecting Patient Autonomy: Reconciling Apparently Conflicting Duties', *Bioethics*, 19(3), 2005: 215–51, at pp 200–21.

[30] s 3(1).

[31] Faden, R R, Beauchamp, T L, *A History and Theory of Informed Consent*, Oxford University Press, 1986, at p 248.

could be argued that the fact that a person is legally competent should be sufficient to generate the assumption that they *are* capable of understanding what they are told. However, if competence is the legal vehicle that triggers respect for autonomy, and is, as it seems to be, in part based on ability to understand, then surely we should scrutinise the actual ability of the person to understand what is being discussed with them, not solely legalistically but also in terms of what they have *actually* understood?

Attributing competence is on its own merely recognition of a particular legal status – it does not imply or guarantee that the competent person will, or can, always make an autonomous decision. The ability to do this would depend on two further factors; first, the communication skills of the doctor and, second, the ability of the patient to understand. Realistically, each of these may be beyond the control of both the patient *and* the doctor, which in turn is relevant to the law's ability to protect autonomy. For example, while it is obviously desirable that healthcare professionals should be excellent communicators, there is probably no way this can be guaranteed. What can be encouraged, however, is acceptance of the need to *attempt* to have a meaningful dialogue. As Katz has said, ' … physicians and patients must learn to converse with one another. Meaningful conversation, however, requires that both are also prepared to trust each other.'[32] While medical professionals can be expected to recognise the importance of the highest standards of communication between doctors and patients, arguably the law cannot *require*, by imposing a legal duty, that doctors actually are, or become, effective communicators.[33]

Nonetheless, since 'the patient's actual understanding seems to be an integral component of the idea of consent … [p]hysicians dedicated to the principles underlying the law of informed consent should take steps to ensure patient understanding even in the absence of a legal requirement.'[34] Legally, it would seem that all that is required is that doctors take 'reasonable and appropriate steps to satisfy themselves that the patient has understood the information … '.[35] This common law position is reinforced by the terms of the Mental Capacity Act 2005 which outlines the need for information to be provided in a manner that encourages or facilitates understanding.[36] This stops short of imposing an obligation, which – while still encouraging dialogue – seems reasonable for practical if not theoretical reasons.

A second consideration in respect of understanding concerns the patient him or her self. Either because of inherent limitations, or perhaps because of

---

[32] Katz, J, *The Silent World of Doctor and Patient*, New York, The Free Press, 1984, at p xxi.

[33] McLean, S A M, *A Patient's Right to Know: Information Disclosure, the Doctor and the Law*, Aldershot, Dartmouth, 1989.

[34] Berg, J W, Appelbaum, P S, Lidz, C W, Parker, L S, *Informed Consent: Legal Theory and Clinical Practice* (2nd edn), Oxford University Press, 2001, at p 67.

[35] *Al Hamwi v Johnston and Another* [2005] EWHC 206, at para 69.

[36] s 3(2).

the existence of illness or anxiety, patients may be thought likely to be unable to understand medical information and use it appropriately. The ability to assimilate and utilise information can depend on intellectual capacity (which need have nothing to do with legal competence), on anxiety or depression levels and even on the extent to which the patient wishes to take control. Thus, a patient can be legally competent yet inherently incapable of understanding all bar the most simple explanation of proposed treatment. This explanation should nonetheless be provided, particularly since, as has been argued, the information informs much more than a purely clinical decision. One additional consideration should be mentioned briefly. As Kukla laments:

> ... bioethicists have focused on how clinicians can get patients to *understand* the information they are giving them so that the patient can make an informed choice. There has been vastly less bioethical concern with whether and when patients will *accept* this information as authoritative, even if they understand it perfectly.[37]

This concern may relate – as so much seems to – to the alleged erosion of trust in the doctor/patient relationship. It is, however, difficult to see how it would be possible adequately to interrogate whether or not the individual has accepted information as 'authoritative'. Fulfilment of this criterion is more likely to hinge on the quality of the relationship between patient and doctor rather than on anything externally testable in law. For that reason, it will not be discussed further here; attention will instead return to the question of understanding.

The mere apprehension or existence of ill health might affect the patient's ability to comprehend what is being imparted to them. While some commentators suggest that patients who are 'nervous, anxious, or distracted' may be less able to understand information,[38] others argue that an alternative consequence is that the control and power potentially generated by the possession of information will in fact help to alleviate anxiety.[39] Avoiding feelings of helplessness or lack of control may, it is argued, result in the possibility 'that patients' depression may be lessened or even avoided if the health care system facilitates their retaining some sense of control, giving them some power in decisions, and helping them acquire some knowledge about their future experiences by providing them with relevant and appropriate information.'[40] Additionally, some research suggests that a moderate

[37] Kukla, Rebecca, 'How Do Patients Know?', *Hastings Center Report*, 37(5), 2007: 27–35, at p 29.

[38] Faden, R R, Beauchamp, T L, *A History and Theory of Informed Consent*, Oxford University Press, 1986, at p 248.

[39] For further discussion, see Buchanan, A, 'Medical Paternalism', *Philosophy & Public Affairs*, 7(4), 1978: 370–90.

[40] Schain, W S, 'Patients' Rights in Decision Making: The Case for Personalism Versus Paternalism in Health Care', *Cancer*, 46, 1980: 1035–41, at p 1035.

elevation of anxiety levels can enhance understanding, and not only might 'a measure of control over one's illness ... be therapeutic and reduce levels of anxiety and depression ... ',[41] it may also have important symbolic value. In any case, even if anxiety is the outcome of information sharing, this does not provide a robust reason for withholding it. It has been argued that '[t]he evidence that patients want information is overwhelming and the mere fact that the receipt of information causes distress does not mean that patients would prefer not to know.'[42]

While understanding the information that is disclosed may be essential to the patient's ability to use the information to make a valid choice, there are also questions to be asked and answered about how this can or should be evaluated in practice. Arguably, while understanding is the ideal, it is difficult to assess. Hutton and Ashcroft for example note that:

> ... there is an epistemological aspect: how can we know whether the patient has understood what they have been told, aside from her telling us? In practice, this means that if a patient gives her consent and signs the consent form, then she is taken to have given informed consent.[43]

The other side of this coin is that it might simplistically be assumed that a patient who *declines* to follow the considered and optimal recommendation of the doctor must have failed to understand what s/he has been told. This (not entirely uncommon) assumption is sometimes utilised to deny that any decision made was, in fact, autonomous and may even be taken as evidence that the person is not truly competent. In any case, even if we accept that understanding is important to the legal validity of the decision made, it is less than clear how we can either ensure it, or even identify its presence or absence. Comprehension is likely to be dependent 'both on the adequacy of the person's understanding of disclosed information and on the adequacy of the professional's grasp of the person's questions and responses ... '.[44] While achieving both is desirable, it is difficult to see how this could be translated into a legal rule.

Assessing the authenticity of understanding is therefore unlikely to be straightforward. At best, we can hope that doctors make real efforts to communicate effectively, that the system facilitates genuine discussion and debate and that patients are ultimately free to make their own decisions in

---

[41] Teff, H, *Reasonable Care: Legal Perspectives on the Doctor–Patient Relationship*, Oxford, Clarendon Press, 1994, at p xxvi.

[42] Parascandola, M, Hawkins, J, Danis, M, 'Patient Autonomy and the Challenge of Clinical Uncertainty', *Kennedy Institute of Ethics Journal*, 12(3), 2002: 245–64, at p 258.

[43] Hutton, J L, Ashcroft, R E, 'Some Popular Versions of Uninformed Consent', *Health Care Analysis*, 8, 2000: 41–52, at p 45.

[44] Faden, R R, Beauchamp, T L, *A History and Theory of Informed Consent*, Oxford University Press, 1986, at p 316.

the light of adequate information and following reflection as to their own interests as well as the clinical recommendations. Kukla argues that:

> In order to understand the relationship between autonomy and knowledge in the domain of health care, we need to see how laypeople's autonomy can be enhanced or compromised in the course of their attempts to collect, understand, and reason about medical information.[45]

However, because understanding and reasoning cannot be subjected to the kinds of tests that competence and quantity of information can be, I would argue that they are of a different order from the other concepts that are central to the process of obtaining or offering a valid consent. In effect, therefore, a more objective way to evaluate the quality of decisions might be to consider the extent to which they can be said to be free or uncoerced; something that is probably more susceptible of proof.

Voluntariness

It is axiomatic that a choice which is coerced or subject to undue influence is not autonomous, and this will be discussed from a legal perspective in more depth in the next chapter. At the theoretical or ethical level, it is self-evident that a person must be in a position that allows for a free decision to be taken; if not, then any purported choice made is scarcely valid (and unlikely, therefore, to be autonomous). Roberts, for example, says:

> Voluntarism is critical for the fulfilment of the idea of informed consent. From an ethical perspective, voluntarism is the principle that embodies respect for the person as a human being, as a self with a personal history and values, and as a moral agent with fundamental rights and privileges in our society.[46]

It also implies that the individual is free from external pressure to make a particular decision. Now, it might be argued that choices in healthcare are technically always influenced by external pressures – for example, the presence of ill health or anxiety and/or the imbalance of power between doctor and patient might work against true freedom of choice. While there is truth in this argument, of course, it is equally the case that we are virtually never free from external influences, yet we nonetheless generally expect and receive respect for our actions (and inactions) outside of the healthcare context. Totally free will, then, is aspirational rather than practical, and where the

[45] Kukla, R, 'How Do Patients Know?', *Hastings Center Report*, 37(5), 2007: 27–35, at p 27.
[46] Roberts, L W, 'Informed Consent and the Capacity for Voluntarism', *Am J Psychiatry*, 159, 2002: 705–12.

influences upon us are not sufficient to overwhelm our ability to decide in a self-governing manner the fact that we are affected by them is not enough to justify disputing either the reality or the value of the decision in question. While, ' ... both substantial understanding and the absence of substantially controlling influences are constituent aspects of autonomous decision making ... ',[47] the bar should not be set impossibly high. As important as understanding, nonetheless, is the requirement that 'actions, like the actions of autonomous states, are free of – that is, independent of, not governed by – controls on the person, especially controls presented by others that rob the person of self-directedness.'[48] As we will see in the next chapter, courts take the issue of voluntariness very seriously indeed.

A second emergent theme relates to the actual context within which decisions are made. Schwab, for example, notes that:

> Formal accounts of autonomy share a relatively abstract conceptual focus, including formal requirements that describe the necessary characteristics or capacities of particular people or particular decision making process. There is a lack of corollary attentiveness to the conditions under which these decisions are made. Such an oversight limits the usefulness of an account for fostering autonomous decisions in healthcare (as well as other areas).[49]

We have already touched briefly on context, and this does not require much further consideration here. However, one contextual issue is worthy of further discussion, and that is the relationship between doctor and patient itself. It is axiomatic that one of the influences most likely to affect the voluntariness of patients' decisions comes from healthcare professionals themselves. Selective omission or overstressing of certain information may be undetectable by the patient, but ultimately controlling of their decisions. While 'it is not common for doctors to minimize the potential benefits of therapy', it 'is equally not common for them to emphasize the risks.'[50] The physician's training and commitment to healing may 'lead to witting or unwitting manipulation of patient decisions so that they conform with the physician's judgments rather than with the patient's self-perceived needs.'[51] While Taylor suggests that ignorance of fact is autonomy-reducing only where it is

[47] Berg, J W, Appelbaum, P S, Lidz, C W, Parker, L S, *Informed Consent: Legal Theory and Clinical Practice* (2nd edn), Oxford University Press, 2001, at p 25.

[48] Faden, R R, Beauchamp, T L, *A History and Theory of Informed Consent*, Oxford University Press, 1986, at p 256.

[49] Schwab, A P, 'Formal and Effective Autonomy in Healthcare', *J Med Ethics*, 32, 2006: 575–79, at p 576.

[50] McLean, S A M, *A Patient's Right to Know: Information Disclosure, the Doctor and the Law*, Aldershot, Dartmouth, 1989, at p 9.

[51] Rosenberg, J A, Towers, B, 'The Practice of Empathy as a Prerequisite for Informed Consent', *Theoretical Medicine*, 7, 1986: 181–94, at p 182.

the result of a deliberate act or omission,[52] this is unlikely to be accepted by, or acceptable to, patients who want to make their own decisions. Whatever the reason for failing to provide information, it can be equally inhibiting of the capacity for autonomous decision-making.

Situationally, of course, it may be expecting too much that patients' decisions in the healthcare setting are anything like as obviously voluntary as, say, the decision to buy a particular car. Decisions about private purchases of consumer goods will very often not require understanding of potentially complex information, nor have the potential gravity of outcome that health-care decisions can have. Berg *et al*, for example, argue that 'the great weight placed on health and longevity is the greatest external threat to autonomy ... ',[53] since we all strive for optimal health and a high quality, long life. The decisions that we take about our healthcare, I would venture, are more important – and therefore potentially more stressful – than the choice between a Bentley and a Ford. Nonetheless, this does not imply that we cannot make autonomous choices; rather, it enhances the need for communication (including both information and clinical recommendations) which can at least assist in helping the patient to reach a conclusion with which they are comfortable.

Of course, the ability to make a truly self-determining choice may be affected by the sheer limitation of available options. Manson and O'Neill note that '[p]atients are typically asked to choose – or refuse – from a very limited menu (often a menu of one item) ... '.[54] Further, as Whitney and McCullough note, doctors make what they call 'silent decisions' all the time.[55] This may in part serve to explain the relative paucity of options to which Manson and O'Neill refer, but it is sometimes argued to be ethically justifiable because, '[i]n each case, the physician makes a decision, grounded in professional integrity, about the ethically justified course of action. The physician then decides not to disclose that decision, for reasons that include the promotion of patient well-being and utilitarian considerations such as saving time.'[56] In agreement, Charles, Whelan and Gafni note that, 'both time and funding constraints can act as disincentives for doctors to explore and respond to patients' preferences regarding the type of partnership they would prefer in the process of making decisions about treatment.'[57] Rosenberg

---

[52] Taylor, J S, 'Autonomy and Informed Consent: A Much Misunderstood Relationship', *The Journal of Value Inquiry*, 38, 2004: 383–91, at p 383.

[53] Berg, J W, Appelbaum, P S, Lidz, C W, Parker, L S, *Informed Consent: Legal Theory and Clinical Practice* (2nd edn), Oxford University Press, 2001, at p 24.

[54] Manson, N C, O'Neill, O, *Rethinking Informed Consent in Bioethics*, Cambridge University Press, 2007, at p 72.

[55] Whitney, S N, McCullough, L B, 'Physicians' Silent Decisions: Because Patient Autonomy Does Not Always Come First', *The American Journal of Bioethics*, 7(7), 2007: 33–38.

[56] Ibid., at p 36.

[57] Charles, C, Whelan, T, Gafni, A, 'What do we mean by partnership in making decisions about treatment?', *BMJ*, 319, 1999: 780–82, at p 782.

and Towers argue that 'the physician's overriding desire to heal may lead to witting or unwitting manipulation of patient decisions so that they conform with the physician's judgments rather than with the patient's self-perceived needs.'[58] Thus, they conclude that '[p]hysicians tend to manipulate or coerce their patients because they work within a biomedical paradigm of medicine that recognizes only cessation or amelioration of disease (a biologic entity) as a treatment goal.'[59] Thus, the actual voluntariness of the patient's decision is contingent on much more than just the usual pressures that affect our daily lives whether we are healthy or ill.

Whether for practical or other reasons, systemic failure to disclose adequate amounts of information to patients has, as we have already seen, generated enthusiasm for the language of human rights in the doctor/patient relationship. This language is commonplace in all situations where people strive for vindication of important values, and is no less relevant in healthcare. Nonetheless, some doubt its actual impact. While doctors are increasingly alert to the rights of their patients, some argue that there is little evidence that this recognition has significantly changed medical behaviour and that the anticipated growth of 'patient power' has not in fact occurred.[60] If so, then the language of rights has failed adequately to penetrate the doctor/patient relationship, despite its wide appeal. This will have an impact both on the informational and the voluntary elements of the patient's decision. Nonetheless, although some commentators disapprove of the use of this language in the doctor/patient relationship, sometimes seeing it as unhelpfully antagonistic, arguments from human rights can in fact serve to enhance rather than damage relationships. Knowles, for example, says that:

> Adopting the language of human rights means moving toward a more expansive understanding of the relationships between human health, medicine and the environment, socioeconomic and civil and political rights, and public health initiatives and human rights.[61]

So, whether or not it has had practical consequences so far, human rights language has the potential both to offer protection to patients and to situate health and healthcare in a broader and more meaningful context.

---

[58] Rosenberg, J A, Towers, B, 'The Practice of Empathy as a Prerequisite for Informed Consent', *Theoretical Medicine*, 7, 1986: 181–94, at p 182.

[59] Ibid., at p 191.

[60] Halpern, S A, 'Medical Authority and the Culture of Rights', *Journal of Health Politics, Policy and Law*, 29(4–5), August–October 2004: 835–52.

[61] Knowles, L P, 'The Lingua Franca of Human Rights and the Rise of a Global Bioethic', *Cambridge Quarterly of Healthcare Ethics*, 10, 2001: 253–63, at p 260.

Expression

Finally, it is obviously necessary that a person can express his or her decision. The Mental Capacity Act includes among those who are not competent someone who is unable 'to communicate his decision (whether by talking, using sign language or any other means).'[62] Much has been written on this subject, albeit more often in terms of *how* the decision is transmitted, even though the manner in which consent (or refusal) is expressed is of little, if any, relevance to the quality or autonomy of the decision. While it is common to obtain written consent for major medical procedures, it is unusual for this to be required for more routine interventions. Neither a signature nor a verbal acquiescence, however, is necessarily sufficient evidence that a valid consent has in fact been given. For example, obtaining a written consent may provide *prima facie* evidence that the patient agreed to what was proposed but it would still be open to the patient to argue, for example, that the signature was provided in the absence of adequate information thereby invalidating the apparent agreement. Buehler argues that 'the two (the process and its documentation) ought never be equated.'[63]

This is equally worth bearing in mind when consent is expressed in other ways. A verbal agreement to, or refusal of, treatment must also be the outcome of more than a ritualistic, formalistic event. It depends also on all of the elements, including information, that have been discussed above. At this point, albeit as something of an aside, I would like to take a pot shot at so called 'implied' consent. It is sometimes argued that, for example the patient who offers an arm to receive an injection without verbalising their consent has both *de facto* and *de jure* provided consent. However, this holds only if the patient does so in knowledge of the risks, benefits and alternatives available, save where that information has been rejected or refused. Coming full circle, then, a critical element in a valid consent is the provision of intelligible information based upon which the patient can make a free and uncoerced decision, irrespective of how that is expressed.

Consent and autonomy

The doctrine of consent, when its constituent elements are carefully considered, offers the patient the opportunity to act autonomously, subject of course to the problem that illness – actual or perceived – along with other external factors, may be said to make full autonomy impossible. Kalbian says that, 'an autonomous chooser is one who acts intentionally, with understanding, and without undue influence or control ... ', but reminds us that 'the health care context often compr[om]ises these very elements that

---

[62] s 3(1)(d).
[63] Buehler, D A, 'Informed Consent – Wishful Thinking?', *Journal of Bioethics*, 1983: 43–57, at p 48.

constitute the autonomous chooser.'[64] This argument, however, has already been discussed and to some extent discounted because *all* social situations have the potential to influence decisions but this does not necessarily mean that people are not, or should not be, free to make choices which are respected. Admittedly the context in which patient and doctor come into contact can put pressure on even the 'mature and intellectually competent' and can affect his or her ability to decide whether or not to accept treatment, which is 'part and parcel of his or her autonomy, of sovereignty over one's own body.'[65] However, this is not to say that we should abandon the attempt to maximise patient autonomy. Were we to do this, we might as well abandon it in every social interaction and for every personal decision. Even if a fully autonomous decision is ultimately unachievable, awareness about, and concern for, patient autonomy can have importance that goes beyond the informational question; for example, it may have a positive influence on the doctor/patient relationship itself by symbolising respect and enhancing trust.

The importance attributed to autonomy means that the historical dominance of medical paternalism has given way to recognition that patients both can and should play a more active role in their healthcare, with doctors acting as expert facilitators – even negotiators – rather than primary decision-makers. White and Zimbelman claim that over time '[t]he moral warrant for informed consent ceased to be understood as located exclusively in beneficence and was seen instead to be substantively derived from the principles of autonomy and respect for persons.'[66] As I have said elsewhere, adherence to these principles requires that doctors and patients communicate with each other, as this is 'a fundamental step in generating a therapeutic atmosphere capable of respecting the rights of the individual patient.'[67] In addition, there is evidence that engaging patients in their own healthcare decisions has both individual and collective benefits, 'since it has been associated with improved health outcomes and enables doctors to be more accountable to the public.'[68] Even if there are contextual and other limitations on the ability of patients to make fully autonomous decisions, practically and symbolically meeting their demands for respect for autonomy has important benefits.

[64] Kalbian, A H, 'Narrative *ART*ifice and Women's Agency', *Bioethics*, 19(2), 2005: 93–111, at p 98.

[65] Brazier, M, 'Patient autonomy and consent to treatment: the role of the law?', *Legal Studies*, 7(2), 1987: 169–93, at p 173.

[66] White, Becky C, Zimbelman, J, 'Abandoning Informed Consent: An Idea Whose Time Has Not Yet Come', *Journal of Medicine and Philosophy*, 33(5), 1998: 477–99, at p 478.

[67] McLean, S A M, *A Patient's Right to Know: Information Disclosure, the Doctor and the Law*, Aldershot, Dartmouth, 1989, at p 5.

[68] Say, R E, Thomson, R, 'The importance of patient preferences in treatment decisions – challenges for doctors', *BMJ*, 327, 2003: 542–45, at p 545.

Goldworth says that '[i]nformed consent is an expression of individual autonomy.'[69] Just as the process of seeking consent 'provides the opportunity for the patient ... to exercise autonomy with respect to the choice to be made ... ',[70] so too it positions him or her in a stronger position within the doctor/patient relationship than was historically the case. At both national and international level, consent is emphasised as the event (or process) which legitimises medical intervention; without it, save in exceptional circumstances such as emergencies, the provision of treatment is deemed illegitimate. Weindling says that '[i]nformed consent has been an axiom of post-World War II clinical research and practice ... ',[71] following the promulgation of the Nuremberg Code which resulted from the Nazi war crimes trials in 1947.[72] It has also become the central plank of the standard clinical encounter, and the 'moral commitment to autonomy and respect for persons finds a legal parallel in the commitment to self-determination.'[73]

While case law on consent to treatment has developed differently in national jurisdictions, the general principle that '[a]n intervention in the health field may only be carried out after the person concerned has given free and informed consent to it ... '[74] is generally accepted as a baseline, and is also enshrined in international declarations. The doctrine of consent is said to be 'founded upon the right to autonomy and the principle of (respect for) autonomy',[75] and was 'stimulated by the need to create a workable doctrine that can accommodate values that to many observers are in an irremediable state of conflict.'[76] The doctrine is designed to ensure that unwanted or un-chosen treatment cannot legitimately be provided, even if it is thought by the clinician to be in the interest of the patient to accept it.[77] Consent law theoretically at least prioritises autonomy over beneficence.

---

[69] Goldworth, A, 'Informed Consent in the Genetic Age', *Cambridge Q of Healthcare Ethics*, 8, 1999: 393–400, at p 393.

[70] Beasley, A D, Graber, G C, 'The Range of Autonomy: Informed Consent in Medicine', *Theoretical Medicine*, 5, 1984: 31–41, at p 33.

[71] Weindling, P, 'The Origins of Informed Consent: The International Scientific Commission on War Crimes, and the Nuremberg Code', *Bull Hist Med*, 75, 2001: 37–71, at p 37.

[72] See the case of *US v Brandt* available at http://nuremberg.law.harvard.edu/php/pflip.php?caseid= HLSL_NMT01&docnum=2&numpages=78&startpage=1&title=Closing+argument+for+the+United+ States+of+America.&color_setting=C (accessed on 10/10/2008).

[73] White, Becky C, Zimbelman, J, 'Abandoning Informed Consent: An Idea Whose Time Has Not Yet Come', *Journal of Medicine and Philosophy*, 33(5), 1998, at p 479.

[74] Convention for the Protection of Human Rights and Dignity of the Human Being with Regard to the Application of Biology and Medicine: Convention on Human Rights and Biomedicine, Oviedo, 4. IV.1997, Chapter II–Consent, Article 5.

[75] Maclean, A, 'Now You See It, Now You Don't: Consent And The Legal Protection of Autonomy', *Journal of Applied Philosophy*, 17(3), 2000) 277–88, at p 277.

[76] Berg, J W, Appelbaum, P S, Lidz, C W, Parker, L S, *Informed Consent: Legal Theory and Clinical Practice* (2nd edn), Oxford University Press, 2001, at p 3.

[77] For further discussion, see Hilliard, B, *The US Supreme Court and Medical Ethics*, St Paul, Mn, Paragon, 2004.

It might, therefore, reasonably be assumed that the growing acceptance of the value of autonomy has been paralleled and enhanced by an increased legal focus on a tightly drawn and coherent doctrine of consent, and there is some evidence that this is so. The consequence has, it is argued, been 'a shift from physician beneficence to patient autonomy as the guiding value of the doctor-patient relationship: the patient was to have an increasingly large, if not the ultimate, say in most treatment decisions.'[78] However, as we will see later, the workings and objectives of the legal doctrine are not identical to the purposes said to be served by, or expected of, the ethical concept of autonomy, nor is the legal approach necessarily engaged in, or even concerned with, the subtleties which are part of the ethical debate on autonomy and its meaning. Yet the content of the legal concept has a profound effect on the parameters of the doctor/patient relationship since it dictates the legal obligations that doctors owe to their patients.[79] By analogy, they also impact on – although they may not be sufficient fully to describe – the ethical obligations of doctors to their patients.

What consent rules may achieve – at least symbolically – is an acknowledgement of the importance of the rights of patients to express and act upon self-determined values and goals, provided that certain criteria, which are discussed further below, are met. Informed decision-making has come to be called 'an orthodoxy of bioethics',[80] from which is derived the authority of 'health care providers to perform certain specified medical interventions on the patient or patient's body.'[81] Moreover, some contend that the requirement to obtain consent 'empowers patients and allows them to take part in critical decision making, as long as they agree to play an active part and have the capacity to do so.'[82] The law therefore hands the responsibility for protecting and enhancing patient autonomy to the doctrine of consent.[83] As O'Neill says, '[w]hat passes for patient autonomy in medical practice is operationalised by practices of informed consent.'[84]

There is, therefore, widespread agreement that a great deal is expected of the doctrine of consent. First, it is expected to protect the patient from unwarranted interventions by insisting that the patient is involved in

---

[78] Baker, L A, '"I Think I Do": Another Perspective on Consent and the Law', *Law, Medicine & Health Care*, 16(3–4), Winter 1988: 256–60, at p 256.

[79] For discussion, see Berg, J W, Appelbaum, P S, Lidz, C W, Parker, L S, *Informed Consent: Legal Theory and Clinical Practice* (2nd edn), Oxford University Press, 2001.

[80] Ells, C, 'Foucault, Feminism, and Informed Choice', *Journal of Medical Humanities*, 24(3/4), Winter 2003: 213–28, at p 219.

[81] Ibid.

[82] Worthington, R, 'Clinical Issues on Consent: Some Philosophical Concerns', *J Med Ethics*, 28, 2002: 377–80, at p 377.

[83] Kukla, R, 'Conscientious Autonomy: Displacing Decisions in Health Care', *Hastings Center Report*, 35 (2), 2005: 34–44.

[84] O'Neill, O, *Autonomy and Trust in Bioethics*, Cambridge University Press, 2002, at p 38.

decision-making, consequent on the provision and reception of appropriate information. Even if it is true that the patient's right to consent has been only 'grudgingly acknowledged by medical professionals',[85] it places obligations on physicians to assist in the facilitation of an appropriate and maximally autonomous decision by their patient. Rosenberg and Towers suggest that this 'requires that the physician use both personhood and past experience to construct a state of mind that can mirror what the patient has communicated of himself or herself.'[86] Second, according to a number of commentators, the doctrine must also act as a substitute for, or measurement of, the necessary trust between patient and doctor. O'Neill notes that:

> Much is demanded of informed consent requirements if they are to substitute for forms of trust that are no longer achievable (or perhaps were never widely achieved, and still less widely warranted), and safeguard the interests of patients who find strangers at their bedside.[87]

As we have already seen, trust is important in the doctor/patient relationship not least because it 'assumes that promises will be kept, that relationships will be dependable and that neither sanctions not rewards are necessary for it to be exercised.'[88] This, Davies argues, is particularly relevant in the case of professionals 'because very often they cannot guarantee success. The most they can do is promise to do their best.'[89] Where doctors are uncertain about outcome, Parascandola, Hawkins and Danis suggest that this even means that 'physicians may need to be extra attentive in order to achieve the same result that they achieve more easily under less challenging conditions.'[90] Trust must be won, and uncertainty is a factor that must also be transmitted as part of the consent process. It seems unarguable that frank engagement with the patient can serve to make the physician worthy of trust, in that it demonstrates respect for the patient and his or her preferences.

If the function of the doctrine of consent is to be the legal protector of autonomy, the primary question must be to what extent can and/or does it achieve this goal? First, we must ask whether its impact on the practice of medicine has been to facilitate or encourage the possibility of autonomy-enhancing practice and behaviour. Piper, for example, argues that it is only a 'meaningful, ethical concept' if it 'can be realized and promoted within the

[85] Waller, Bruce, N, 'The Psychological Structure of Patient Autonomy', *Cambridge Quarterly of Healthcare Ethics*, 11, 2002: 257–65, at p 257.

[86] Rosenberg, J A, Towers, B, 'The Practice of Empathy as a Prerequisite for Informed Consent', *Theoretical Medicine*, 7, 1986, at p 184.

[87] O'Neill, O, *Autonomy and Trust in Bioethics*, Cambridge University Press, 2002, at p 39.

[88] Davies, M, *Medical Self-Regulation: Crisis and Change*, Aldershot, Ashgate, 2007, at p 89.

[89] Ibid., at p 90.

[90] Parascandola, M, Hawkins, J, Danis, M, 'Patient Autonomy and the Challenge of Clinical Uncertainty', *Kennedy Institute of Ethics Journal*, 12(3), 2002: 245–64, at pp 246–47.

boundaries of good medical practice … '.[91] Its actual impact on medical practice is disputed, however. For some, the need to obtain informed consent is merely a legalistic intrusion into the good practice of medicine. For others, by seemingly encouraging the separation of patient and doctor the doctrine can affect the dynamic between them, threatening the mutuality of the enterprise.[92]

At one level, then, the doctrine of consent could be seen as confrontational rather than facilitating. By reshaping the doctor/patient relationship, and theoretically placing the patient in a potentially antagonistic position vis-à-vis medical practitioners and their advice, it might be seen as counter-productive – at least in terms of optimal clinical outcome. On the other hand, it has been said that '[i]nformed consent can lead to better patient-physician relationships, better physician understanding of the patient's illness, and better patient adherence to treatment recommendations.'[93] But can, or does, it result in truly autonomous decisions being made?

Making autonomous decisions

While it is possible that the mechanics and processes of obtaining a valid consent do serve a purpose in terms of the protection of autonomy, it remains to be seen whether or not they can also ensure that choices made are *in fact* autonomous, which presumably is the ultimate goal. Ensuring that patients have authorised clinical interventions may at face value seem to make the link between autonomous decisions and the consent doctrine, but is this the reality? O'Neill notes that '[b]y insisting on the importance of informed consent we *make it possible* for individuals to choose autonomously, however that is to be construed. But we in no way guarantee or require that they do so.'[94] While consent rules may serve the purpose of deflecting the urge to paternalism, the mere fact that the requirements for consent are met does not answer the question whether or not specific decisions made by a patient 'reflect what a person truly values, wants, or believes … '.[95] If the decision as well as the person is to be autonomous it should reflect the individual's life priorities and values.

---

[91] Piper, A, 'Truce on the Battlefield: A Proposal for a Different Approach to Medical informed Consent', *The Journal of Law, Medicine & Ethics*, 22(4), Winter 1994: 301–13, at p 307.

[92] For discussion, see Ackerman, T F, 'Medical Ethics and the Two Dogmas of Liberalism', *Theoretical Medicine*, 5, 1984: 69–81.

[93] Veerapen, R J, 'Informed Consent: Physician Inexperience is a Material Risk for Patients', *Journal of Law, Medicine & Ethics*, Genetics and Group Rights, Fall 2007: 478–85, at p 478.

[94] O'Neill, O, *Autonomy and Trust in Bioethics*, Cambridge University Press, 2002, at p 2.

[95] Dodds, S, 'Choice and Control in Feminist Bioethics', in MacKenzie, C, Stoljar, N (eds), *Relational Autonomy: Feminist Perspectives on Autonomy, Agency and the Social Self*, New York, Oxford University Press, 2000, 213–35, at p 217.

If otherwise autonomous individuals make decisions which are based on misunderstandings or on overt or covert denial of choice resulting from withholding of information that *would* have been important to that particular patient or would result in a choice which is in ultimate (albeit possibly unintentional) contradiction of their values, the consequences are potentially extremely serious. The presence of any or all of these limitations on autonomous choice can prevent the making of decisions that are truly reflective of the 'self-governance' that is said to be central to the value of autonomy.[96] Just making a decision is not necessarily an exercise of autonomy. Wilson says, ' ... it is clear that we cannot let just any old choice count as autonomous if we are going to claim that all autonomous choices are intrinsically worthy of respect.'[97] Indeed, within the medical profession itself it has been recognised that '[e]thically it is important to be sure that the choices people make when signing a consent form really do reflect their settled will.'[98]

Of course, we could challenge this. It could for example be argued that it is sufficient that people are given the *opportunity* to make an autonomous decision even if in the long run it turns out not to have been the one they would have made had it been fully autonomous. Expecting a truly autonomous choice might, in fact, prove to be too demanding a standard to set, thereby precluding many decisions from being respected. Beasley and Graber, for example, say:

> To be one hundred percent autonomous ... would require one to have a fully articulated set of life goals that is totally coherent and comprehensive and to make *all* life-decisions on the basis of deliberation by reference to these goals. This leaves no room at all, for example, for action on the basis of the whims of the moment. It is clear that this is an impossible goal in practice – and, indeed, there might be questions about whether so fully rational an approach to life is really desirable, in the final analysis.[99]

Faden and Beauchamp appear to agree with this, saying that the apparent need to 'chain informed consent to *fully or completely* autonomous decision-making stacks the deck of the argument and strips informed consent of any meaningful place in the practical world, where people's actions are rarely, if ever, fully autonomous.'[100] Thus, we may need to inquire whether or not we

[96] Goldworth, A, 'Informed Consent in the Genetic Age', *Cambridge Q of Healthcare Ethics*, 8, 1999: 393–400.

[97] Wilson, J, 'Is Respect for Autonomy Defensible?', *J Med Ethics*, 33, 2007: 353–56, at p 354.

[98] RCOG Ethics Committee Position Paper 2: November 2002, *Patient and Doctor Autonomy within Obstetrics & Gynaecology*, available at http://www.rcog.org.uk/resources/Public/doc/Ethics_patient_autonomy.doc (accessed on 24/10/2007), transcript, p 3.

[99] Beasley, A D, Graber, G C, 'The Range of Autonomy: Informed Consent in Medicine', *Theoretical Medicine*, 5, 1984: 31–41, at p 33.

[100] Faden, R R, Beauchamp, T L, *A History and Theory of Informed Consent*, Oxford University Press, 1986, at p 240.

are asking for standards of autonomy, or autonomous decision-making, in healthcare that we do not, and never would, expect in other areas of life. True, the decisions we make about our healthcare are often of singular importance, but so too are many of the other decisions we make which are seldom – if ever – subject to the same level or kind of scrutiny.

Setting standards for autonomy in healthcare that are too high might not only make it practically impossible to regard *any* decision as truly autonomous (opening the door wide to the reintroduction of paternalism), but could also make it easier to justify failure to share the information which is central to the patient's sense of self – of control (however ephemeral) over his or her own destiny – because, tested against this standard, autonomous decisions would never be possible. These concerns militate against setting the bar too high. If the doctrine of consent has any value in offering 'the opportunity for the patients ... to exercise autonomy ... ',[101] then it must be more than a merely symbolic one, even if there are inherent problems in identifying a truly autonomous decision. Such, as they say, is life – inside and outside of medicine and healthcare. Few decisions are totally free, as both relational and individualistic accounts of autonomy would concede. We are all influenced by circumstances irrespective of our preferred view of what it means to be autonomous and of what autonomous decisions consist. The question then is not *whether* we are influenced by external considerations but rather what is the *extent* of that influence?

Moreover, the critique that denies the possibility of patients ever making an autonomous decision arguably over-emphasises the role played by clinical information, by assuming that this is the most significant element in patients' decision-making. In other words, the fact that the patient can never be as 'educated' as the physician, nor will they necessarily understand the full ramifications of their choices in a clinical sense,[102] does not mean that their decisions are non-autonomous. As we have said, patients are able – uniquely so – to balance personal values and interests with clinical considerations. Moreover, since patients can competently reject the provision of information and still make a legally valid decision, it must be the case that their interests can be advanced even in the absence of complete understanding of the clinical information. Indeed, in Faden and Beauchamp's research, even though patients felt that being given clinically relevant information had increased their decision-making confidence, it was not the primary basis for the choices they made. As many as 93% of the patients in their study 'reported deciding on a treatment option even before hearing the disclosure.'[103] Thus, while

---

[101] Beasley, A D, Graber, G C, 'The Range of Autonomy: Informed Consent in Medicine', *Theoretical Medicine*, 5, 1984: 31–41, at p 33.

[102] For an interesting further discussion of these points, see Hutton, J L, Ashcroft, R E, 'Some Popular Versions of Uninformed Consent', *Health Care Analysis*, 8, 2000: 41–52.

[103] Faden, R R, Beauchamp, T L, 'Decision-Making and Informed Consent: A Study of the Impact of Disclosed Information', *Social Indicators Research*, 7, 1980: 313–36, at p 327.

clinical information is obviously relevant, it is not necessarily the single most important consideration when making personally authentic decisions. Rather, the provision of information and efforts to render it intelligible are symbolic as much as practical routes to enhancing the quality of the doctor/ patient relationship and facilitating the making of a genuinely autonomous decision.

Conclusion

The assessment that a person is legally competent, implying that s/he is autonomous and therefore that his or her decisions are worthy of respect, does not in and of itself mean that the ensuing decision will be an autonomous one – which might arguably be the most important consideration. After all, it might be asked, what is the point of valuing (and agonising over) autonomy if it is just a sham – a philosophical concept that has no bearing on the real world? More than a basic evaluation of competence seems necessary to decide whether or not a competent person has acted autonomously. In an ideal world it is likely that everyone would both agree with this and strive to achieve it, but is it actually attainable?

Despite the difficulties of fully satisfying the various elements of consent, it is still commonly claimed both to facilitate and to respect the expression of patient autonomy. By demanding the provision of information, possibly some level of understanding and legal competence to reach autonomous, uncoerced decisions, the doctrine of consent claims to prioritise respect for patient autonomy, and to position it as the dominant value in law as in bioethics. This, it is said, shows respect for patients' rights – a concept that has grown exponentially in importance in the last decades. Thus, '[i]ncreased recognition and respect for patients' rights and insistence on the ethical importance of securing their consent are now viewed as standard and obligatory ways of securing respect for patients' autonomy.'[104] However it must be asked what kind of autonomy is protected by the doctrine of consent and what is the extent of any protection offered?

The emphasis of the consent doctrine is said to be very much on the individual. Even though it is accepted that the individual is in a relationship with the doctor and others, the aim of the law of consent is to ensure adherence to its constituent requirements of competence, information, voluntariness and expression, on the assumption that doing this enables an autonomous decision to be made. A decision made by a competent person is supposed to be respected regardless of its impact on others unless demonstrable harm is the result. For example, respect for the decision of Mr C to reject treatment that his doctors believed to be life-saving could have been

---

[104] O'Neill, O, *Autonomy and Trust in Bioethics*, Cambridge University Press, 2002, at p 2.

justified in part because it affected only (or primarily) him, given that he had satisfied the other tests as to competence, voluntariness and understanding.[105] However, this was not in fact the justification used – the effect of his decision on others was not considered; rather, once the required elements were established he was free to make whatever choice he wished even if it was likely to lead to his death. In other words, a highly individualistic model of autonomy was applied even when the outcome could have been incredibly serious.

Manson and O'Neill, however, identify what they call 'two levels of distortion' in the way consent is conceptualised in relation to autonomy.[106] The first, they say is the 'assumption that informed consent is justified as a means to securing autonomy.'[107] From their perspective:

> The standard *justification* of informed consent stresses the *conveyance or transfer of information* (*from* researcher or clinician, *to* research subject or patient), sees this information as material for individual decision-making, and insists that individual decision-making (autonomous choice) *ought* to be respected. This line of thinking distorts informed consent by downplaying or hiding both the complexity of informed consent transactions and the numerous purposes they serve.[108]

In other words, the kind of 'autonomy' which is protected by the primacy given to information disclosure is essentially empty; devoid of ethical merit or content. Of course, Manson and O'Neill's view depends on a particular account of autonomy that need not be accepted, but it has undoubtedly been influential. And, of course, there are other critiques of the consent doctrine, one of which arises from the apparent differences between 'the goals highlighted by the ethical theories ... and the practical effects of the current system.'[109] For some, even if primarily symbolic, it is the focus on the individual and his/her rights that in and of itself supplies the ethical content of the consent doctrine as it manifests itself in law. Again, this approximates most closely to the individualistic approach to autonomy, which 'makes sense of the doctrine of informed consent in terms of the patient's civil rights.'[110] This allows the patient to decide – in the absence of paternalism – which is a benefit 'because the physician's values have no place in the actual

---

[105] *Re C (adult: refusal of medical treatment)* (1993) 15 BMLR 77.

[106] Manson, N C, O'Neill, O, *Rethinking Informed Consent in Bioethics,* Cambridge University Press, 2007, at p 34.

[107] Ibid.

[108] Ibid., at p 34.

[109] Berg, J W, Appelbaum, P S, Lidz, C W, Parker, L S, *Informed Consent: Legal Theory and Clinical Practice* (2nd edn), Oxford University Press, 2001, at p 147.

[110] Kuczewski, M and McCruden, P J, 'Informed Consent: Does it Take a Village? The Problem of Culture and Truth Telling', *Cambridge Q of Healthcare Ethics,* 10, 2001: 34–46, at p 36.

treatment decision.'[111] This approach squares more closely than does that of Manson and O'Neill with the assumption that the value of the consent doctrine lies in its respect for self-governing, self-determining and self-regarding decisions. However, we still have to resolve the underlying conundrum of how to translate autonomy from aspiration into decisional reality. As Schwab has said:

> Even if we suppose that a desire is formally autonomous, because every decision is subject to the biases of human decision making, some or many of people's choices will not reflect their autonomously formed desires. The desire may be formally autonomous, but the decisions may not reflect the desire.'[112]

This assertion is clearly at odds with an approach that evaluates decisions from the fundamental presumption that 'human beings have a distinctive capacity for making choices in light of personal values and goals ... ',[113] which simply because of that capacity ought to be respected. Other arguments downplay the importance of autonomy, claiming that it 'ought not ... be taken as a starting point or absolute ordering principle in medicine. Rather, it should be seen as part of the goal of treatment, one of the goods of the patient, to be promoted but not to the total exclusion of other goods.'[114] This would rearrange the balance between autonomy and other values, such as beneficence, and would in addition lend support to the place of informed persuasion. Kelley, for example, says that in medicine it is 'perfectly compatible' with the doctrine of consent 'for a physician to try to persuade a patient by pointing out the possibly dire consequences of the patient's irresponsible behaviour.'[115] This is unproblematic, of course, so long as this persuasion does not cross the line that demarcates professional advice from undue influence.

No one doubts that physicians have a complicated role to fulfil. On the one hand, they are trained to provide treatment when there is hope of success; on the other, they are increasingly encouraged to prioritise the autonomy of their patients. There is, therefore, a need to find a balance between 'a physician's obligation to protect the patient's health through beneficence and the physician's obligation to respect the patients' autonomy.'[116] This, however,

---

[111] Ibid., at p 36.

[112] Schwab, A P, 'Formal and Effective Autonomy in Healthcare', *J Med Ethics*; 32, 2006: 575–79, at p 577.

[113] Morreim, H, 'Three Concepts of Patient Competence', *Theoretical Medicine*, 4, 1983: 231–51, at p 232.

[114] Pellegrino, E D, Thomasma, D C, 'The Conflict Between Autonomy and Beneficence in Medical Ethics: Proposal for a Resolution', *Journal of Contemporary Health Law and Policy*, 3(23), 1987: 23–46, at p 31.

[115] Kelley, M, 'Limits on Patient Responsibility', *Journal of Medicine and Philosophy*, 30, 2005: 189–206, at p 194.

[116] King, J S, Moulton, B W, 'Rethinking Informed Consent: The Case for Shared Medical Decision-Making', *American Journal of Law & Medicine*, 32, 2006: 429–501, at p 435.

is not a straightforward calculation, and it may be seen as a hindrance to good medical practice. For example, it has been said that:

> ... the triumph of patient autonomy raised a new set of ethical quandaries. Many clinicians fear that strict observance of patient autonomy may override good medical judgment, encourage moral detachment on the part of the physician, and even work against the patient's best interests.[117]

Those clinicians who are concerned about this may be said to repeat the mistake of assuming that what is right for the patient, what their interests are, is essentially correlative to 'best *medical* interests', a position that has already been criticised. Further, it is surely debatable whether the result of the 'triumph' of autonomy would necessarily be to encourage the 'moral detachment' of the doctor. It is equally plausible that by paying attention to the individual's personal interests clinicians may become closer to their patients and correspondingly seen as more worthy of trust, thereby potentially facilitating the making of a truly autonomous decision by the patient.

From a theoretical perspective, achieving the ideal of autonomy – or more accurately, recognising a truly autonomous decision – is obviously not uncomplicated. From the legal perspective, it is arguably even more difficult. In particular, the need to elaborate a normative formula that will ensure consistency of application, and the certainty which people can legitimately expect of the law, may make it difficult to accommodate the subtleties and nuances of the ethical debate, or to inquire into the autonomy quotient of the decision. Of course, this may be no bad thing. Kristinsson, for example, suggests that ' ... the preoccupation with self-determination might be nothing more than a widespread and fashionable obsession, lacking in rational justification.'[118] On the other hand, patients (and others) may disagree. The growth of the patients' rights movement has seen attention focused firmly on the individual's right to determine his or her own healthcare decisions, and it seems unlikely that this is merely a whim. Nonetheless, a parallel movement has begun to develop in some quarters that seems to be little more than an attempt to rehabilitate the notion of beneficence (even paternalism) as a complementary or even supererogatory principle. Pellegrino and Thomasma describe beneficence as a 'principle that prompts physicians to cite their moral commitments and personal support for patients beyond

---

[117] Bulger, R E, Bobby, E M, Fineberg, H V (eds), *Society's Choices: Social and Ethical Decision Making in Biomedicine*, Committee on the Social and Ethical Impacts of Developments in Biomedicine, Division of Health Sciences Policy, Institute of Medicine, National Academy Press, Washington, DC, 1995, at p 35.

[118] Kristinsson, S, 'Autonomy and Informed Consent: A Mistaken Association?', *Medicine, Health Care and Philosophy*, 10, 2007:253–64, at p 255.

just respecting their rights.'[119] When not equated with paternalism – as it sometimes is – this is of course a beneficial component of the doctor/patient relationship but there is no reason why it should be placed in opposition to respect for autonomy. Indeed, it can function as a complement to autonomy – not its enemy.

In evaluating how the law manages consent in practice, it will be necessary to bear in mind three critical issues that have emerged from the discussion so far. First, autonomy could simply be described as the ability to make decisions, based on adequate information. Second, the growing view that autonomy is or should be a more relational concept needs to be considered as do the consequences of adopting this position. If, as some communitarian and feminist arguments would advocate, decision-making should be influenced by other-regarding considerations, how – and to what extent, if at all – can the formulae of the law reflect this? Finally, can or should the law accommodate the concept of beneficence in its consideration of protecting autonomy rights? In an attempt to consider these questions, the next chapter will analyse the most important cases on consent.

This will require the unpicking of a number of judicial statements, as judges are not always clear on the ethical bases for their decisions. As Coggon puts it:

> It is rare for a judge to provide an explicit, philosophical investigation of autonomy. This is both unsurprising and understandable. Perhaps it is even desirable. Many bioethicists seem to have made something of a religion of autonomy, and were judges to follow too assiduously a specific doctrinal approach, they may well be open to the sort of criticism that they are employed to judge the law and not questions of ethics. On the other hand, when judges make claims regarding the moral neutrality of their judgements, it is not hard in some circumstances to be rather cynical of their alleged capacity to divorce matters of ethical theory from matters of legal theory.[120]

By scrutinising the reasons – where identifiable – for the way in which consent laws have developed, and by interrogating judicial decisions, it may be possible to clarify what the law actually takes autonomy to mean, and the extent to which, if at all, it takes account of the rich ethical debate surrounding its meaning and role. Moreover, it should be possible to discover whether or not the consent doctrine in law is truly concerned with *any*

---

[119] Pellegrino, E D, Thomasma, D C, 'The Conflict Between Autonomy and Beneficence in Medical Ethics: Proposal for a Resolution', *Journal of Contemporary Health Law and Policy*, 3(23), 1987: 23–46, at p 45.

[120] Coggon, J, 'Varied and Principled Understandings of Autonomy in English Law: Justifiable Inconsistency or Blinkered Moralism?', *Health Care Anal*, 15, 2007: 235–55, at p 236.

identifiable concept of autonomy; does it indeed amount to the legal side of the ethical coin as is so often claimed? Does the law of consent really respect or reflect patient autonomy? At least one commentator is unconvinced, saying that ' ... the conflation of autonomy with consent robs the former of much of its meaning and strips it of much of its ethical credibility.'[121] We will see.

---

[121] Laurie, G, *Genetic Privacy: A Challenge to Medico-Legal Norms*, Cambridge University Press, 2002, at p 184.

Chapter 3

Consent, autonomy and the law

Law is essentially a set of rules; courts are not necessarily the ideal place for an ethical battleground. This is not to say that law never engages with complex and divisive ethical issues – obviously it often has to – but rather that it needs an appropriate framework and workable guidelines in order to function with internal logic and consistency. This generally means that courts operate on the basis of adherence to principle and/or precedent. Since courts are arranged in hierarchies, previous decisions can carry considerable – sometimes definitive – weight. When confronted with new situations, judges will either try to identify precedent to guide them or, as is particularly true in Scotland whose law owes much to its Roman Law heritage, will apply long established principles to novel problems. In terms of consent to treatment, however, there is – in the case of competent adults at least[1] – no difference between the various United Kingdom jurisdictions. Each starts with the presumption that the competent adult has a right to make his or her own healthcare decisions, and even to reject optimal medical advice. This, as we have seen, is said both to derive from and to reflect the law's declared prioritisation of autonomy.

It has emerged from our previous discussion, however, that while it seems relatively easy to identify the autonomous person, it is much less easy to decide whether or not a decision is truly autonomous. Allmark, for example, says that while being autonomous is a *sine qua non* of an autonomous act, on the other hand 'it is not always the case that an act performed by such an agent is autonomous.'[2] The ability to make an autonomous choice, however, will in large part hinge on fulfilling the criteria identified in the previous chapter – such as information disclosure and voluntariness.[3] Without the

---

[1] For the position in respect of children, see Elliston, S, *The Best Interests of the Child in Healthcare*, Routledge/Cavendish, 2007.

[2] Allmark, Peter, 'An Aristotelian Account of Autonomy', *The Journal of Value Inquiry*, 42, 2008:41–53, at p 43.

[3] For further discussion, see Marta, J, 'Whose Consent Is It Anyway? A Poststructuralist Framing of the Person in Medical Decision-Making', *Theoretical Medicine and Bioethics*, 19, 1998: 353–70.

luxury of space and time for academic debate, the courts must nonetheless reach a decision that at least *prima facie* satisfies the law's commitment to respect for autonomy. This the law does through the requirement to obtain consent before medical treatment can be provided. Either unaware of, or perhaps functionally unable to address, the concerns already canvassed about the real value of consent in respecting truly autonomous choice, courts have over the years fashioned their own position which will be considered in the remainder of this chapter.

The primary aim of this discussion is to work out what criteria are used by the law to identify the validity of consent itself, and – more importantly – to evaluate whether or not the concept of consent as developed in law bears any relationship to the concept of autonomy. However, of course, it must be recognised immediately that there could well be some divergence between the goal(s) served on the one hand by the concept of respecting autonomy and on the other by those of the judiciary in dispensing 'justice' using the law of consent to treatment. Moreover, from the perspective of the aggrieved patient, while disrespecting his or her autonomy is an important issue, there may be additional purposes served by raising an action based on an allegedly flawed consent – for example, obtaining compensation, naming and shaming the doctor, receiving an apology or simply trying to ensure that lessons are learned for the future. Since these are also legitimate aims, it is obviously important that the action available to the aggrieved patient is appropriate to meeting their interests or needs. As different legal actions require different kinds of proof, it is worth briefly considering this question as it can play a significant part in shaping – even circumscribing – the law's ability to protect the autonomy of the patient.

Assault/battery or negligence?

Simply put, any touching without consent amounts to battery, trespass or assault. In some cases, unconsented touching might even attract criminal liability and technically, even within the context of healthcare, criminal prosecution is possible. However, this is extremely rare in medicine and would require the elements of a criminal offence – such as the requisite *mens rea* – to be both present and established to the satisfaction of the court. Although it is clear that some medical behaviour – for example, surgery – could, in another context, and without the beneficent intentions normally attributed to the doctor, satisfy the criminal threshold, the special circumstances of healthcare render it non-criminal if consented to. As Lord Templeman said in the case of *R v Brown*, '[s]urgery involves intentional violence resulting in actual or sometimes serious bodily harm but surgery is a lawful activity.'[4] It is not just the consent that makes surgery non-criminal, since

---

[4] [1993] 2 All ER 75, at p 79.

consent to a crime does not generally exculpate the perpetrator,[5] it is also the fact that surgery is *prima facie* not a crime in and of itself. In the same case, for example, Lord Mustill (dissenting) commented that in some cases the 'reason why the perpetrator of the harm is not liable is not because of the recipient's consent, but because the perpetrator has acted in a situation where the consent of the recipient forms one, but only one, of the elements which make the act legitimate.'[6] Although there have been occasional cases in which the criminal liability of a physician has been established,[7] they are so insignificant numerically as to need no further consideration here.

It is non-criminal (civil) actions which are generally regarded as appropriate where it is alleged that there has been an unconsented touching in medicine. These can be found in the law of battery, trespass to the person (in Scotland, assault), or in the tort or delict of negligence. Negligence will be considered later, but for the moment it is actions based in assault that will be discussed. Schultz points out that there are distinct advantages for the aggrieved individual in being able to pursue their claim using the concept of battery or assault,[8] not least that this kind of action 'establishes an uncompromising baseline of protection for patients' self-determination.'[9] In addition, there need be no actual harm caused by the act; what matters is the violation of the person's bodily integrity (or autonomy). On the other hand, not every medical act involves the 'touching' which would be necessary to sustain an action based on battery/assault – the example most commonly given to illustrate this point is the prescription of therapeutic drugs. In addition, this kind of action 'does not, and cannot, cover cases where the failure to have proper regard for the right [of the patient to make the decision] involves the provision of no therapy, or failure to disclose therapeutic alternatives.'[10] There are also policy reasons which militate against the use of battery or assault-based actions against healthcare professionals, not least that – with only very rare exceptions – the doctor's intention (even if misguided) is beneficent. Labelling doctors as criminals is also something that courts are reluctant to do, for reasons which are obvious. Doctors will usually treat their patients without criminal intent and with the aim of benefiting them.

It is, therefore, now accepted in most jurisdictions that the appropriate action where it is alleged that patients' 'right to know' has been infringed and the validity of the choice taken is in doubt is based in negligence rather

---

[5] See, for example, *R v Donovan* [1934] 2 KB 498.

[6] Ibid., at p 103.

[7] *R v Cox* (1992) 12 BMLR 38.

[8] Schultz, M M, 'From Informed Consent to Patient Choice: A New Protected Interest', *The Yale Law Journal*, 95(2), December 1985: 219–99.

[9] Ibid., at p 224.

[10] McLean, S A M, *A Patient's Right to Know: Information Disclosure, the Doctor and the Law*, Aldershot, Dartmouth, 1989, at p 167.

than battery or assault. In the United Kingdom, this was clarified in the case of *Chatterton v Gerson* where the judge said:

> I think justice requires that in order to vitiate the reality of consent [for an assault case] there must be a greater failure of communication between doctor and patient than that involved in a breach of duty if the claim is based on negligence.[11]

The standard of information disclosure required in a negligence action, therefore, is less strict than that required in assault analysis, potentially making it more difficult for patients to succeed in proving their allegations. This shift from assault to negligence has also occurred in other jurisdictions. In the United States, for example, this was made clear in cases such as *Cobbs v Grant*,[12] leading to a situation where the evaluation of patients' claims is inseparable from the duties of the doctor. This immediately shifts the focus away from patient's interests (or rights) and towards what is professionally acceptable behaviour (albeit ultimately subject to legal control and scrutiny). While '[t]he patient's interest in autonomy is conceded basic protection under battery rules ... ',[13] under negligence rules 'the autonomy interest tends to be seen as either mainly symbolic or highly aberrational ... or as largely redundant to protections under competence-regulating negligence rules ... '.[14]

There are obvious consequences to this. Whereas unconsented-to touching is all that needs to be shown in battery/assault analysis, when the patient must raise the action in negligence 'the plaintiff must prove not only the breach of duty to inform but that had the duty not been broken she would not have chosen to have the operation.'[15] Hidden in this analysis is what has probably been one of the most contentious questions; that is, how is the patient to establish breach of duty unless the duty itself is clearly and coherently defined in law? While the second question – that of causation – can also be highly problematic to establish, the preliminary question rests on establishing just what the doctor's duty to the patient actually is. In legal discourse, the answer to this question has generally focused on the extent of the disclosure required to make a consent 'real'; not necessarily from the patient's perspective, but from a position with which the law, as an instrument of social policy, is comfortable. Thus, not only is the focus on autonomy which is said to underpin the law watered down by the move from assault to negligence, it is further affected by the imperative that judges accommodate policy and other considerations. Although, battery analysis may seem to be

---

[11]   (1980) 1 BMLR 80, per Bristow, J, at p 89.

[12]   8 Cal 3d 229 (1972).

[13]   Schultz, M M, 'From Informed Consent to Patient Choice: A New Protected Interest', *The Yale Law Journal*, 95(2), December 1985: 219–99, at p 229.

[14]   Ibid.

[15]   *Chatterton v Gerson* (1980) 1 BMLR 80, per Bristow, J, at p 89.

preferable from the patient's perspective (at least in some cases), Skegg says that, 'there is no likelihood of the tort of battery playing more than a very minor role in matters of "informed consent".'[16]

Information (unless refused) is, of course, central to both consent and to the making of an autonomous decision. Harris and Keywood describe the function of the law in this area as twofold. First, 'it provides guidance to doctors concerning the lawful discharge of their professional obligations to the patient.'[17] It allows – in theory at least – doctors to know what they need to tell patients while seeking their consent to treatment. The second function is said to be that 'it acts to ensure that patients receive sufficient information to enable them to exercise informed choices about their care.'[18] In theory, this is true, but there is a need to explore *how* the law actually works to see whether it is also the case in reality.

Consent to treatment: the cases

As we have seen, except where the patient chooses *not* to receive it, in order to make a valid or autonomous choice the patient has to be provided with sufficient information to enable them to decide. The doctor's corresponding obligation to disclose derives from the very fact of the consultation; patients seek out medical advice because they do not have clinical expertise (or they do not have the relevant clinical knowledge). Their ability to make an autonomous decision, therefore, rests firmly on the extent to which they are made aware of the consequences of their choice. In what follows, some of the most important cases on this issue will be considered.

The doctor's general duty to his or her patients was first described in the United Kingdom in modern times in the Scottish case of *Hunter v Hanley*.[19] In this case, it was noted that '[i]n the realm of diagnosis and treatment there is ample scope for genuine difference of opinion … '.[20] Accepting this, essentially uncontroversial, assertion led the judge in that case to conclude that 'one man clearly is not negligent merely because his conclusion differs from that of other professional men … '.[21] This test was restated, and unarguably strengthened, in the English case of *Bolam v Friern Hospital Management Committee*,[22] which was heard a couple of years later. In his judgement in this case, McNair, J. reformulated and recast the *Hunter* test in this way:

[16] Skegg, P D G, 'English Medical Law and 'Informed Consent': An Antipodean Assessment and Alternative', *Medical Law Review*, 7, summer 1999: 135–65, at p 143.
[17] Harris, J, Keywood, K, 'Ignorance, Information and Autonomy', *Theoretical Medicine*, 22, 2001: 415–36, at p 421.
[18] Ibid.
[19] 1955 SC 200.
[20] Ibid., at p 217.
[21] Ibid.
[22] (1957) 1 BMLR 1.

' ... a doctor is not guilty of negligence if he has acted in accordance with a practice accepted as proper by a responsible body of medical men (*sic*) skilled in that particular art.'[23] Perhaps most importantly, McNair opened a defence to doctors that was to shape many of the cases that followed; namely, that negligence cannot be established if there is a body of responsible medical opinion that agrees with the doctor in question, even if there are many more who would not agree, and even if the number of doctors making up this body of opinion is vanishingly small.[24] The *Bolam* test was accepted unequivocally in a number of subsequent cases, such as *Maynard v West Midlands RHA*,[25] where Lord Scarman said:

> It is not enough to show that there is a body of competent professional opinion which considers that theirs was a wrong decision if there also exists a body of professional opinion, equally competent, which supports the decision as reasonable in the circumstances.[26]

While there may be a certain sense in clinical (operational) matters – which are beyond the comprehension of 'mere' judges – being decided by reference to what other experts believe to be acceptable (even if not optimal) behaviour, it might reasonably be assumed that issues which require not the exercise of clinical expertise, but rather only transmission of the knowledge generated by it, would be subject to a different test. Any faint hope that *Bolam* might be circumvented or discredited in information disclosure cases was, however, effectively dashed in what became the leading case in this area; *Sidaway v Bethlem Royal Hospital Governors and others*.[27] Because of the enduring importance of this case, it is worth considering the judgements in some depth.

Although the facts of this case are well known, they will be briefly restated here in order to contextualise the judgements of Their Lordships. Mrs Sidaway, who suffered from persistent pain in her back and shoulders, was advised by her surgeon, Mr Falconer – who had died before the House of Lords heard the case – to undergo surgery on her spinal column. While he had apparently warned her about the risk of damage to a nerve root, he had allegedly failed to alert her to the possibility of damage to the spinal cord. While the former was a more statistically likely side-effect (estimated at about 1–2%), the latter was estimated at less than 1%. However, although the result of either risk eventuating would be serious, the consequences should the latter occur were obviously more so. When this statistically lesser, but personally more serious, risk did eventuate, Mrs Sidaway sued, claiming that Mr Falconer's failure to give her this information was a breach of his

---

[23] Ibid., at p 5.
[24] *De Freitas v O'Brien* (1995) 25 BMLR 51.
[25] [1985] 1 All ER 635.
[26] Ibid., at p 638.
[27] (1985) 1 BMLR 132.

duty of care to her. There was no allegation that the operation itself was negligently performed.

Although their Lordships reached the same decision as to liability – there was none – they did so by somewhat different routes. Lord Diplock appeared to be the judge most firmly wedded to the relevance and applicability of *Bolam*. Although it was argued for Mrs Sidaway that the clinical (operational) duty of care and the duty to provide information could be separated, Lord Diplock held that the decision as to what should be disclosed was 'as much an exercise of professional skill and judgment as any other part of the doctor's comprehensive duty of care to the individual patient, and expert medical evidence on this matter should be treated in just the same way.'[28] There was, he asserted ' … no convincing reason … that would justify treating the *Bolam* test as doing anything less than laying down a principle of English law that is comprehensive and applicable to every aspect of the duty of care owed by a doctor to his patient in the exercise of his healing functions as respects that patient.'[29]

Lords Keith and Bridge were in agreement, with their joint judgement being delivered by Lord Bridge. For them, the decision about what to tell patients so that they can make a rational choice whether or not to undergo a particular treatment 'must primarily be a matter of clinical judgment.'[30] While agreeing, therefore, that this means the *Bolam* test is the appropriate one to be applied by courts, this did not, Lord Bridge asserted, involve 'the necessity 'to hand over to the medical profession the entire question of the scope of the duty of disclosure, including the question whether there has been a breach of that duty'.'[31] Therefore, it would remain open to the courts to 'come to the conclusion that disclosure of a particular risk was so obviously necessary to an informed choice on the part of the patient that no reasonably prudent medical man would fail to make it.'[32]

Lord Templeman took a slightly different position. While not rejecting the *Bolam* test outright, he emphasised the need for doctors to give patients sufficient information to allow them to make a 'balanced judgment if the patient chooses to make a balanced judgment.'[33] Rather than seeing this as a matter solely to be judged by medical evidence, Lord Templeman preferred the view that although the patient is not 'entitled to know everything', neither is 'the doctor entitled to decide everything.'[34]

It was, of course, Lord Scarman's judgement that provoked the most interest at least among academic commentators, since it rejected the

[28] Ibid., at p 151.
[29] Ibid., at p 150.
[30] Ibid., per Lord Bridge, at p 155.
[31] Ibid.
[32] Ibid., at p 156.
[33] Ibid., at p 159.
[34] Ibid.

traditional reliance on *Bolam* and adopted a seemingly more radical account. Unlike his fellow judges, Lord Scarman situated the issue squarely in the arena of patient's rights, and concluded that '[t]he doctor's duty arises from his patient's rights.'[35] This represented a significant departure from his colleagues, who seem to have begun their deliberations from consideration of the doctor's duties rather than the patient's rights. Instead, Lord Scarman was clear that:

> It would be a strange conclusion if the courts should be led to conclude that our law, which undoubtedly recognises a right in the patient to decide whether he will accept or reject the treatment proposed, should permit the doctors to determine whether and in what circumstances a duty arises requiring the doctor to warn his patients of the risks inherent in the treatment which he proposes.[36]

The obligation of the courts, accordingly, was to ensure that medical opinion about the interests of the patient was not allowed 'to override the patient's right to decide for himself whether he will submit to the treatment offered him.'[37] While this focus on patient's rights was a breath of fresh air, particularly for those who had argued that there was a difference between the operational and the informational aspects of healthcare provision, it failed to carry the day, and for many years subsequent cases by and large continued to prefer the *Bolam* formulation on matters pertaining to information disclosure. Indeed, in the case of *Gold v Harringey Health Authority*,[38] the *Bolam* test was also applied to the question of consent to elective treatment, apparently closing the door on further argument. Although Jackson points out that using this so-called professional test in matters relating to what information should be disclosed is problematic because, 'this is not a question which requires clinical expertise.',[39] it seemed that the law was settled.

Meantime in other jurisdictions, some movement was apparent. Lord Scarman, in *Sidaway*, actually based his argument on the test enunciated in the US case of *Canterbury v Spence*.[40] Although this test is not accepted in every US state, it is utilised in a significant number[41] and has proved to be

---

[35] Ibid., at p 145.

[36] Ibid., at p 139.

[37] Ibid., p. 140.

[38] [1987] 2 All ER 888.

[39] Jackson, E, '"Informed Consent" to Medical Treatment and the Impotence of Tort', in McLean, S A M (ed), *First Do No Harm: Law, Ethics and Healthcare*, Aldershot, Ashgate, 2006, 273–86, at p 279.

[40] 464 F2d 772 (DC Cir 1972).

[41] See King, J S, Moulton, B W, 'Rethinking Informed Consent: The Case for Shared Medical Decision-Making', *American Journal of Law & Medicine*, 32, 2006: 429–501, who note at p 430 'Currently, the states are almost evenly split between two types of standards for informed consent – the physician-based standard, effective in 25 states, and the patient-based standard, effective in 23 states and the District of Columbia.'

highly influential. It serves as a firm reminder of the famous words of Mr Justice Cardozo in the case of *Schloendorff v Society of New York Hospitals*, where he said that '[e]very human being of adult years and sound mind has a right to determine what shall be done with his own body ... '[42] While times have moved on since *Schloendorff* was decided this statement is emblematic of the law's purported aspiration to protect autonomy. Some four decades later, in what was probably the first real 'informed consent' case, *Salgo v Leland Stanford*,[43] the court said:

> A physician violates his duty to his patient and subjects himself to liability if he withholds any facts which are necessary to form the basis of an intelligent consent by the patient to the proposed treatment.[44]

The decision in *Canterbury v Spence*, while also relatively elderly, remains worthy of consideration since it has certainly played an iconic and influential role in commentary on the issue of consent. There are two main aspects of this case that have generated interest. First, is the court's definition of the test to be used to decide on what patients should be told; whereas in the United Kingdom the *Bolam* test relies on what has been called the 'prudent doctor' test, *Canterbury* seems to take the issue of patients' rights more seriously, based in the idea that it is the patient's right to self-determination which, 'shapes the boundaries of the duty to reveal.'[45] This means that 'the test for determining whether a particular peril must be divulged is its materiality to the patient's decision: all risks potentially affecting the decision must be unmasked. And to safeguard the patient's interest in achieving his own determination on treatment, the law must itself set the standard for adequate disclosure.'[46]

On the other hand, the second important issue deriving from this case – which is less friendly to patients' rights – was judicial recognition of the so-called 'therapeutic privilege', which was also endorsed by Lord Scarman in *Sidaway*. The *Canterbury* court, describing the patient's dependence on the doctor for information as 'well-nigh abject ... '[47] declared that there were 'formidable obstacles to acceptance of the notion that the physician's obligation to disclose is either germinated or limited by medical practice.'[48] Nonetheless, the court accepted that in 'carefully circumscribed'[49] situations the doctor might be entitled to withhold information for 'therapeutic

[42] 105 NE 92 (NY, 1914).
[43] 154 Cal App 2d 560.
[44] Ibid., at p 578.
[45] 464 F2d 772 (DC Cir 1972), at para [41].
[46] Ibid., at para [41].
[47] Ibid., at para [31].
[48] Ibid., at para [23].
[49] Ibid., at para [49].

purposes'.[50] Most certainly, however, these would not include 'the paternalistic notion that the physician may remain silent simply because divulgence might prompt the patient to forego therapy the physician feels the patient really needs.'[51]

In Canada, in the case of *Reibl v Hughes*[52] the court also accepted that negligence was the appropriate action in consent cases, saying that ' ... actions of battery in respect of surgical or other medical treatment should be confined to cases where surgery or treatment has been performed or given to which there has been no consent at all or where, emergency situations aside, surgery or treatment has been performed or given beyond that to which there was consent.'[53] In *Hopp v Lepp*[54] the court noted that obtaining consent gives ' ... protection to his surgeon or physician only if the patient has been sufficiently informed to enable him to make a choice whether or not to submit to the surgery or therapy.'[55]

In Australia, the leading case is that of *Rogers v Whitaker*.[56] In this case, the Australian court moved decisively away from the *Bolam* standard, and this was subsequently confirmed in the case of *Chappel v Hart*.[57] In *Rogers v Whitaker*, Mrs Whitaker had been blind in one eye for some time. She was advised by her surgeon to have surgery on the eye, which he hoped would improve her sight. Mrs Whitaker repeatedly asked questions about the risks of the surgery and was not informed of the risk of sympathetic ophthalmia, which in fact eventuated, leaving her virtually blind. Noting that the *Bolam* test would lead to a different conclusion, the court held that it was necessary to disclose such information that 'a reasonable person in the patient's position, if warned of the risk, would be likely to attach significance to it or if the medical practitioner is or should reasonably have been aware that the particular patient, if warned of the risk, would be likely to attach significance to it'.[58] The court was concerned to describe a duty to disclose which would enable patients to make their own decisions about treatment, since the ability to make a decision is 'in reality, meaningless unless it is made on the basis of relevant information and advice'.[59]

---

[50] Ibid.
[51] Ibid.
[52] [1980] 2 SCR 880.
[53] Ibid., at pp 890–91.
[54] [1980] 2 SCR 192.
[55] Ibid., at p 196.
[56] (1992) 175 CLR 479. For valuable commentaries on this case, see Chalmers, D, Schwartz, R, 'Rogers v Whitaker and Informed Consent in Australia: A Fair Dinkum Duty of Disclosure', *Medical Law Review*, 1, Summer 1993: 139–59; Tickner, K, 'Rogers v Whitaker – Giving Patients a Meaningful Choice', *Oxford Journal of Legal Studies*, 14(1), 1995: 109–18; Skene, L, Smallwood, R, 'Informed consent: lessons from Australia', *BMJ*, 324, 2002: 39–41.
[57] (1998) 156 ALR 517.
[58] (1992) 175 CLR 479, at p 490.
[59] Ibid., at p 489.

In *Chappel v Hart*, Mrs Hart was advised to have surgery for the removal of a pharyngeal pouch in her oesophagus. She questioned the surgeon about possible risks to her vocal cords, and was assured that this was a common operation. In the event, her vocal cords were damaged and she claimed that she would not have agreed to the operation had she been aware of the risks, or at least she might have sought a more experienced surgeon. The court concluded that the surgeon's failure to disclose the information prevented Mrs Chappel from making a decision that might have minimised risk. Freckleton comments that, following these and subsequent Australian cases it 'is clear that medical opinion will have only a modest role to play in determining whether a given health care practitioner has acted negligently in giving advice about the risks of treatment.'[60]

It is, however, not just in other jurisdictions that the law has moved on, albeit perhaps more radically; in the United Kingdom, small – but not unimportant – changes have emerged. In the case of *Bolitho v City and Hackney Health Authority*,[61] a case which it should be noted was not about the provision of information, the strict *Bolam* test was modified by the House of Lords. In this case, the question hinged on the treatment of a two year old boy who was left severely brain damaged following respiratory problems. Although a doctor had been summoned on two occasions prior to this final episode, no doctor had attended. On his behalf, his mother argued first that the failure to attend was negligent, and second that had the doctor attended and intubated her son, the damage could have been avoided (the question of causation).

In concluding on this case, Lord Browne-Wilkinson noted the terms of the *Bolam* test, and observed that the opinion of the medical experts called by both sides differed as to whether or not Patrick should have been intubated. In a variation on the test, Lord Browne-Wilkinson declared that the courts must be satisfied not just whether other doctors would or would not have taken the same action as the doctor whose behaviour is under scrutiny, but also that the expert opinions on which courts rely had 'a logical basis.'[62] In reaching this conclusion, he relied on earlier cases, such as *Hucks v Cole*,[63] which proposed that '[t]he court must be vigilant to see whether the reasons given for putting a patient at risk are valid in the light of any well-known advance in medical knowledge, or whether they stem from a residual adherence to out-of-date ideas ... '[64] In other words, courts have long held themselves able to scrutinise expert evidence rather than simply accept it even if they seem to have been reluctant to do so.

---

[60] Freckleton, I, 'The new duty to warn', *AltLJ*, 4, 1999, available at http://www.austlii.edu.au/au/journals/AltLJ/1999/4.html (accessed on 1/5/2008), at p 6.

[61] (1997) 39 BMLR 1.

[62] Ibid., at p 9.

[63] (1968) reported at (1993) 4 Med LR 393.

[64] Ibid., at p 9.

Further, in *Pearce v United Bristol Healthcare NHS Trust*,[65] Lord Woolf, MR said:

> In a case where it is being alleged that a plaintiff has been deprived of the opportunity to make a proper decision as to what course he or she should take in relation to treatment, it seems to me to be the law ... that if there is a significant risk which would affect the judgment of a reasonable patient, then in the normal course it is the responsibility of a doctor to inform the patient of that significant risk, if the information is needed so that the patient can determine for him or herself as to what course he or she should adopt.[66]

Although *Pearce* might seem to add an additional caveat to the routine acceptance of the *Bolam* test, namely the need to disclose risks that are 'significant' to the patient, its actual impact is not clear. It does, however, entail some consideration of the patient's interests, which the *Bolam* test does not do. *Pearce* is, in fact, not the first time that UK courts have declared themselves committed to the protection of patient autonomy, although in the earlier cases they have also simultaneously endorsed the *Bolam* test. For example, in the earlier case of *Re T (adult: refusal of medical treatment)*[67] the court had been clear as to what considerations were of paramount importance:

> The right to determine what shall be done with one's own body is a fundamental right in our society. The concepts inherent in this right are the bedrock upon which the principles of self-determination and individual autonomy are based. Free individual choice in matters affecting this right should ... be accorded very high priority.[68]

Nonetheless, this so-called 'right' was still evaluated within the constraints imposed by the *Bolam* case – not as a stand-alone interest that the patient may hold. Other cases too have reiterated the position that it is for the competent adult to make his or her own decisions about medical treatment, based – if patients so choose – on the information provided by the doctor. Nonetheless, they have done so within a decisional framework that has been constrained by the *Bolam* test. Since this test – even if weakened by *Pearce* – is concerned with doctors' duties rather than patients' rights, and despite the rhetoric about concern for these rights, the very framework of the law is essentially inimical to their vindication. UK law on consent has some way to go before it can truly be seen as *in fact* being the legal equivalent of respect for autonomy.

---

[65] (1998) 48 BMLR 118.
[66] Ibid., at p 124.
[67] (1992) 9 BMLR 46.
[68] Ibid., at p 63.

In addition, there seems to be little agreement as to precisely what needs to be disclosed and with what goal in mind. As an example, in *Chatterton v Gerson*, the court declared that 'a real risk of a misfortune inherent in the procedure ... '[69] must be disclosed. In the Canadian case of *Hopp v Lepp, supra*, the court indicated that not only should doctors ' ... generally, ... answer any specific questions posed by the patient as to the risks involved', but they should also 'without being questioned, disclose to [the patient] the nature of the proposed operation, its gravity, any material risks and any special or unusual risks attendant upon the performance of the operation.'[70] And in *Reibl v Hughes*, also referred to above, the court said:

> Merely because medical evidence establishes the reasonableness of a recommended operation does not mean that a reasonable person in the patient's position would necessarily agree to it, if proper disclosure had been made of the risks attendant upon it, balanced by those against it.[71]

From *Canterbury*, it would seem that the information that must be disclosed is that which would enable the patient to make an 'intelligent' choice.[72] What these different formulations mean in general terms for the obligation to disclose is less than obvious. What we can see, however, is that no judge has yet suggested that *all* available information should be offered to the patient. In addition, even the most patient-centred test places emphasis on the nature of the patient's decision – 'intelligent' or 'balanced' for example – suggesting that it is not information disclosure for its own sake that is important in law; rather, it is steering patients towards a particular kind of decision that matters. The level of disclosure required by the law of consent is apparently not absolute but rather just enough to allow patients to make 'intelligent', 'informed' or 'balanced' decisions. Arguably, this falls short of meeting the *prima facie* requirements of the ethical concept of autonomy.

One final UK case warrants consideration – *Chester v Afshar*.[73] Like *Chappel v Hart*, which was referred to earlier, this case hinged on the question of causation. In each of these cases, the question to be resolved was whether or not, had the patient been informed of the risk, they would have proceeded with the surgery. In *Chappel*, the court was inclined to believe that had Mrs Chappel been alerted to the risk, she might well have sought an alternative, more experienced, surgeon. In other words, she may well have proceeded with surgery, but not at that time and not with that doctor. In *Chester*, the patient indicated only that she would not have had the surgery *at that time* if

---

[69] (1980) 1 BMLR 80, at p 91.
[70] [1980] 2 SCR 192, at p 210.
[71] [1980] 2 SCR 880, at p 899.
[72] 464 F2d 772 (DC Cir 1972), at para [41].
[73] [2004] UKHL 41.

she had been warned of these risks. She did not deny that she would have undergone the surgery; rather she claimed that she would have waited before agreeing to it. In other words, the risk was essentially the same, but she would have preferred the opportunity to consider her options and delay the surgery. In a decision which raised a few eyebrows, but which must have brought heart to patients, the court found for the patient. Interestingly, this was done on the basis that 'justice' required that a remedy be made available.

Lord Steyn, for example, said that, ' ... as a result of the surgeon's failure to warn the patient, she cannot be said to have given informed consent to the surgery in the full legal sense. Her right of autonomy and dignity can and ought to be vindicated by a narrow and modest departure from traditional causation principles.'[74] He continued that '[t]his result is in accord with one of the most basic aspirations of the law, namely to right wrongs.'[75] Lord Hope took a similar line, declaring that 'the law which imposed the duty to warn on the doctor has at its heart the right of the patient to make an informed choice as to whether, and if so when and by whom, to be operated on.'[76] As he said, '[t]he function of the law is to enable rights to be vindicated and to provide remedies when duties have been breached. Unless this is done the duty is a hollow one, stripped of all practical force and devoid of all content.'[77] Devaney points out that this decision nonetheless 'leaves the courts with the difficult job of determining who is telling the truth and doctors with the delicate task of determining how much information their duties demand patients should be given.'[78] Despite initially seeming to argue that nothing has really changed following *Chester*, Devaney – perhaps surprisingly – then concludes that '[a]ll that is new is that patient autonomy really rules.'[79]

So, what can be gleaned from this brief discussion of these cases? In some, the content and extent of the duty to disclose were effectively decided by reference to what doctors believed to be appropriate. The United Kingdom for some years essentially stood alone in adopting this position – until the cases of *Pearce* and now *Chester*, which seem to have moved the law in the direction of the 'prudent patient' rather than the 'prudent doctor' test and to have reinforced the basic concept that the doctors' duties flow from the patients' rights, not the other way round. Indeed, Meyers suggests ' ... it may be that *Chester* will prove to be more noteworthy for defining the scope of the doctor's duty to warn his or her patient of the risks inherent or special in the treatment being proposed ... No longer can the reasonable doctor

---

[74] Ibid., at para 24.

[75] Ibid., at para 25.

[76] Ibid., at para 86.

[77] Ibid., at para 87.

[78] Devaney, S, 'Commentary: Autonomy Rules OK Chester v Afshar', *Medical Law Review*, 12, Spring 2005: 102–7, at p 107.

[79] Ibid.

standard of *Bolam*, as applied in the disclosure of risk concept in *Sidaway*, be said to be the law.'[80] In Australia, considering the cases of *Rogers* and *Chappel*, Freckleton suggests that the primary consequence of these decisions, as arguably may now be the case in the United Kingdom following *Chester*, is that:

> Technical proficiency henceforth will be only part of the health care practitioner's necessary arsenal of skills. It must be accompanied by sophisticated communication skills, and this is an important step forward for consumers ... The doctor must engage in 'real dialogue' with the patient.[81]

Of course, whether or not this is an accurate conclusion depends on whether or not these cases have an impact on actual practice. Skegg suggests that even were UK courts to follow the Canadian and Australian approach 'the interests of the overwhelming majority of patients would be totally unaffected.'[82] This, he argues is because '[m]ost doctors and other health professionals would not know of that decision, much less understand it; even fewer would change their practice in consequence.'[83] If true, the ability of the law to change clinical practice is relatively minimal, a suggestion that seems to be borne out by Robertson's research in Canada, which showed that even following the landmark case of *Reibl v Hughes* 'plaintiffs lose in the vast majority of informed consent cases.'[84]

Even if the practice of clinicians were changed by legal decisions, the test emerging from these more recent cases remains objective in nature. In this very real sense, it will not reflect individual autonomy. While welcoming Freckleton's view that they emphasise the need for 'real dialogue', the aggrieved patient might nonetheless conclude that the standard that emerges from them is still not ideally suited to the protection of his or her own autonomy. The individual patient will have interests and needs which might bear little relationship to the 'prudent patient', however conceptualised. Autonomy is essentially a personal concept, which is supposed to take account of the individual's own interests and concerns – not those of some homogenised, fictional character. Yet, it is very much the common pattern of law to establish and develop general concepts such as the 'reasonable man' (or the 'prudent patient') in order to adjudicate on disputes.

---

[80] Meyers, D, '*Chester v Afshar*: Sayonara, Sub Silentio, *Sidaway?*', in McLean, S A M (ed), *First Do No Harm: Law, Ethics and Healthcare*, Aldershot, Ashgate, 2006, 255–71, at p 270.

[81] Freckleton, I, 'The new duty to warn', *AltLJ*, 4, 1999, available at http://www.austlii.edu.au/au/journals/AltLJ/1999/4.html (accessed on 1/5/2008), at p 6.

[82] Skegg, P D G, 'English Medical Law and 'Informed Consent': An Antipodean Assessment and Alternative', *Medical Law Review*, 7, summer 1999: 135–65, at p 146.

[83] Ibid.

[84] Robertson, G B, 'Informed Consent: 20 Years Later', *Health Law Journal Special Edition*, 2003: 153–59, at p 154.

There are, of course, reasons for not utilising a subjective test. Not only would such a test leave healthcare professionals wide open to the hindsight of the patient who has suffered harm, it would also potentially cripple the healthcare system. As was said in the case of *Reibl v Hughes* ' ... to apply a subjective test to causation would ... put a premium on hindsight, even more than would be put on medical evidence in assessing causation by an objective standard.'[85] Thus, the court in this, and other, cases endorsed the 'reasonable patient test', which, it has been suggested 'emphasizes patient autonomy by requiring that risk disclosure be conducted to satisfy what an ordinary reasonable person in the patient's particular position would want to know.'[86] Whether or not this objective test actually does emphasise autonomy is debatable, and arguably seems unlikely. While it may be more likely than the 'prudent doctor' test at least to engage with autonomy, it clearly cannot take account of the individual's specific interests.

Not only, then, do the tests applied in law – even when they move away from over-emphasis on what doctors do – fail to take account of the individual patient, the retention of the concept of therapeutic privilege still permits non-disclosure even of information that the patient might feel would have been important to his or her own decision. This allows for the omission of certain information if the doctor believes it would harm the patient to provide it, for example by making them anxious or distressed. However, in a study conducted with family planning patients, Faden and Beauchamp found that, while the courts have expressed concern that disclosure of certain information might raise anxiety 'there was no evidence that disclosed information produced such negative consequences. Patients receiving the information were no more anxious than patients who were not so informed.'[87] Nonetheless they also concede that '[d]isclosed information could have different consequences where the patient is in a more serious condition.'[88] Whether this is true or not is moot, and – as I (and others) have already argued – making patients anxious does not provide an overwhelming argument against disclosure.

Buchanan persuasively critiques the issue of potential harm resulting from disclosure.[89] He claims that there are three arguments used to justify non-disclosure, two of which are concerned with the alleged avoidance of harm to the patient. These he calls the Prevention of Harm Argument and the Contractual Version of the Prevention of Harm Argument.[90] The Prevention of

---

[85] [1980] 2 SCR 880, at p 898.

[86] Veerapen, R J, 'Informed Consent: Physician Inexperience is a Material Risk for Patients', *Journal of Law, Medicine & Ethics, Genetics and Group Rights*, Fall 2007: 478–85, at p 478.

[87] Faden, R R, Beauchamp, T L, 'Decision-Making and Informed Consent: A Study of the Impact of Disclosed Information', *Social Indicators Research*, 7, 1980: 313–36, at p 332.

[88] Ibid., at p 332.

[89] Buchanan, A, 'Medical Paternalism', *Philosophy & Public Affairs*, 7(4), 1978: 370–90.

[90] Ibid., at p 377.

Harm argument runs as follows: the doctor's duty is to prevent or minimise harm, disclosure of certain information will harm the patient, therefore the doctor can withhold it. Buchanan argues that this common justification is fundamentally flawed for several reasons. One of these is that it omits the important criterion of how it is to be calculated that disclosure would cause more harm than the failure to provide it would do. The doctor, Buchanan says, 'must judge that withholding the information will result in less harm on balance than divulging it.'[91] However, he argues that making a decision of this sort is not only one that requires sophisticated reasoning of a type that is probably beyond most physicians, but that it also is a '*moral* evaluation of the most basic and problematic kind.' (original emphasis).[92] Even assuming that such judgements are reasonable or feasible, Buchanan continues that they would depend on 'a profound knowledge of the most intimate details of the patient's life history, his characteristic ways of coping with personal crises, his personal and vocational commitments and aspirations, his feelings of obligation toward others, and his attitude toward the completeness or incompleteness of his experience.'[93] This, he concludes, is implausible at best.

The Contractual Version of the Prevention of Harm argument is based on the idea that the doctor/patient relationship is contractual in nature and includes terms that authorise the doctor to minimise harm to the patient. Thus, if the doctor decides that disclosure would cause harm, s/he is contractually obliged to withhold it. While vulnerable to the same arguments as the non-contractual version, Buchanan notes further major objections to this account; namely, that people do not in fact believe that this *is* the nature of the doctor/patient relationship and even if some do, this does not effectively justify a general approach to (non-)disclosure. In any case, even if such a contract did exist, it would be constrained by the general law of contract, which would entitle a patient to withdraw from it if its terms are not being met. How, Buchanan asks, could the patient know whether or not the withholding of information vitiates the contract unless s/he knows that the information has been withheld?[94]

Whatever the consequence of disclosure might be, there is also reason to be concerned that courts might endorse the application of the therapeutic privilege principle not to prevent harm following directly from the information, but rather where 'disclosure would result in no harm other than refusal of the treatment ... '.[95] This, says Simpson, should not be permitted.[96]

[91] Ibid., at pp 377–78.

[92] Ibid., at p 381.

[93] Ibid., at pp 381–82.

[94] Ibid., see discussion at pp 384–85.

[95] Simpson, R E, 'Informed Consent: From Disclosure to Patient Participation in Medical Decisionmaking', *Northwestern University Law Review*, 76, 1981: 172–207.

[96] Ibid.

Simpson also points out that while '[t]he stated purpose of the therapeutic privilege is to generate the disclosure level most conducive to the patient's health ... ', in fact what has occurred is that 'its immediate effect is to permit the physician to withhold vital information from the patient.'[97]

It is also interesting to note how many qualifiers of the term 'decision' or 'choice' are used in the judgements highlighted. The choice to be enabled by disclosure should be, variously 'intelligent', 'rational', 'balanced' and so on. Unfortunately, the cases are less than clear as to whether these are all the same *kind* of choice, and equally therefore they do not provide any satisfactory details about just what doctors *must* disclose. While it might be reasonable to assume that direct questions should be answered honestly,[98] it cannot be said that, in any of the jurisdictions considered, there is an unequivocal account of just what the patient is entitled to be told. This takes us back, therefore, to the question of just what the law is either attempting or able to achieve in this area.

Disclosure, consent and the law

It has already been suggested in Chapter 2 that at a theoretical level the legal doctrine of consent lacks credibility in a number of ways as a protector of autonomy. From what has emerged from a brief consideration of the case law, it seems that the translation of the ethical concept of autonomy into the law using the vehicle of consent law further highlights the dissonance between the ethical importance of respect for autonomy and the fundamental processes and goals of the law. In part this is because the law has both purposes and constraints which may not lend themselves to equivalence with the ethical concept. And, as we have seen, this is so even when courts officially pronounce that respecting autonomy is the principle reason for providing information and seeking consent. Lord Donaldson, for example, has declared that '[t]he patient's interest consists of his right to self-determination – his right to live his own life how he wishes, even if it will damage his health or lead to his premature death',[99] and in the same case, Dame Elizabeth Butler-Sloss declared that '[t]he right to determine what shall be done with one's own body is a fundamental right in our society.'[100] Yet this right to self-determination or autonomy will be vindicated only partially, if at all, when current, established legal tests are applied to the process of seeking consent and to evaluation of the decision taken.

Nonetheless, the purpose of the law in this area has repeatedly been expressed as being to support and protect the patient's right to make

---

[97] Ibid., at p 201.

[98] But see *Blyth v Bloomsbury Health Authority* [1993] 4 Med LR 151 (CA).

[99] *Re T (adult: refusal of medical treatment)* (1992) 9 BMLR 46, at p 59.

[100] Ibid., at p 63.

autonomous healthcare decisions. As Kukla says, 'we can roughly translate the principle of respecting patient autonomy into the principle of protecting and promoting patients' ability to make and act upon free, informed decisions resulting from capable and uninfluenced deliberation.'[101] But this is indeed only a 'rough' translation, despite the rhetoric to the contrary. The UK Department of Health says that a valid consent is one 'given voluntarily by an appropriately informed person ... who has the capacity to consent to the intervention in question.'[102] Or, as Maclean says, '[t]he legal rules of consent are founded upon the right to autonomy and the principle of (respect for) autonomy.'[103] 'Informed consent', says Worthington, 'empowers patients and allows them to take part in critical decision making, as long as they agree to play an active part and have the capacity to do so.'[104] Yet as we have seen there is a poor fit between the ethical concept of autonomy and the legal rules of consent. In reality, both in 'simple' consent cases, and in the more contentious ones that will be discussed in later chapters, the law's engagement with patients' decisions and medical obligations does not satisfy the lofty aspiration of respecting and/or protecting autonomy. First, while apparently espousing what might be seen as equivalent to the individualistic model of autonomy,[105] policy issues are superimposed so that the individual patient him or her self is removed from the equation, to be replaced with the 'reasonable' or 'prudent' patient (or, worse, with a test based on the 'reasonable' doctor). The reasons for this have been briefly touched upon, and they result in a position that is less than satisfactory for the patient who wants to have his or her *individual* choices vindicated in law. Indeed, far from the concept of individual autonomy being given flesh in law, policy (and perhaps other less evident considerations) mandates that an objective assessment be utilised.

Second, the law has a history of deference to the medical profession that has often worked to prioritise the concept of professional beneficence (which sometimes seems indistinguishable from paternalism) in the courts' scrutiny of the quality of patients' decisions. Medicine is a highly valued profession, and its practitioners have a unique societal status. Teff, for example, notes that '[m]edicine is generally considered supreme among professions – one of the very few walks of life in which people are so totally identified with their

---

[101] Kukla, R, 'Conscientious Autonomy: Displacing Decisions in Health Care', *Hastings Center Report*, 35 (2), 2005: 34–44, at p 35.

[102] *Reference Guide to Consent for Examination or Treatment*, London, Department of Health, 2001, at p 4, para 1.

[103] Maclean, A, 'Now You See It, Now You Don't': Consent And The Legal Protection of Autonomy', *Journal of Applied Philosophy*, 17(3), 2000: 277–88, at p 277.

[104] Worthington, R, 'Clinical Issues on Consent: Some Philosophical Concerns', *J Med Ethics*, 28, 2002: 377–80, at p 377.

[105] For further discussion, see Kuczewski, M and McCruden, P J, 'Informed Consent: Does it Take a Village? The Problem of Culture and Truth Telling', *Cambridge Q of Healthcare Ethics*, 10, 2001: 34–46.

work that they are routinely addressed by their professional title, in and out of working hours.'[106] In addition, as Katz notes, courts have been 'hesitant to intrude on medical practices', which he says is in part because '[t]heir impulse to foster individual self-determination collided with an equally strong desire to maintain the autonomy of the profession, both for the sake of the profession and for the "best interests" of patients.'[107] One of the United Kingdom's most senior judges, Lord Woolf, reflecting on the alleged deference of the law to medicine, cautioned firmly against it, although he also argued that this traditional attitude was disappearing. He said, ' ... it is unwise to place any profession or other body providing services to the public on a pedestal where their actions cannot be subject to close scrutiny. The greater the power the body has, the more important is this need.'[108] Despite his view that deference is on the decrease, Teff's assertion that 'English law has endorsed this approach to a much greater extent than other comparable systems ... '[109] still resonates. As I have argued elsewhere, '[o]n numerous occasions, courts in the United Kingdom have chosen rather to prioritise the good of medicine at the expense of the rights of patients – the therapeutic rather than the personal imperative.'[110]

Moreover, medicine itself is a discipline with schizophrenic tendencies in this area. While doctors surely recognise the value of respecting patient autonomy, Tauber notes that while '[r]espect for the person ... is implicit in the professional role ... ', nonetheless the 'ethic of compassion regards autonomy as only one of a number of moral principles governing the caring relationship among which it finds beneficence a more resonant expression of medicine's fundamental ethos'.[111] These two concepts seem difficult to reconcile. If doctors do in fact respect the patient's autonomy interests and rights, then 'compassion' is not a relevant justification for unduly influencing patients towards making a particular decision. To be sure, it is permissible to persuade, but not to coerce; while the latter is antagonistic to autonomy, the former is not. Although, Parascandola, Hawkins and Danis point out that '[t]he obligations of physicians are defined in terms of at least two, sometimes competing, ethical goals – beneficence and respect for autonomy',[112]

---

[106] Teff, H, *Reasonable Care: Legal Perspectives on the Doctor-Patient Relationship*, Oxford, Clarendon Press, 1994, at p 85.

[107] Katz, J, *The Silent World of Doctor and Patient*, New York, The Free Press, 1984, at p 59.

[108] Lord Woolf, 'Are the Courts Excessively Deferential to the Medical Profession?', *Medical Law Review*, 9, Spring 2001: 1–16, at p 15.

[109] Teff, H, *Reasonable Care: Legal Perspectives on the Doctor-Patient Relationship*, Oxford, Clarendon Press, 1994, at p xxiii.

[110] McLean, S A M, 'Talking to patients – Information Disclosure as "Good" Medical Practice', in Westerhall, L and Phillips, C (eds), *Patients Rights – Informed Consent, Access and Equality*, Stockholm, Nerenius & Santerus, 1994, 171–89, at p 185.

[111] Tauber, A I, 'Sick Autonomy', *Perspectives in Biology and Medicine*, 46(4) (autumn), 2003: 484–95, at p 486.

[112] Parascandola, M, Hawkins, J, Danis, M, 'Patient Autonomy and the Challenge of Clinical Uncertainty', *Kennedy Institute of Ethics Journal*, 12(3), 2002: 245–64, at p 247.

the greater of these should be respect for autonomy, not least because respecting autonomy could equally be described as incorporating beneficence.

On the other hand, as Buchanan has suggested, it is unknown whether failing to facilitate autonomous behaviour even as an act of compassion is in fact beneficent. It could equally be argued to be harmful to the patient who values his or her right to bodily integrity. To make any sense, the account that clearly distinguishes beneficence from respect for autonomy must have implicit in it the assumption that beneficence is equivalent to accepting the medical recommendation, in which the exercise of autonomy might not result. The patient, therefore, has only one authentic choice available – to accept the clinical decision. Yet, this would surely mean that autonomy is irrelevant. Why then does the law continually hold it out as the primary consideration?

There are formidable – even perhaps intelligible – reasons why both healthcare and legal professionals might be tempted to balance autonomous decisions with the ethos of beneficence, which remains an important ethical and professional commitment of doctors. Much, however, depends on how beneficence is conceptualised. If seen as equivalent, or at least similar, to the concept of paternalism, it will inevitably conflict with the idea that patients are uniquely qualified to make decisions *about and for themselves*. Paternalism crudely put implies that 'doctor knows best', while the decisions that patients want to make depend on more than the expertise (rightly) claimed by healthcare professionals which is central to their recommendations. As Tauber notes:

> ... autonomy's dominance has been widely regarded as both a judicial and philosophical problem, not only because its practical application must be balanced with other moral tenets, but because patient expectations and physician responsibilities are oriented by the dominance of one principle or another as determined by a complex sociology of clinical practice.[113]

It is, therefore, no simple task to balance professional ethics and practice with patient expectations or claims – not even for patients themselves. Teff, for example, notes that insistence on patients' rights is problematic as it can turn 'what may have been a caring and amicable relationship into an adversarial one, inimical both to constructive dialogue and their own future health.'[114] On the other hand, this is not an inevitable consequence of a rights-dominated medical interaction. Respecting patients' rights – even the

---

[113] Tauber, A I, 'Sick Autonomy', *Perspectives in Biology and Medicine*, 46(4), (autumn), 2003: 484–95, at p 487.

[114] Teff, H, *Reasonable Care: Legal Perspectives on the Doctor-Patient Relationship*, Oxford, Clarendon Press, 1994, at p 115.

right to make the 'wrong' decision – may, as I have suggested earlier, instead serve to build and reinforce a relationship based on trust. On the other hand, the mere apprehension that one is not being told the truth or the full facts – whether true or not – is enough to damage that trust and may even *generate* the adversarial relationship that Teff wants to avoid.

Yet beneficence still holds considerable authority in medical thinking and practice and often is used as an argument to justify avoiding the perceived tensions which can result from respecting patient autonomy. Beneficence, however, as I have suggested could be conceptualised differently – it could, for example, be that a beneficent action is one that is intimately linked with autonomy rather than at odds with it. This, however, would require the active engagement of the doctor in helping the patient to make an autonomous decision – the sharing of relevant information, and the attempt to make it intelligible, are therefore beneficent and autonomy enhancing at the same time. If beneficence is interpreted as a value designed to help enhance autonomy rather than restrict it, there is no conflict between doctors' obligations and patients' rights. The duty on the doctor is to ensure that adequate information is disclosed to the patient to enable a decision to be made and that the patient is assisted, where possible, to understand that information, albeit coupled with clinical recommendations. This would, at least in theory, allow patients to make a choice based on their own assessment of what serves their interests. Maximising and reinforcing the disclosure obligation would also help to avoid the problem, identified by Bridson *et al*, that even full disclosure of 'risks, benefits, and alternatives, may yet fail to be patient centred if made in ignorance of what a compliant patient truly wants.'[115] Exploring the interests of the patient and teasing out their values satisfies the interests of both beneficence and respect for autonomy, while avoiding the pitfalls of a return to paternalism.

In the previous chapter two other important aspects of consent were raised. First, was the question of understanding. The provision of information, it is said, must be more than 'merely a means of avoiding a trip [to] the courtroom', otherwise it risks being 'done in a formulaic manner which does not achieve the objectives of providing the information ... '.[116] Jones notes that there is an increasing tendency for courts to emphasise the issue of comprehension. Courts, he says, are increasingly making it 'clear that risk-disclosure is meant to be a process of *communicating* information. Simply telling the patient about risks without making any attempt to see that the patient has understood the information can be negligent.'[117] Nonetheless. he says that

---

[115] Bridson, J, Hammond, C, Leach, A, Chester, M R, 'Making consent patient centred', *BMJ*, 327, 2003: 1159–61, at p 1161.

[116] Jones, M A, 'Informed Consent And Other Fairy Stories', *Medical Law Review*, 7, Summer 1999: 103–34, at p 130.

[117] Ibid., at p 118.

'the basic structure of the law remains strongly defendant-oriented and paternalistic.'[118] As we have seen, the test derived from the case of *Re C*[119] and essentially adopted into English Law by the terms of the Mental Capacity Act 2005, places some emphasis on understanding. In *Re C*, despite the fact that C was suffering from paranoid schizophrenia, it was held that he had 'understood and retained the relevant treatment information, that in his own way he believes it, and that in the same fashion he has arrived at a clear choice',[120] and this was sufficient to require respect for his decision.

Doubts about the ability of patients to understand medical information have also been used to justify limiting what is disclosed to them. An example of this can be found in the third of Buchanan's arguments, which he calls the Argument From the Inability to Understand.[121] This presumes that 'the physician is justified in withholding information when the patient ... is unable to understand the information.'[122] Buchanan, however, points to a number of counter arguments. For example, he says, this position is based on 'dubious and extremely broad psychological generalizations ... '.[123] Second, it omits to take account of the disabling impact of the institution in which patients find themselves, making failure to understand a 'self-fulfilling prophecy'.[124] Finally, he argues that ' ... it is a mistake to maintain that the legal duty to seek informed consent applies only where the physician can succeed in adequately informing [patients].'[125] While the doctor may have an obligation to try to *ensure* understanding, this is not a legal duty and is not fundamental to the obligation to seek consent. No matter how important patient understanding may be for the ability to make an autonomous decision, it is a condition that it would be extremely difficult for the law to evaluate and a requirement that it could scarcely enforce. Consent rules, therefore, once again seem somewhat distant from respect for autonomous decisions.

Finally, we come to the issue of voluntariness. It was indicated in the previous chapter that the law takes this very seriously, and this can be seen most clearly from the case of *Re T*.[126] In this case, a pregnant woman had been injured in a road traffic accident. Following a discussion with her mother, who was a Jehovah's Witness, she signed a form refusing blood transfusion should this become necessary. Following an emergency caesarean section, her condition deteriorated and she was in need of a transfusion. A Declaration

---

[118] Ibid., at p 123.

[119] *Re C (adult: refusal of medical treatment)* (1993) 15 BMLR 77.

[120] Ibid., at p 82.

[121] Buchanan, A, 'Medical Paternalism', *Philosophy & Public Affairs*, 7(4), 1978: 370–90, especially at pp 386–87.

[122] Ibid., at p 386.

[123] Ibid.

[124] Ibid.

[125] Ibid.

[126] *Re T (adult) (refusal of medical treatment)* (1992) 9 BMLR 46, CA.

authorising transfusion was obtained and upheld in the Court of Appeal. Although the case was ultimately decided on different grounds, the question of voluntariness was raised, as it was postulated that her refusal might have resulted from the coercive or undue influence of her mother. Were there evidence that T's will had been overcome by this, her choice would not have been seen as authentic and therefore not autonomous. Family pressure, of course, is not the only way in which patients can be influenced to act against what they might see as their autonomy interests. Failure to provide necessary information can also be coercive of patients but it seems that the selective (non-)provision of information by doctors has not generally been sufficient to convince courts to declare the subsequent choice invalid. For the moment, concern about autonomy reducing factors in patients' decisions seems to have been reserved for cases where religious beliefs are thought to have prevented the making of a free choice,[127] where the patient's situation is inherently coercive, such as where the patient is in prison[128] and where the patient's condition is inimical to the exercise of free will, such as in the case of anorexics.[129] As these can be seen as 'special groups' they will not be further explored here.

Consent in practice

It is evident that there are very different approaches to the meaning and importance of consent in the medical setting. On the one hand is the notion that consent is the mechanism whereby the right of the autonomous person to make self-regarding choices in determining their healthcare is translated from ethical rhetoric to legal reality. On the other, is the view that consent is a mechanistic, but rather empty, vehicle to protect doctors from liability. By going through the motions of involving patients, physicians remain free to usurp the patient's real right to choose; to act autonomously. Whereas Baker suggests that 'the rise of the legal doctrine of informed consent brought with it a shift from physician beneficence to patient autonomy',[130] still others believe that the claims made for the doctrine of consent are 'exaggerated'.[131] Given what has gone before, it might seem that the latter impression is the more accurate. Genuine protection for patients' autonomous decisions depends on the ability of the law to operate in such a way as to vindicate

---

[127] See, for example, the case of *Re E (a minor)* [1994] 5 Med LR 73.

[128] See, for example, *Freeman v Home Office (No 2)* [1984] 1 All ER 1036; *Secretary of State for the Home Department v Robb* [1995] 1 All ER 677.

[129] *Riverside Mental Health Trust v Fox* (1993) 20 BMLR 1; *Re C (detention: medical treatment)* [1997] 2 FLR 180.

[130] Baker, L A, '"I Think I Do": Another Perspective on Consent and the Law', *Law, Medicine & Health Care*, 16(3–4), Winter 1988: 256–60, at p 256.

[131] O'Neill, O, 'Some limits of informed consent', *J Med Ethics*, 29, 2003: 4–7, at p 2.

them, yet it would appear that there are limitations – both mechanistic and theoretical – on the law's ability to do this.

In terms of the mechanistic or operational difficulties, the move from assault to negligence immediately placed the rights of the patient in potential competition with other principles which are regarded as more important. Policy issues, such as the alleged imperative to protect medical professionals from unwarranted challenge, immediately stand between the patient and vindication of his or her autonomy rights. Equally, the fundamental rules of the negligence action seem ill-suited to the focus on individual choice that respect for autonomy would presumably demand. Thus, the law of consent is functionally unable *in practice* to operate in such a way as to recognise fully that '[t]he decision whether or not to accept risks is the personal and important right of the patients, and can be, and often is, independent even of medically optimal advice ... '.[132]

Additionally, the law develops through the decisions of judges, based on their understanding of the standards established by precedent and their interpretation of the value to be given to interests which can sometimes be in conflict with each other. Thus, in the United Kingdom it was many years before blind adherence to the *Bolam* test – a test which made the task for the patient virtually impossible – was challenged, and until the judgement in *Chester v Afshar*,[133] causation also remained a very significant obstacle to patient success. While other jurisdictions, such as Canada, Australia and some US states moved away from the *Bolam* type of approach earlier than did the United Kingdom, even in these countries the test applied, while not physician-focused, is equally not entirely patient-centred. In as much as the law needs rules that can be applied in each situation, it is probably intelligible that courts cannot listen to each individual's claims about what his or her own particular preferences would have been. Even where courts moved away from exclusive contemplation of the doctor's behaviour, they developed in its place the 'objective patient' test, which also homogenised decision-making, reducing the inquiry – as is routinely the case in tort law – to presumptions about what the reasonable or prudent patient would want to know; not what that *particular* patient wanted. It is difficult to see how this kind of test could in fact protect or foster individual autonomy. Rather, it promotes the development of a generalised standard which is inherently inimical to the individual patient and, *ex hypothesi*, to respect for actual autonomy.

Indeed, as we have seen, evidence from Canada suggests that, even following the leading case of *Reibl v Hughes*,[134] the success rate of cases where

---

[132] McLean, S A M, *A Patient's Right to Know: Information Disclosure, the Doctor and the Law*, Aldershot, Dartmouth, 1989, at p 176.

[133] [2004] UKHL 41.

[134] [1980] 2 SCR 880.

patients challenge doctors over 'informed' consent remains virtually the same as before *Reibl* was decided. Robertson's research, however, suggests that causation now lies at the heart of most failures and he sees some cause for optimism because of this as it 'may be an indication that the legal standard is having a positive impact on medical practice.'[135] If so, then the apparent relaxation of the test for causation in cases such as *Chester v Afshar* may be of tangible benefit to patients in the United Kingdom, but there is no clear evidence that in general doctors are *in fact* telling patients what they want, and need, to know. Schneider suggests that the reality is that ' ... lawmakers have essentially established rules intended to hold medicine to its own standards and then mostly left the system to work unmolested.'[136] Also, as we have seen, Halpern says while courts have emphasised the need for patients to be informed and active participants in healthcare decisions, this has not been mirrored in the 'realities of patient care'.[137]

In addition, it has been argued that the law on consent did not start from a neutral position, but rather from one that was informed by 'a literature to which doctors and medical ethicists contributed crucially.'[138] If so, then it is perhaps unsurprising that the law's understanding of autonomy does not necessarily equate with that espoused by ethicists (whichever form of definition they prefer). Kukla, for example, says that:

> ... while bioethicists know that the concept of informed consent does not exhaust the rich concept of autonomy, many still take it as a governing assumption that in the practical domain of health care, concerns about autonomy can be translated into concerns about self-determination, which can in turn be translated into concerns about informed consent.[139]

If the law of consent is, as I have suggested, unable to take meaningful account of the concept of autonomy, its role is arguably reduced to what has been called a ritualistic rather than organic one.[140] Moreover, Waller suggests that 'the current process of gaining informed consent may subtly shape patient passivity, a passivity that threatens both physical and psychological well-being.'[141] While the law of consent may perform a symbolic function in

---

[135] Robertson, G B, 'Informed Consent: 20 Years Later', *Health Law Journal Special Edition*, 2003: 153–59, at p 159.

[136] Schneider, C E, 'Void for Vagueness', *Hastings Center Report*, January–February 2007: 10–11, at p 10.

[137] Halpern, S A, 'Medical Authority and the Culture of Rights', *Journal of Health Politics, Policy and Law*, 29(4–5), August–October 2004: 835–52, at p 840.

[138] Schneider, C E, 'Void for Vagueness', *Hastings Center Report*, January–February 2007: 10–11, at p 10.

[139] Kukla, R, 'Conscientious Autonomy: Displacing Decisions in Health Care', *Hastings Center Report*, 35 (2), 2005: 34–44, at p 35.

[140] Tauber, A I, 'Sick Autonomy', *Perspectives in Biology and Medicine*, 46(4), (autumn), 2003: 484–95, at p 485.

[141] Waller, B N, 'Patient Autonomy Naturalized', *Perspectives in Biology and Medicine*, 44(4), (autumn), 2001: 584–93, at p 285.

reminding doctors that patients need information, it does not seem to be able to *insist* that information disclosure is made to a standard that would satisfy the patient seeking to make an autonomous decision, nor indeed the concept of autonomy itself.

Conclusion

There are powerful and important reasons to respect the autonomous decision of an autonomous (competent) person. These focus on and are derived from the right that many patients want to claim – that is, to be decision makers in their own cause. However, despite the recognition in both ethics and law of the importance of this right, not only do ethicists not agree on what are the characteristics of an autonomous decision, but the law has developed in such a manner as to be systemically incapable, or perhaps unwilling, to find a formula that can support the preferred account. While it would seem that there has been some change in the way in which doctors approach the process of seeking patient consent, given a more clear understanding that information is necessary to the patient who is being invited to make a decision, courts continue to rely on traditional principles to assess their decisions.

The cases, according to Faden and Beauchamp, have focused 'entirely on whether disclosures about undesirable outcomes or risks have been made, and, if not, whether they represent tolerable outcomes under the circumstances or whether knowledge of them would have altered the patient's intentions and behavior.'[142] While this is important, it is also the case that the person whose ability to decide is adjudicated upon is not the instant patient, but rather an imagined conglomerate of *all* patients, reduced to a kind of lowest common denominator. In an ideal world, judges would use the law to reinforce the fundamental value of patient autonomy. To the contrary, however, courts have devised a system that has arguably been overly concerned not with prioritising patient rights, but rather with balancing them with other, often policy based, considerations. While this may not, in any abstract sense, be wrong, it nonetheless presents a major obstacle to encouraging and/or vindicating truly autonomous decisions.

However, it is worth reminding ourselves that doctors may in any event be more influenced by what their professional bodies say – such as the General Medical Council's recent publication *Consent: patients and doctors making decisions together*[143] and guidance from the British Medical Association – than by what emerges from the courts. Jones suggests that case law 'can never be a comprehensive framework' ... and that the guidance from professional bodies 'can be both more specific and more likely to be read and acted upon by

---

[142] Faden, R R, Beauchamp, T L, *A History and Theory of Informed Consent*, Oxford University Press, 1986, at p 247.

[143] London, General Medical Council, 2008.

doctors.'[144] This is not to say that the law is entirely without value in this area. Annas points out that – however much we may criticise the concept of consent – it was 'not a concept that had been promoted or embraced by medicine or medical ethics: it had to be imposed on medicine by law.'[145] It is paradoxical that once embraced by the professions, the importance of respect for autonomy seems to have been taken more seriously by them than by the law. Having said that, however, it is the law and not professional guidance that is the ultimate arbiter of physician's behaviour and for that reason, if for no other, we can and should expect it to pay serious attention to the importance of self-determination and autonomous decision-making. However, the rituals, rules, policies and idiosyncrasies of the law seem ill-suited to recognising its centrality. Patients' decisions about healthcare are intensely and highly personal yet the law seems unable or unwilling to prioritise their significance for the patient in the face of apparently competing values. As Teff says, '[t]he optimum choice of treatment is not necessarily that which is conventionally deemed medically best, even when such a judgement can confidently be made.'[146] In light of the concerns highlighted about the ability of the doctrine of consent to vindicate individual autonomy, it is probably unsurprising that Jackson should conclude that, ' … there is an increasing need to think seriously about abandoning the pretence that tort law offers any protection at all to patients' interests in access to information about their medical treatment.'[147] In other words, the law of consent is not inherently capable of fully – perhaps even partially – vindicating patient autonomy.

However, in the absence of an obvious alternative, it will remain to the law that we must turn to ensure that our informational and decisional rights are recognised. In this chapter, we have analysed cases that outline what the law purports to do and questioned what it achieves in reality. What has emerged is a theoretical commitment to respect for what I referred to earlier as the 'individualistic' concept of autonomy, albeit, it has been argued, rather ineffectually. In fact, despite what it says, the law has distanced itself in the 'true' or 'pure' consent cases we have examined from any concept of autonomy that focuses on the individual *qua* individual, preferring – or perhaps forced – to consider the hypothetical reasonable doctor or reasonable patient. It would seem, then, that the doctrine of consent, or 'informed' consent has little in reality to offer in protecting individualistic autonomy. Nor would

---

[144] Jones, M A, 'Informed Consent And Other Fairy Stories', *Medical Law Review*, 7, Summer 1999: 103–34, at p 106.

[145] Annas, G J, *American Bioethics: Crossing Human Rights and Health Law Boundaries*, Oxford University Press, 2005, at p 97.

[146] Teff, H, *Reasonable Care: Legal Perspectives on the Doctor-Patient Relationship*, Oxford, Clarendon Press, 1994, at p 123.

[147] Jackson, E, '"Informed Consent" to Medical Treatment and the Impotence of Tort', in McLean, S A M (ed), *First Do No Harm: Law, Ethics and Healthcare*, Aldershot, Ashgate, 2006, 273–86, at p 28.

proponents of relational autonomy necessarily be satisfied. Although the policy considerations that shape the law on consent are external to the patient, they are not obviously the kind of concerns that this model wants to see incorporated into autonomy. They do not *prima facie* concern lives in the context of society; rather they prioritise lives in the context of the doctor/patient relationship – a mere microcosm of the community of which the individual is a part.

If so, this is likely to have an impact on other areas where people want to claim a right to make their own decisions. It will, therefore, be of interest to consider whether the courts and/or the law have appropriately utilised the concept of autonomy and whether they have been consistent in their application of the rules they have developed about consent in specific, and problematic, situations. Each of the topics in the chapters that follow involves a situation in which the right to exercise one's individual autonomous choice is of critical importance, yet where there are also potentially other (relational) interests at stake. By evaluating the law's response to these difficult and problematic situations, we can further interpret the value actually given to autonomy in law and assess the extent to which (if at all) the apparent moral superiority of the relational account turns out to be real.

Chapter 4

Autonomy at the end of life

It is generally agreed that the corollary of the right to consent to treatment is the right to refuse it. While choosing to accept recommended therapy can be an affirmation of the patient's autonomy, so too can be his/her decision to avoid or reject it. Both are about self-determination or control over our lives, which, as Frey says, ' ... is one of the most important goods we enjoy.'[1] While rejecting treatment may seem in some cases to be irrational, especially when there is hope of palliation or cure, there may be reasons – possibly unknown to healthcare professionals – that lead people to make the decision not to accept it. As Charlesworth says:

> The essence of liberalism is the moral conviction that, because they are autonomous moral agents or persons, people must as far as possible be free to choose for themselves, even if their choices are, objectively speaking, mistaken.[2]

For Dworkin, acceptance of the individual's right to be self-determining serves a vitally important function in that it 'makes self-creation possible. It allows each of us to be responsible for shaping our lives according to our own coherent or incoherent – but, in any case, distinctive – personality.'[3] Thus, in making independent decisions about our future, we are affirming our own view of who we are and how we should live (and in this case die). In so doing, according to Hoffmaster, we also liberate ourselves from the 'tragedy and suffering that vulnerability can mean ... '.[4]

In some cases the consequences of refusing treatment may be relatively trivial. Failure to accept a prescription for sleeping pills may cause harm, but

---

[1] Frey, R G, 'Distinctions in Death', in Dworkin, G, Frey, R G, Bok, S, *Euthanasia and Physician-Assisted Suicide: For and Against*, Cambridge University Press, 1998, 17–42, at p 17.

[2] Charlesworth, M, *Bioethics in a Liberal Society*, Cambridge University Press, 1993, at p 4.

[3] Dworkin, R, *Life's Dominion: An Argument about Abortion and Euthanasia*, London, HarperCollins, 1993, at p 224.

[4] Hoffmaster, B, 'What Does Vulnerability Mean?', *Hastings Center Report*, March–April 2006: 38–45, at p 42.

it may also mean only that insomnia persists for longer than it otherwise would. In other cases, however, rejecting medically recommended treatment may result in serious injury or damage – even death. In consequence, while we may be relatively unperturbed by the former decision, we may be seriously troubled by the latter. Nonetheless, as we will see, in some situations the choice of an individual – even if it results in death – will be respected 'because we acknowledge his right to a life structured by his own values.'[5]

Part of that life is, of course, death. Sadly, we will all die and we live our lives in the sure and certain (albeit often subliminal) knowledge that this is so. Just as we take seriously how we dispose of our property after death, we have what Dworkin would call a 'critical interest' in how we die. People's critical interests, he says, are 'interests that it does make their life genuinely better to satisfy, interests they would be mistaken, and genuinely worse off, if they did not recognize.'[6] Critical interests stand in contrast with 'experiential interests', which contribute to the quality of life 'because and when they feel good'.[7] In healthcare, especially in situations where death might result from the choice made, critical interests are of immense importance because '[t]hey represent critical judgments rather than just experiential preferences.'[8] They are authentic choices of the individual concerned and reflect deeply held values. In respecting self-determined decisions about medical treatment we are vindicating the 'critical judgements' that people make. Arguably, nowhere is this more important or 'critical' than in situations where the judgement concerns matters of life and death – or perhaps more accurately, matters of death.

While it is almost certainly the case that most people value every second of their lives, there are some for whom life has become intolerable and/or unwanted. We may not understand why this is so, nor may we believe that in their circumstances we would feel the same way, but the value attributed to one's own life is a highly personal matter which is not susceptible of second-guessing by others. Having said that, the state, through the vehicle of the law, claims an interest in preserving life; an interest that, in most countries throughout the world, means that the law prohibits assisted dying (either assisted suicide or voluntary euthanasia). Killing is universally regarded as wrong, although in states where assisted dying and/or voluntary euthanasia have been legalised, a distinction is drawn between *unlawful* killing (universally prohibited) and what might be termed *lawful* killing (which is permissible within limits). Even in those countries which have resisted the legalisation of assisted dying, there are sub-categories of life-ending behaviour

[5] Dworkin, R, *Life's Dominion: An Argument about Abortion and Euthanasia*, London, HarperCollins, 1993, at p 224.

[6] Ibid., at p 201.

[7] Ibid., at p 201.

[8] Ibid., at p 202.

which do nonetheless allow for the bringing about of some deaths. This can arise in cases where, for example, the person is in a permanent vegetative state,[9] or an infant is so ill or disabled that treatment is regarded as futile or unduly burdensome.[10] Since these cases manifestly do not and cannot hinge on the question of autonomy, they will not be considered in depth here, although reference will be made to them where relevant.[11]

Although the law in the United Kingdom, as in most other jurisdictions, does not permit the deliberate taking of life, there are some legal devices that do result in bringing about the end of someone's life. For example, using the principle of double effect, doctors may knowingly (but, it is claimed, unintentionally) bring about the death of a patient by increasing doses of analgesia. Broadly, this principle permits the end (the patient's death) so long as the intention is the relief of pain, not the death itself.[12] There are many reasons to question this doctrine, but since – again – the decision is generally that of the doctor, albeit in some cases the patient may be involved,[13] this will also not be dealt with further in this discussion. This example shows that while doctors cannot lawfully respond to a direct request for assistance to die in many jurisdictions, they nonetheless 'can assist patients to die, even in situations where no such request is made.'[14] However paradoxical this may appear to be in light of what follows, it is an important point to bear in mind when considering what is – or should be – the law's response when assistance in dying is requested. It is particularly important to bear this in mind when analysing the claims of opponents of legalised assisted dying that bringing about death is *never* acceptable.

Of specific interest in this chapter are situations where the person has a voice and seeks to exercise it; in other words, to prioritise their autonomy at the end of life. The first example to be considered arises when an individual wishes to refuse life-sustaining or life-saving medical treatment. At least theoretically standing in direct confrontation with the person's wishes is the state's interest in preserving life, encapsulated in the principle of the sanctity of life. Pretty obviously, this principle holds that all human life – irrespective of its condition – is sacred and inviolable; in other words, it can never be deliberately taken. As Lord Hoffmann has said, adherence to this principle 'explains why we think it is almost always wrong to cause the death of another

---

[9] *Airedale NHS Trust v Bland* (1993) 12 BMLR 64.

[10] See, for example, *Re Wyatt (a child) (medical treatment: parents' consent)* [2004] Fam Law 866.

[11] However, for further consideration, see McLean, S A M, *Assisted Dying: Reflections on the Need for Law Reform*, Routledge-Cavendish, 2007; Huxtable, R, *Euthanasia, Ethics and the Law: From Conflict to Compromise*, Routledge-Cavendish, 2007.

[12] *R v Adams* [1957] Crim LR 365.

[13] *R v Cox* (1992) 12 BMLR 38.

[14] Freeman, M, 'Death, Dying, and the Human Rights Act', *Current Legal Problems*, 52, 1999: 218–38, at p 232.

human being, even one who is terminally ill or so disabled that we think if we were in his position we would rather be dead ... '.[15]

However, courts have also made it clear that the principle of the sanctity of life is sometimes defeasible since it is 'only one of a cluster of ethical principles which we apply to decisions about how we should live.'[16] In the case of *Re T* Lord Donaldson went even further, saying:

> The patient's interest consists of his right to self-determination – his right to live his own life how he wishes, even if it will damage his health or lead to his premature death. Society's interest is in upholding the concept that all human life is sacred and that it should be preserved if at all possible. *It is well established that in the ultimate the right of the individual is paramount* (emphasis added).[17]

In the case of *Airedale NHS Trust v Bland*, Lord Goff also explicitly declared that 'the principle of the sanctity of human life must yield to the principle of self-determination.'[18] Thus, it would seem that in principle individuals are free to make decisions even where they fly in the face of clinical recommendations and even when they conflict with the state's avowed interest in preserving life. Whether they are always respected is another matter, as we will see, and the attitude of the law seems to depend not primarily on respect for self-determination, nor on the competent expression of the individual's wishes, but rather on issues that are essentially contextual or situational, no matter how they are actually justified.

Rejecting life-saving or life-sustaining treatment

Were there any remaining room for doubt about the standing of a competent refusal of life-sustaining treatment – which legally speaking there should not have been – this was fully clarified in the case of *Re B (adult: refusal of treatment)*.[19] In this case, the doctors attending to Ms B refused to acquiesce in her request that life-sustaining ventilation be discontinued. Ms B was, therefore, forced to take the matter to law. Her circumstances were that she suffered a haemorrhage of the spinal column in her neck in 1999. Later in the same year she executed a living will or advance directive, which indicated that should she suffer a life-threatening condition, or become permanently mentally impaired or unconscious in the future, she would not wish any life-sustaining treatment to be left in place. In 2001, she suffered an

---

[15] *Airedale NHS Trust v Bland* (1993) 12 BMLR 64, at p 96.
[16] Ibid.
[17] *Re T* (1992) 9 BMLR 46, at p 59.
[18] *Airedale NHS Trust v Bland* (1993) 12 BMLR 64, at pp 111–12.
[19] (2002) 65 BMLR 149.

intramedullary cervical spine cavernoma, which left her tetraplegic. The doctors caring for her did not believe that the advance directive was sufficiently specific to be triggered by her situation, but Ms B repeatedly asked that the ventilation be turned off. Doubts about her capacity were resolved and she was found to be legally competent. Despite her insistent requests that the ventilator be switched off, and the making of another advance directive, her doctors refused to follow her wishes. Instead, they offered her the option of a move to another hospital where she might be weaned off the ventilator. This was rejected by Ms B. Since recovery was admittedly impossible, Ms B wanted the right to choose death over continued existence in her present condition, while at the same time intimating that she would, of course, have chosen life if she believed it would have been tolerable.

Ultimately, the judge accepted that Ms B's choice had been competently made, and agreed that it was her right to make it. She said:

> If mental capacity is not in issue and the patient, having been given the relevant information and offered the available options, chooses to refuse the treatment, that decision has to be respected by the doctors. Considerations that the best interests of the patient would indicate that the decision should be to consent to treatment are irrelevant.[20]

Ms B's autonomy was thereby respected, and her doctors were – unusually – found liable in trespass for their failure to accede to her wishes. It is worth noting, however, that although refusal of treatment is said to be a patient's right – not just because of consent laws but also because it is an assault on the patient to continue or provide treatment that has not been agreed to – in this case Ms B's rights were not regarded as absolute by her doctors who used their own morals to prevent her from exercising them. Essentially, therefore, the judgements of others were sufficient to ensure that Ms B, rather than being free to exercise her own autonomy, was forced through a series of medical and legal hoops to win the right to choose. However, in the case of Re AK, it was made clear that doctors cannot provide treatment, even if it maintains life, where the patient 'has let it be known that he does not consent and that such treatment is against his wishes.'[21]

It seems entirely logical that refusal of treatment should be honoured, in recognition of the fact both that it is an expression of the competent individual's autonomy rights and that treatment without consent is an assault. Death is not always a fate to be avoided. Indeed, decisions that will inevitably result in death are lawfully taken in some cases by third parties, even where the patient is not competent, and their views are not known. For

---

[20] Re B (adult: refusal of treatment) (2002) 65 BMLR 149, per Dame Elizabeth Butler-Sloss, at p 174.
[21] Re AK (2000) 58 BMLR 151, per Hughes, J, at p 156.

example, in the *Bland* case,[22] where the young man in question was not competent to express any wishes, the court allowed doctors to withdraw life-sustaining treatment; a situation mirrored in the law of other jurisdictions. Further, where people have declared in advance that they do not wish life-sustaining treatment should certain circumstances arise this, too, is respected. This is now enshrined in law in England and Wales by the terms of the Mental Capacity Act 2005,[23] and is the law in many other jurisdictions. For example, in the US case of *Cruzan v Director of Missouri Department of Health*[24] the court accepted that an individual is entitled to make an advance refusal of life-sustaining treatment, although it was also held that the state can impose evidentiary and procedural requirements in testing the validity of such a refusal in order to establish the veracity of the claim that this is indeed what the person would have wanted. It would be ironic were the law to permit bringing about death in these cases, but refuse to support the person's own competently and contemporaneously expressed wishes.

To return to the case of *Ms B*, one important conclusion can be drawn. While naturally preferring life in the abstract, her decision was designed to bring about her death. She was not simply choosing non-treatment; she actively and consciously knew that her decision would inevitably result in death, and indeed was aware that there was an alternative regime which could have preserved her life, albeit that it would not improve her condition. Despite the reluctance of her doctors to abide by her decision, both the law and the guidance from the General Medical Council now make it clear that competent adult patients 'have the right to refuse treatment even where refusal may result in harm to themselves or in their own death, and doctors are legally bound to respect their decision.'[25]

Equally interesting, particularly given the way the law treats the issue of an affirmative consent, once Ms B's competence was established no further inquiry was made into her decision. On the other hand, when patients argue that they would have rejected treatment had they been fully informed,`their assertion is subjected to close inquiry including a generalisation about what information the reasonable patient would have needed or the prudent doctor would have disclosed. Where the treatment is rejected, even if the inevitable outcome is death, only competence seems to be at issue which might seem strange given the gravity of the consequences. As Orentlicher notes:

> ... since treatment withdrawals *typically* involve morally justified deaths, the law permits all persons to refuse life-sustaining treatment

[22] (1993) 12 BMLR 64.

[23] s 24.

[24] 497 US 261 (1990).

[25] *Withholding and Withdrawing Life-prolonging Treatments: Good Practice in Decision-making*, London, General Medical Council, 2002, at para 13.

without trying to decide whether the decision to die is morally justified in each case (original emphasis).[26]

Unlike in the case where affirmative consent is at issue, the patient who chooses to bring about their death by rejecting treatment is the focus of the inquiry. No consideration of what the 'prudent patient' would choose is engaged in. The individual choice is prioritised over all other considerations. Evidence of legal competence is enough to mandate respect for the decision and questions about the 'reasonableness' of the decision are not raised. Nor, indeed, is there any inquiry made into what information has been disclosed to the patient. Despite the seriousness of the outcome, and the widespread prohibition on bringing about death, a refusal of treatment is evaluated by reference to competence alone, yet as Orentlicher says, '[o]ne can kill ... by withdrawing treatment.'[27] Indeed, as Lord Browne-Wilkinson noted in the *Bland* case, in UK law bringing about death may be lawful even when *mens rea* is present – which would normally render the action (or sometimes even omission) criminal. As he said, ' ... the whole purpose of stopping artificial feeding is to bring about the death of Anthony Bland.'[28] Not every 'assisted' death is then regarded as 'wrong', whatever the rhetoric of the law.

The explanation for this seemingly paradoxical situation is evident in the argument bruited in the *Bland* case (and others) that the difference between act and omission – between killing and 'letting die' – is of critical importance. I have argued elsewhere that this is essentially a distinction without a morally relevant difference.[29] Rather, it is a device to render some deaths legally acceptable, while allowing the law to continue to assert that it will never sanction the knowing or deliberate termination of a life. In essence, what adherence to this distinction has done is to obfuscate the debate. As Beauchamp says:

> The terms 'letting die' and 'killing' function to obscure more than to clarify what happens when a physician provides a patient with the means to escape the ravages of an illness ... this distinction as it has been used in many quarters of bioethics is fatally flawed as a means of treating the major problems of the right to die and physician-assisted death that face medicine and society today. For over thirty years this distinction has done more to cloud than to clarify the issues.[30]

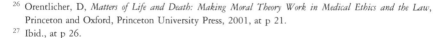

[26] Orentlicher, D, *Matters of Life and Death: Making Moral Theory Work in Medical Ethics and the Law*, Princeton and Oxford, Princeton University Press, 2001, at p 21.

[27] Ibid., at p 26.

[28] (1993) 12 BMLR 64, at p 127.

[29] McLean, S A M, *Assisted Dying: Reflections on the Need for Law Reform*, Routledge-Cavendish, 2007.

[30] Beauchamp, T L, 'The Right to Die as the Triumph of Autonomy', *Journal of Medicine and Philosophy*, 31, 2006: 643–54, at p 650.

Grayling supports this assertion, saying that 'withholding treatment is an act, based on a decision, just as giving treatment is an act, based on a decision.'[31] Orentlicher comments that ' ... we cannot assume for any *particular* act or omission that there is or is not moral culpability. In some cases, an omission is as reprehensible as an act.'[32] By analogy, an act can be every bit as acceptable as an omission. Nonetheless, the House of Lords, for example, continued to hold to the apparent distinction between the two – in my view simplistically – saying '[t]he right to refuse medical treatment is far removed from the right to request assistance in dying.'[33] Despite this, Lord Mustill in the case of *Airedale NHS Trust v Bland*[34] expressed his concern at using this alleged distinction as a basis for decision-making, noting his concern that 'however much the terminologies may differ, the ethical status of the two courses of action is for all relevant purposes indistinguishable.'[35]

Despite this, while the latter (assisted dying) is prohibited, the former (refusing life-sustaining medical treatment) is not, the presumption apparently being that the former simply allows a 'natural' death to occur, thereby not implicating the doctors or other healthcare professionals in a criminal act. Yet, what is special about a 'natural' death? As Davies says, '[t]he idea that there is something praiseworthy about enduring unrelievable suffering until a 'natural' death occurs should not be thrust upon someone who sees no point in such a course of action.'[36] Further, Orentlicher disputes the argument that there is a difference between a 'natural' death and one brought about with assistance, saying:

> Whether a death is natural also is not helpful in distinguishing treatment withdrawal from suicide assistance. Patients who have received artificial ventilation, kidney dialysis, or cancer chemotherapy are no longer able to die a 'natural' death. A natural death occurs only when a person has received no treatment for the illness that ultimately proves fatal. Accordingly, patients who die when treatment is withdrawn also die an unnatural death. Indeed, inasmuch as medical treatment changes a patient's death from its "natural" course, assisted suicide may bring the patient's death closer to what it would have been naturally (i.e., as it would have been without medical treatment).[37]

---

[31] Grayling, A C '"Right to die"', *BMJ*, 330, 2005: 799, at p 799.

[32] Orentlicher, D, *Matters of Life and Death: Making Moral Theory Work in Medical Ethics and the Law*, Princeton and Oxford, Princeton University Press, 2001, at p 30.

[33] *House of Lords Select Committee on Medical Ethics*, HL Paper 21–1, 1994, at para 236.

[34] (1993) 12 BMLR 64.

[35] Ibid., at p 132.

[36] Davies, J, 'Altruism towards the end of life', *J Med Ethics*, 19, 1993: 111–13, at p 113.

[37] Orentlicher, D, *Matters of Life and Death: Making Moral Theory Work in Medical Ethics and the Law*, Princeton and Oxford, Princeton University Press, 2001, at p 29.

Price notes the ephemeral nature of the distinction between refusal of treatment and active assistance in dying, saying that '[e]ven if the treatment refusal is an omission, it is the cause of death where this is the known and inevitable consequence of the patient's decision.'[38] Indeed, while Singer concedes that it might be psychologically easier for doctors to 'let' someone die rather than actually 'helping' them to do so, he also argues that they really must ask themselves whether there is a real difference between the two.[39] As Otlowski notes, ' ... the distinction between active and passive euthanasia and the underlying acts/omissions doctrine is most problematic and unsatisfactory ... the distinction is of debatable moral and philosophical significance.'[40] If these commentators are right, then the law has developed artificial and disingenuous rules to differentiate the situations from each other, presumably to serve policy-based purposes. One of these might be to avoid an increase in the number of cases where people might choose death, with the possible implications this might have on society. However, the scope of treatment rejections could also be immensely wide. As has been said, '[w]ithholding a ventilator from a patient with pneumonia or withholding a transfusion from a patient with a sudden loss of blood can result in the death of someone who could be restored to good health.'[41] Thus, 'treatment withdrawal can bring about the death of an essentially healthy person.'[42] Jackson notes that anyone – irrespective of their clinical condition – who refuses life-sustaining treatment must have that choice respected, even if the patient 'wants to refuse life-prolonging treatment for bizarre or illogical reasons, or even for no reason at all ... '.[43]

In treatment refusal cases, then, what matters is that the person is legally competent; no inquiry is made, or is apparently seen as necessary, into the reasons for choosing death. What matters is that the patient's decision is a reflection of his or her self-determined judgement. This is, of course, entirely in line with the law of consent which prohibits unconsented touching, and the law of assault. Not everyone is satisfied, however, with the position adopted by the law. Callahan, for example, disputes the value of choice pure and simple, unless it is 'complemented and undergirded by rich cultural and moral resources and incentives to exercise [it] wisely ... '.[44] Otherwise, he

---

[38] Price, D T, 'Assisted Suicide and Refusing Medical Treatment: Linguistics, Morals and Legal Contortions', *Medical Law Review*, 4, Autumn 1996: 270–99, at pp 287–88.

[39] Singer, P, *Rethinking Life and Death: The Collapse of our Traditional Ethics*, New York, St Martin's Griffin, 1994.

[40] Otlowski, M F A, *Voluntary Euthanasia and the Common Law*, Oxford, Clarendon Press, 1997, at p 12.

[41] Orentlicher, D, *Matters of Life and Death: Making Moral Theory Work in Medical Ethics and the Law*, Princeton and Oxford, Princeton University Press, 2001, at p 31.

[42] Ibid.

[43] Jackson, E, 'Whose Death is it Anyway?: Euthanasia and the Medical Profession', in Holder, J, O'Cinneide, C and Freeman, M (eds), *Current Legal Problems 2004*, 57: 415–42, at p 420.

[44] Callahan, D, *The Troubled Dream of Life: In Search of a Peaceful Death*, Washington DC, Georgetown University Press, 2000, at p 36.

suggests, the right to choose 'can be vacuous.'[45] This sounds very much like an appeal to what has been termed a 'relational' account of autonomy, that considers decisions to be genuinely autonomous only when they take account of the contextual nature of human existence. However, who is to say, and how would we know, whether or not account has been taken of context and relationships? In any case, ' ... autonomy does not entail that the individual be an island of independence, distanced in a radical way from the company of others, indeed, the opposite is the case: we cannot conceive of agent autonomy in isolation from the social context in which the autonomous agent comes into being.'[46] Also, it must be asked how we could differentiate between a relational and an individualistic decision? While Callahan's assertion that we should be considering '*how* or *what* we choose', rather than the fact that 'we have a right to choose'[47] is appealing in some ways, it is virtually impossible to translate this into reality unless we investigate every treatment refusal so intensely as to deny the value of any kind of choice, and thereby the importance of autonomy itself.

People who want to embark on a path towards death by rejecting life-sustaining treatment have their decisions treated with respect. Their desire not to continue with a life that (for them) is undignified allows them to choose a death that is dignified (for them). Cassel argues that '[a]ddressing this need for dignity might be more profoundly significantly human than all the other caring that physicians do.'[48] Doctors who accede to a request for treatment withdrawal are, in effect, offering their patients both trust and respect. This, it could be argued, is the supreme act of caring. While watching patients die must be uncomfortable, especially where treatment is available, respect at the end of life is likely to be of great importance to the patient. This was recently highlighted by the decision of 13-year-old Hannah Jones to refuse a life-saving heart transplant.[49] Although the hospital involved with Hannah's care originally sought legal clarification of their position, once satisfied that she was competent, they did not oppose her choice. Like it or not, the law's approach to choosing death by omission adopts a strictly individualistic account of autonomy, preferring to focus on competence rather than the outcome of the decision and thereby recognising the importance of individual self-determination. It might be assumed, then, that *any* choice to die would be routinely accepted with no inquiry made beyond the issue of legal capacity. However, as we will see, competence is by

[45] Ibid.

[46] Oshana, M A L, 'The Autonomy Bogeyman', *The Journal of Value Inquiry*, 35, 2001: 209–26, at p 221.

[47] Callahan, D, *The Troubled Dream of Life: In Search of a Peaceful Death*, Washington DC, Georgetown University Press, 2000, at p 36.

[48] Cassel, C K, 'Physician-assisted suicide: Progress or peril?', in Thomasma, D C and Kushner, T (eds), *Birth to Death: Science and Bioethics*, Cambridge University Press, 1996, 218–30, at p 222.

[49] For discussion of this case, see McLean, S A M, http://blogs.bmj.com/bmj/2008/11/14/sheila-mclean-whose-decision-is-it-anyway (accessed on 3/12/2008).

no means the only consideration taken into account when an individual wishes to die, but is incapable of doing so without assistance.

Choosing an assisted death

Patients who refuse or reject life-sustaining treatment are *in reality* choosing death. That they would rather live than die if their condition were different does not distinguish them from others who need help to die – in fact, this is the principle characteristic that they have in common. Where there is life-sustaining treatment to reject, and the individual makes the choice to refuse it in the knowledge that it will bring about death, neither doctors nor the law can or will stand in their way. There are, however, others who share the same desire to end their suffering but who need help to effectuate it – help, that is, beyond the withdrawal or withholding of medical treatment. If the significant issue is the individual's competence, as it seems to be when treatment refusal is involved, then it would *prima facie* be reasonable to assume that those who need more active help to vindicate their decisions would be equally entitled to have their choice to die respected. However, while treatment refusals are accepted as valid – indeed they are binding on doctors – people who (competently) request active assistance in dying will find that their legal competence is not sufficient in most jurisdictions to render their decision lawful.

It is instructive to inquire as to why this should be the case. Choosing to die is not in itself outlawed. Suicide is not a crime and deliberate decisions to reject life-sustaining treatment are routinely accepted as legally valid. The law's stance in these cases is, then, essentially individualistic. Even if a person's death has consequences for third parties – as it will where the person has a social network – this is not taken to be legally relevant and the individual's decision will be respected; any harm resulting from their death is insufficient to overturn the presumption that the individual's self-determined decisions prevail. Given what has been said about treatment withdrawal, it might be concluded that it is not the outcome – death – that is the primary concern of the law. Rather, it is the offering of respect for individual autonomy that matters. If so, then individuals should be free to make their own life and death decisions, unencumbered by anything more than an inquiry into their competence. However, this would be a simplistic assumption, as we will see. When individuals require active assistance to satisfy their desire to control their own death, considerations beyond the question of competence are used to stand in their way. Perhaps the paradigmatic case is that of Diane Pretty. While there are others, this is probably the best known and most thoroughly argued case, and will therefore be used as an exemplar of the law's approach in the United Kingdom.

Diane Pretty was suffering from motor neurone disease – a degenerative condition that ultimately results in physical inability to swallow, breathe and so on, but leaves the intellect unimpaired. The person becomes effectively trapped in a useless body, all too aware of the indignity and distress caused by this but unable to do anything about it. For Diane Pretty, this future was unacceptable; she wished to ensure that she would not be obliged to live through such an unpleasant, indeed terrifying, end to her life. Knowing that she would be unable to kill herself when her life deteriorated to the point at which she no longer wished to survive, she wanted the Director of Public Prosecutions (DPP) to agree in advance not to prosecute her husband should he assist her to die at the time of her choosing. Should he help her, he would be in direct breach of s. 2(1) of the Suicide Act 1961.[50] Leaving aside the question as to whether or not the DPP could competently enter into such an agreement, and although this case is unusual in that Mrs Pretty wanted her husband rather than a physician to assist in her death, the arguments she offered in challenging the law's prohibition of assisted suicide are instructive, as are the judgements of the courts. Having failed to win her case in the domestic courts, Mrs Pretty finally sought a decision from the European Court of Human Rights, whose judgement forms the basis of what follows.[51]

Mrs Pretty sought to use a number of articles of the European Convention on Human Rights, incorporated into UK law by the Human Rights Act 1998, to challenge the validity of the 1961 Act and the refusal of the DPP to guarantee not to prosecute her husband should he assist her to die. She first invoked the terms of Article 2 – the right to life. She argued that although this right was principally intended to protect people from third parties it should also be read as encapsulating freedom of choice. On her argument, '[w]hile most people want to live, some want to die, and the article protects both rights. The right to die is not the antithesis of the right to life but the corollary of it, and the state has a positive obligation to protect both.'[52] She further argued that the 1961 Act placed her, and people in similar situations, in a position that amounted to a breach of Article 3 – the right not to be subjected to inhuman and degrading treatment. Unlike Article 2, this right is not subject to any permissible derogations. Mrs Pretty argued that:

(1) Member states have an absolute and unqualified obligation not to inflict the proscribed treatment and also to take positive action to prevent the subjection of individuals to such treatment ... (2) Suffering attributable to the progression of a disease may amount to such treatment if the state can prevent or ameliorate such suffering and does not do so ... (3) In denying Mrs Pretty the opportunity to bring her suffering

---

[50] This Act does not apply in Scotland, where the appropriate charge would almost certainly be culpable homicide, although technically a murder charge could be brought.

[51] *Pretty v United Kingdom* (2002) 66 BMLR 147.

[52] Ibid., at p 155.

to an end the United Kingdom ... will subject her to the proscribed treatment ... (4) since ... it is open to the United Kingdom under the Convention to refrain from prohibiting assisted suicide, the Director [of Public Prosecutions] can give the undertaking sought without breaking the United Kingdom's obligations under the Convention. (5) If the Director may not give the undertaking, s 2 of the 1961 Act is incompatible with the Convention.[53]

She also argued that Article 8 of the Convention – the right to private and family life – was in support of her right to make her own decisions about her death. This right is generally referred to as the one which protects autonomy, which, in Mrs Pretty's submission, should include her right autonomously to choose death (albeit with assistance). Article 9, the right to freedom of thought, conscience and religion, was also argued to protect her right to choose to follow her own principles, which included support for assisted dying. Finally, she argued that her Article 14 right not to be discriminated against was breached by the terms of the 1961 Act.

The European Court of Human Rights was, however, not persuaded by Mrs Pretty's arguments. While recognising that some member states have decriminalised assisted dying, from the Court's perspective this did not mean that a state's failure to do so was in breach of the Convention. What Mrs Pretty would have had to establish was that 'the United Kingdom is in breach of the Convention by failing to permit it or would be in breach of the Convention if it did not permit it.'[54] This, according to the judge was an 'untenable' contention.[55] Further, Mrs Pretty's argument that what she was seeking was different from euthanasia was rejected. For the Court, if it could be argued that self-determination in situations such as this was conferred by Article 2, 'it would necessarily follow in logic that such a person would have a right to be killed at the hands of a third part without giving any help to the third party and the state would be in breach of the Convention if it were to interfere with the exercise of that right.'[56] This conclusion it would not accept, thus effectively dismissing her Article 2 and Article 3 arguments. As to Article 8, this, according to the Court 'protects the physical, moral and psychological integrity of the individual ... ' but 'there is nothing to suggest that it confers a right to decide when or how to die.'[57] As for Article 9, while accepting that Mrs Pretty was indeed free to hold to her own principles and morals, nonetheless 'her belief cannot found a requirement that her husband should be absolved from the consequences of conduct which, although

[53] Ibid., at pp 159–60.
[54] Ibid., at p 159.
[55] Ibid.
[56] Ibid., at p 156.
[57] Ibid., at p 163.

it would be consistent with her belief, is proscribed by the criminal law.'[58] Since none of her other Convention articles was engaged, it was not necessary to consider Article 14.

On the face of it, the singular factual difference between Ms B and Mrs Pretty is the fact that Ms B was able to effectuate her decision by rejecting treatment, whereas Mrs Pretty needed active assistance to die. The so-called acts/omissions doctrine has already been referred to and it has been suggested that it is thoroughly unsatisfactory. Nonetheless, it seemingly continues to carry weight in the eyes of the law. The question is why? The answer may be found not just from within the doctrine itself, but also from extraneous considerations which are used to bolster the claim that killing in an active manner is always wrong, without exploring whether or not bringing about death in other ways (for example by removing life-sustaining treatment) is morally equivalent. It is certainly possible that healthcare professionals may feel more comfortable 'assisting' a person to die by not interfering (except of course where the treatment needs to be physically removed) than they would if they were actively involved (for example, by providing a lethal injection or a prescription for medication), but this in and of itself is not sufficient to make the difference between the two morally relevant. Indeed, as I have argued elsewhere 'any ethical difference between killing and letting die – real or perceived – could equally hinge on whether or not the death was chosen or imposed.'[59] In other words, if there is a difference between the two situations it would depend on the voluntariness of the choice, rather than on how it is effectuated.

Battin argues that the acts/omission distinction 'does not succeed in carrying the moral weight often placed on it.'[60] While Williams postulates that application of the distinction might produce the 'right resolution', she also argues that 'the method by which that result is achieved is defective when it is based on an untenable fabrication which relies, to a great extent, on judicial intuition and preconceived categorisations of what is acceptable and what is not.'[61] In fact, both killing and letting die can be conceptualised as either 'right' or 'wrong'; each can be justified in specific circumstances. Letting die through neglect can be every bit as wrong as active killing; equally active killing may be justified in self-defence. So, if there is no evident moral distinction between some (or any) cases of actively assisted deaths and those brought about passively, what remains of the argument against legalisation of both (or neither, of course)? Arguably, the answer must be – very little, if anything.

[58] Ibid., at p 169.

[59] McLean, S A M, *Assisted Dying: Reflections on the Need for Law Reform*, Routledge-Cavendish, 2007, at p 93.

[60] Battin, M, *The Least Worst Death: Essays in Bioethics on the End of Life*, Oxford University Press, 1994, at p 19.

[61] Williams, G, *Intention and Causation in Medical Non-Killing: The Impact of Criminal Law Concepts on Euthanasia and Assisted Suicide*, Routledge-Cavendish, 2007, at p 56.

However, it is at this point that additional considerations intrude into the debate. One such consideration relates to the alleged effect that allowing people to choose an assisted death would have on others. For example, the House of Lords Select Committee on Medical Ethics[62] expressly referred to this, voicing their concern that legalising assisted dying would send an inappropriate message to people who are vulnerable. Rather than 'obliquely' encouraging such people to choose death, the message that should be sent is to 'assure them of our care and support in life.'[63] Precisely so, but the Select Committee fails to explain why there should be any link between allowing competent people to seek assistance in dying and accepting as valid a coerced or pressurised 'request' from someone who is acting non-autonomously. Nor does the Committee explain the ethical difference between removing life-sustaining treatment and helping another to die. The Committee's report *asserts* this difference but provides no intellectual justification for its existence. Additionally, since this report was written, there is some empirical evidence that would seem to refute the assumptions they took as gospel. Contrary to their apprehension, legalisation of assisted suicide in the US state of Oregon has not resulted in the weak and the vulnerable being singled out; on the contrary, the carefully documented evidence from that state points to the conclusion that it is the strong-willed, educated individual who is more likely to seek an assisted death.[64] In its eighth report, the Oregon Department of Human Services reported that the most common concerns were 'a decreasing ability to participate in activities that make life enjoyable (89%), loss of dignity (89%) and losing autonomy (79%).'[65] Recent evidence does suggest that some patients requesting assisted dying may be suffering from depression, although it was also found that the majority of those receiving an assisted death do not suffer from a depressive disorder.[66] While this research would suggest that it might be wise to seek proper psychiatric evaluation in order to ensure patient competence, it does not argue against legalisation of assisted dying. The requirement for psychiatric evaluation is in fact part of the Oregon legislation, and is also required by the recent legislation that has legalised physician assisted dying in the US state of Washington.[67]

Nonetheless, concerns similar to those expressed by the Select Committee were repeated at some length in the European Court of Human Rights'

[62] Cm 2553 (1994).

[63] Ibid., at p 49, para 239.

[64] See for example, Eighth Annual Report on Oregon's Death with Dignity Act, Oregon Department of Human Services, 9 March 2006, available at http://egov.oregon.gov/DHS/ph/pas/docs/year8.pdf (accessed on 9/3/2007). The report from year 9 shows a similar pattern – available at http://egov. oregon.gov/DHS/ph/pas/docs/year9.pdf (accessed on 4/8/2008).

[65] Ibid.

[66] Ganzini, L, Goy, E R, 'Prevalence of depression and anxiety in patients requesting physicians' aid in dying: cross sectional survey', *BMJ*, 337, 2008: a1682.

[67] Dyer, C, 'Washington state legalises physician assisted suicide', *BMJ*, 337, 2008: a2480.

judgement in Diane Pretty's case. Indeed, the Court postulated that, for example, the elderly might seek assisted dying, not because they actually wanted to die but rather 'from a desire to stop being a burden on others.'[68] Leaving aside the question as to whether or not the desire not to be a burden is, or might be, a relevant concern for the elderly or those otherwise deemed to be vulnerable, both the Select Committee and the Court of Human Rights are essentially using a sleight of hand in order to maintain the *status quo*. Their failure to attend to the difference between competent choice and pressurised or coerced decisions results in a flawed argument, and while harm to third parties might be a legitimate reason to constrain individual behaviour, the harm referred to here is entirely speculative and could equally be prayed in aid when people refuse life-sustaining treatment. Moreover, their argument seems to slide from adopting an individualistic account of autonomy in treatment refusal decisions to a more relational model when death must be actively assisted, allegedly based on fears about the effect of respect for individual choice on third parties.

As I have said, unless individuals live a life that is totally without human contact, their death will likely have a negative impact on those who care for them, but whether this is sufficiently important to de-legitimise their choice to die is surely moot. In any case, every death of a socially situated individual is likely to cause grief to third parties; the fact that it was chosen arguably makes no ethical or legal difference. Although Meisel argues that in such cases 'the patient's interests are not the sole interests involved ... ',[69] it is debateable how much weight should be given to the interests that others might have in our choices. As the court said in the US case of *Compassion in Dying v State of Washington*:[70]

> Those who believe strongly that death must come without physician assistance are free to follow that creed, be they doctors or patients. They are not free, however to force their views, their religious convictions, or their philosophies on all other members of a democratic society, and to compel those whose values differ from theirs to die painful, protracted, and agonizing deaths.[71]

There is one further, and important, reason to doubt the value of the distinction drawn in law between treatment rejection/refusal and assisted dying. If pressure can be brought to bear on people to ask for an assisted death, and if this were a sufficient reason to outlaw it, then surely common sense

[68] (2002) 66 BMLR 147, at p 169.
[69] Meisel, A, 'Ethics and Law: Physician-Assisted Dying', *Journal of Palliative Medicine*, 8(3), 2005: 609–21, at p 610.
[70] 79 F3d 790 (9th Cir 1996) 810.
[71] Ibid., at p 839.

dictates that the same pressure could result in a person refusing life-sustaining treatment? Jackson argues that worries about the existence of pressure to choose death could be 'equally or perhaps even more true when death is achieved by treatment withdrawal.'[72] Yet as Parker notes, while this is probably true, nobody is demanding that there should be 'comparative research into treatment withdrawals and assisted suicide.'[73] Indeed, he also argues that, even if it were found that 'treatment withdrawals were subject to similar abuses and failures to safeguard autonomous requests for withdrawal, it is doubtful whether anyone would suggest that treatment withdrawal should be criminalized.'[74] This is because of the fundamental prohibition on interfering with competent choice and the prohibition of assault.

Jackson further questions the differential treatment of rejection of therapy and requests for assisted dying, pointing out that if we can claim to know that Ms B was competent, then surely the same evaluation would be equally possible had she required more active assistance.[75] In other words, if competence is the key to legitimising decisions, it makes no sense to hold that we can identify it in once case (treatment withdrawal) but not in another (a request for assistance in dying). In addition, Dworkin points out that '[i]f a physician can manipulate the patient's request for death, he can manipulate the patient's request for termination of treatment.'[76] The importance of voluntariness, then, is the same in each case and if it can be tested in one situation it can surely be tested in the other. Further, as Price points out, the pretence that a patient's rejection of life-sustaining treatment is not a decision to commit suicide means that 'the doctor's actions (encouragement as well as assistance) are in all instances outside the control of the criminal law.'[77] Yet, decisions to reject life-sustaining therapy are not scrutinised for any of the characteristics – such as mistakes on the part of the person rejecting the treatment, or the influence of others on their decision – that are typically used to deny the option of an assisted death to someone whose choice to die may be every bit as reasoned as that of those who do not require (active) assistance and whose desire to avoid a continued undignified or unwanted life is likely to be every bit as strong.

[72] Jackson, E, 'Whose Death is it Anyway? Euthanasia and the Medical Profession', in Holder, J, O'Cinneide, C and Freeman, M (eds), *Current Legal Problems 2004*, 57: 415–42, at p 429.

[73] Parker, M, 'End Games: Euthanasia Under Interminable Scrutiny', *Bioethics*, 19 (5–6), 2005: 523–36, at p 533.

[74] Ibid.

[75] Jackson, E, 'Whose Death is it Anyway? Euthanasia and the Medical Profession', in Holder, J, O'Cinneide, C and Freeman, M (eds), *Current Legal Problems*, 57, 2004: 415–42.

[76] Dworkin, G, 'Public Policy and Physician-Assisted Suicide', in Dworkin, G, Frey, R G and Bok, S, *Euthanasia and Physician-Assisted Suicide: For and Against*, Cambridge University Press, 1998, 64–80, at p 67.

[77] Price, D T, 'Assisted Suicide and Refusing Medical Treatment: Linguistics, Morals and Legal Contortions', *Medical Law Review*, 4, Autumn 1996: 270–99, at p 292.

A similar pattern emerges from other jurisdictions. In Canada, for example, perhaps the most significant case was that of *Rodriguez v Attorney General of Canada and another, British Columbia Coalition of People with Disabilities and others intervening*.[78] This case involved a woman of 42 years of age who was suffering from amyotropic lateral sclerosis, with a life expectancy of 2 to 14 months. She wanted to obtain a physician assisted death at a time of her choosing, and petitioned the court to declare that she had a right to do so under the terms of the Canadian Charter of Rights and Freedoms. Her argument was based on various rights outlined in the Charter, and like Mrs Pretty she challenged the terms of the legislation – in this case the Canadian Criminal Code – that prohibits aiding and abetting a suicide. In a very close judgement, she ultimately lost her case. In the United States, cases such as *Washington v Glucksberg*[79] have also paralleled the decision in Diane Pretty's case, clarifying that there is no constitutional bar on states legislating against assisted dying. In *Vacco v Quill*,[80] it was further held that states can distinguish between withdrawing treatment and assisted dying without violating the Equal Protection Clause of the Fourteenth Amendment.

It is evident that considerations beyond autonomy – or at least beyond the individualistic account of it – are taken to be important when a person wishes to die with active assistance, but not when a person's chosen death is brought about by omission. Yet, can it really be argued that the doctor who offers a prescription (which a patient may or may not take) or gives a lethal objection is somehow more closely involved in the death of their patient than is the doctor who removes the ventilation that sustains life? However illogical, the doctor in the first case would in many countries be guilty of a crime, while the second would not be. And if society is in some way harmed by permitting the former, then surely it is equally harmed by the latter?

The individual and the community

While I would argue that the apparent conflict between the individual choosing an assisted death and the community's interests is a fabricated tension, it is one which nonetheless seems real to many people. Magnusson, for example, says:

> ... regardless of religious belief, many opponents of legalised euthanasia are simply more 'communitarian' in outlook, believing that individual freedoms and interests should be tempered by communal values, social goals, and traditional constraints. Euthanasia, in contrast, is atomistic in

---

[78] (1993) 50 BMLR 1.
[79] 521 US 702 (1997).
[80] 521 US 793 (1997).

its philosophy, an affirmation of individual moral freedom in a world lacking moral absolutes.[81]

The arguments against respecting a competent request for an assisted death sometimes focus, therefore, not on the individual but rather on the impact of its permissibility on the community (or specific parts of it). For the House of Lords Select Committee on Medical Ethics, 'the issue of euthanasia is one in which the interest of the individual cannot be separated from the interest of society as a whole.'[82] Miller, while agreeing that the 'liberal-individualistic argument' has merit, nonetheless believes that the issue should be viewed 'in terms of reciprocal *responsibilities* between dying patients and their caregivers and the *responsibility* of society not to abandon dying patients to intolerable suffering.'[83] Meisel believes that people other than the individual him or her self 'have an interest in the patient's well-being and an interest in defining what counts as well-being.'[84] Even if we accept this, on what ground these concerns trump the interest of the individual in self determination is not clear. In the absence of evidence that distinguishes the right to commit suicide or refuse life-sustaining treatment clearly from an actively assisted death, the purported interest of third parties in determining how others should be permitted to exercise their autonomy is problematic at best.

The law seems to be that suicide and rejecting life-sustaining treatment – each of which as I have argued also has social and community effects – are lawful irrespective of the reasons for the decisions or their consequences. Whatever the effect of this choice on others, the individual's decision is paramount. However, apparently assisted dying is seen as qualitatively different. Primarily this would seem to depend on the application of the acts and omissions doctrine, which I have already criticised, on the postulated effects on others and also, it would appear, on the notion that legalising assisted dying will place us firmly at the top of a slippery slope (which apparently allowing treatment rejection will not).

Concerns for the elderly, the disabled and those otherwise perceived as vulnerable are routinely dragged out as evidencing why we should not permit assisted dying, ignoring the autonomy based arguments rehearsed above and also the fact that they could lawfully choose death by rejecting treatment. The reason given is that these groups might be pressurised or coerced into choosing an assisted death. In the case of assisted dying the slippery slope argument is said to have two main consequences. First, it is

---

[81] Magnusson, R S, *Angels of Death: Exploring the Euthanasia Underground*, Yale University Press, 2002, at p 37.

[82] Cm 2553 (1994), at para 237.

[83] Miller, F G, 'A Communitarian Approach to Physican-Assisted Death', *Cambridge Q of Healthcare Ethics*, 6, 1997: 78–87, at p 79.

[84] Meisel, A, 'Ethics and Law: Physician-Assisted Dying', *Journal of Palliative Medicine*, 8(3), 2005: 609–21, at p 610.

argued, legalising assisted dying sends a message to vulnerable people that they are not valued, resulting in unnecessary decisions to die earlier than they might otherwise prefer. Second, the argument would run, allowing assisted dying might eventually lead to a situation where the voluntary leads to the involuntary – raising the spectre of a 'duty' to die. Each of these arguments is important, and will be considered in what follows.

The first has already been briefly canvassed. The purported danger that allowing the competent exercise of self-determination in seeking an actively assisted death will have a negative impact on those who are already deemed vulnerable in society is widely argued for by, for example, disability rights activists. The UK's Disability Rights Commission (DRC) has expressed these concerns forcefully, reiterating their anxiety that people with disabilities are already undervalued and discriminated against in healthcare provision; how easy, they speculate, would it be disproportionately to target the disabled were assisted dying to be legalised?[85] Shakespeare, on the other hand, believes that the social model of disability (widely embraced in the United Kingdom and elsewhere) prevents the disability rights lobby from fully engaging with 'debates about illness, impairment and the end of life. It could be argued that a social model philosophy enables some to disengage from troubling questions about bodies and mortality.'[86] One fundamental problem with the DRC's position is that, while discrimination undoubtedly does exist in respect of people with disabilities, there is neither evidence nor reason to believe that allowing people to choose an assisted death will in fact disproportionately target them. As Burgess says, ' … those who regard voluntary euthanasia as a step onto a slippery slope that will (probably) lead to disaster have so far failed to make out a case that is at all convincing. Detailed empirical evidence is required and detailed empirical evidence is conspicuously lacking.'[87] Additionally, as with the second implication of the slippery slope argument, this seems to ignore the question of self-determination. Surely, we do not wish to suggest that the mere existence of disability is enough to mean that people are not capable of making self-regarding, autonomous decisions?

Another group widely thought of as vulnerable are the elderly. Here, the argument is that allowing assisted dying would 'put pressure on people … to end their lives so as not to be a burden or a nuisance to others … '.[88]

---

[85] Disability Rights Commission, Assisted Dying Policy Statement, 20/1/2006, available at http://www. drc-gb.org/library/policy/health_and_independent_living/assisted_dying_policy_statement.aspx (accessed on 29/8/2006).

[86] Shakespeare, T, Submission to the House of Lords Select Committee on the Assisted Dying for the terminally Ill Bill, at para 2.7 (personal communication); available in Volume II of the report, 254 (with Alison Davies).

[87] Burgess, J A, 'The great slippery-slope argument', *J Med Ethics*, 19, 1993: 169–74, at p 171.

[88] Shand, J, 'A Reply to Some Standard Objections to Euthanasia', *Journal of Applied Philosophy*, 14(1), 1997: 43–47, at p 43.

Shand counters this concern in two ways. First, he suggests, there may be 'nothing wrong with the decision to end one's life based on the opinion that one will be a burden – one may indeed be a burden ... it may be perfectly reasonable not to want to be a burden.'[89] Equally, he argues that failure to legalise assisted dying may mean that 'many people feel forced to go on living when they would rather die.'[90] In any case, people in Ms B's position might equally dread being a burden but that would not be enough to allow doctors to continue to force treatment on her.

The second fear of the slippery slope is that respecting an autonomous choice to have an assisted death will somehow mean that choosing death will become a duty rather than a right. There is, however, no logic in the assertion that allowing people to choose will inevitably lead to forcing them to do so. If a lawful assisted death is circumscribed by the need to make a competent, autonomous decision – as with a choice for treatment withdrawal (which may also be influenced by the perceived impact on others of continuing to live) – then it is a right not a duty: if it is autonomous, then it will be legally respected, if not, then it will not be, since a decision is not an exercise of autonomy if it is coerced or unduly influenced. In the end, Dworkin suggests that ' ... slippery slope arguments ... are very weak ones. They seem only disguises for deeper convictions that actually move most opponents of euthanasia.'[91] In reality, there is no fundamental difference between assisted suicide and treatment withholding or withdrawal. Rather, '[i]n each case, the patient's interest in self-determination gives the patient a right to die, whether by refusing treatment, having treatment withdrawn, or accepting the assistance of a physician.'[92]

Still, however, there are those who believe that the impact on the community of legalising assisted dying must not be underestimated, and that – where conflict arises – the rights of the individual 'may have to give way to those larger community interests.'[93] Yet opponents of legalisation have failed to explain why a form of individualistic autonomy is accepted – even mandated – in some cases (treatment refusal), but a more relational model is applied in others (active assisted dying). Indeed, Smith suggests that legalising assisted dying 'could actually provide a greater opportunity to involve at least the immediate community. Pre-death rituals are particularly important ... '.[94] In fact, there is some evidence that relatives of people who die an

---

[89] Ibid., at p 44.

[90] Ibid., at p 43.

[91] Dworkin, R, 'When is it right to die?', *New York Times*, 5 May 1994.

[92] 'Physician Assisted Suicide and the Right to Die with Assistance', *Harv L Rev*, 125, 2001: 2001–40, at p 2040.

[93] Smith, S W, 'Some Realism about End of Life: The Current Prohibition and the Euthanasia Underground', *American Journal of Law & Medicine*, 33, 2007: 55–95, at p 75.

[94] Ibid., at p 76.

assisted death are likely to manage that death better,[95] presumably in part because the death has been the subject of discussion and is recognised as the honest and competent choice of the individual concerned to avoid further suffering.

The distinction between acts and omissions is untenable in logic; the slippery slope argument does not work. Opponents of legalisation are not, however, without one further argument. One final trump card, they would argue, is that a decision to have an assisted death can never be autonomous, and that therefore opponents of legalisation are not ignoring autonomy, nor attempting to recast it in a relational form, but are rather concerned that autonomy does not lie at the heart of the decision. Society, therefore, has not just an interest in preventing the legalisation of assisted dying but in fact a duty to protect people from the grave consequences of a choice which is not in fact real or authentic.

Autonomy and the end of life

Dworkin says that '[e]very day, rational people all over the world plead to be allowed to die. Sometimes they plead for others to kill them.'[96] But can such pleas be regarded as truly autonomous? It must be conceded that some people will be driven to seek death as a result of factors which might be susceptible of change. For example, the individual who is suffering from depression might be persuaded to accept treatment and may then find a new value in life – it may even become desirable once more. Still others, however, might wish to reject treatment that could restore their sense of well-being, and this they would be entitled to do unless they were deemed incompetent. Therein lies the rub. Does depression always equate to incompetence? As Woodman asks ' ... doesn't anyone who is about to die feel some degree of depression? And who decides whether the sadness that they feel is clouding their judgement or heightening their understanding of their situation?'[97] Indeed, unrelieved, or perhaps rather unrelievable, depression might be a very good reason to choose death. Who is to say that Ms B was not depressed by her condition – by her contemplation of a future that was either ventilator-dependent or, if weaned off the ventilator, offered nothing but permanent paralysis and dependency? Yet her decision to orchestrate her own death, with the assistance of the doctors who removed the ventilator and would need to provide sedation to ensure that her death was peaceful, was

---

[95] Swarte, N B, Marije, L et al, 'Effects of euthanasia on the bereaved family and friends: a cross sectional study', *BMJ*, 327, 2003: 189.

[96] Dworkin, R, *Life's Dominion: An Argument about Abortion and Euthanasia*, London, HarperCollins, 1993, at p 179.

[97] Woodman, S, *Last Rights: The Struggle Over the Right to Die*, New York and London, Plenum Trade, 1998, at p 189.

not unlawful. Indeed, her doctors were compelled to comply with it. Who can say that the young man struggling with a degenerative condition who finally signals his desire for treatment to be discontinued when he could no longer communicate verbally, was not depressed? Yet his decision too was respected in law.[98]

The law has recognised that even the existence of mental illness is not inevitably sufficient to negate the validity of a decision which could result in death.[99] While the question of competence is central to whether or not an act is autonomous, it cannot simplistically be assumed that people who are depressed, mentally ill, or whatever, are always incompetent. It equally cannot be assumed that people who choose death are not competent simply because of the choice itself. If such an assumption were made, then Ms B would have been forced to continue to live, irrespective of her wishes, as would AK. If Ms B's decision is autonomous, then so too is the decision of someone else whose circumstances differ from hers only in the degree and type of assistance they need to effectuate their wishes. The difference between killing and letting die, then, is less obvious than some would have us believe. In fact, Parker suggests that:

> Most opponents of euthanasia appear to have conceded that the con-ceptual debate concerning the bare moral difference between killing and letting die has now been decided against them. Once this concession is made, different arguments are required if one wishes to continue to resist change.[100]

This requires a level of ingenuity. If none of the arguments considered *supra* actually works, how are opponents of legalisation to mount a strong case against it? Here, two further arguments based on physicians themselves are sometimes brought into play. First, it might be argued, doctors just like anyone else are entitled to respect for their own autonomy and should not be coerced into participating in assisted dying if they disapprove of it. This must be conceded, but it has no relevance to the debate. A so-called conscience clause, common in jurisdictions where assisted dying is lawful, routinely protects doctors from being forced to participate. Additionally, as Jackson points out, for those doctors who support their patients' right to make such decisions, 'the absolute prohibition of euthanasia unreasonably fetters clinical discretion.'[101] Prohibition of assisted dying may affect the autonomy rights of doctors too.

[98] *Re AK* (2001) BMLR 151.
[99] *Re C (Mental Patient: Medical Treatment)* (1993) 15 BMLR 77.
[100] Parker, M, 'End Games: Euthanasia Under Interminable Scrutiny', *Bioethics*, 19(5–6), 2005: 523–36, at p 535.
[101] Jackson, E, 'Whose Death is it Anyway? Euthanasia and the Medical Profession', in Holder, J, O'Cinneide, C and Freeman, M (eds), *Current Legal Problems*, 57, 2004: 415–42, at p 417.

Second, it could be argued that it is inimical to the ethics of medicine that doctors should participate in the death of their patients. After all, the aim of medicine surely is to cure, not to kill? Based in the Hippocratic prohibition on killing this might seem a strong argument. Yet, it could also be argued that '[f]or medical law to be reinforcing Hippocratic values rather than promoting optimum patient care, or enhancing autonomy, is now deeply anachronistic.'[102] Arguably, in any case, whether or not responding to a competent request for assistance in dying is seen *by doctors* as compatible with medical ethics (and there is no unanimity on this) the weight given to their opinions is disproportionate, particularly where the conscience clause provides an 'opt out' option. In any case:

> ... the moral principle that doctors must not kill their patients makes no practical sense in the light of our willingness to accept the medical profession's extensive and routine involvement in the shortening of patients' lives, but it nevertheless continues to have extraordinary symbolic resonance.[103]

Indeed, the apparent rejection of assisted dying by the medical professions (at least in the majority of countries, it would seem) has been described as potentially 'self-serving in its emphasis on a professional scrupulosity that seems blind to the expressed needs of the patients.'[104] And, of course, not all doctors are opposed to legalisation or to participation in the assisted death of their patients, even though their professional associations may be.

A final sub-set of the argument that focuses on the role of clinicians concerns the question of trust, which has already been briefly discussed. Some would argue that allowing doctors to participate actively in bringing about the end of their patient's life, even following a competent request, will destroy (or at least damage) the trust which is so essential to the doctor/ patient relationship. To be sure, if decisions are taken *by doctors* rather than patients, this would be a genuine concern. However, if legalisation is based on respect for autonomy, then it is the patient who makes the decision, and as Shand says, '[t]he trust between patient and doctor is that the doctor will *do his best* for the patient; it begs the question to assume that this will consist in not carrying out acts of euthanasia.'[105] Patients who fear that doctors will breach their trust by bringing about their death when this is not what they want have no more reason to be concerned when assisted dying is legalised

---

[102] Ibid., at p 416.

[103] Ibid., at p 436.

[104] Cassel, C K and Meier, D E, 'Morals and Moralism in the Debate Over Euthanasia and Assisted Suicide', *New England Journal of Medicine*, 323(11), 1990: 750–52, at p 751.

[105] Shand, J, 'A Reply to Some Standard Objections to Euthanasia', *Journal of Applied Philosophy*, 14(1), 1997: 43–47, at p 46.

than where it is not. Doctors already engage proactively with the death of their patients – both lawfully and unlawfully. It is unclear why allowing those who wish to die but need assistance to exercise their autonomy would render anyone more vulnerable to bad, illegal or unscrupulous conduct by doctors.

For the moment in the United Kingdom and many other countries, the fact that doctors are formally precluded from acceding to a competent request for assistance in dying has resulted in a situation where some people choose to travel abroad – most commonly to Switzerland – to obtain the help they need. The authenticity of their decisions is arguably reinforced by the determination and organisation required to make such a trip. It is also evidenced by the fact that they may carry through their decision even when they fear that any loved ones who travel with them will be prosecuted. In two recent cases, for example, the possibility of prosecution became the subject of legal investigation. In the case of *R (on the application of Purdy) v Director of Public Prosecutions & Anor*,[106] Debbie Purdy sought judicial review of the failure of the DPP to issue specific guidance on the circumstances in which a prosecution under the relevant section of the Suicide Act 1961[107] would be brought. Although she was unsuccessful in arguing that her Article 8 Convention right was engaged by this alleged failure, the court expressed 'great sympathy for Mrs Purdy, her husband and others in a similar position who wish to know in advance whether they will face prosecution for doing what many would regard as something that the law should permit, namely to help a loved one to go abroad to end their suffering when they are unable to do it on their own.'[108] Additionally, the parents of Daniel James who accompanied him to Switzerland to obtain an assisted death were also subjected to police questioning and faced the possibility of prosecution.[109] Interestingly, the decision that no prosecution would in fact be undertaken was made not on the basis that there was insufficient evidence to do so, but rather that it would not be in the public interest to charge the parents.[110] Sadly, for people in this situation, political reluctance to review the law and iron out existing inconsistencies will maintain this uncertainty in times of tragedy.[111] Even though no prosecution has to date been undertaken in these circumstances, the Purdy court and the Crown Prosecution Service's decision in Daniel James' case held out the possibility that it might yet be: all this, while it would seem that the tide of public opinion is moving in

---

[106] [2008] EWHC 2565 (29 October 2008).

[107] This Act does not apply in Scotland.

[108] [2008] EWHC 2565, at para 84.

[109] 'Player's assisted suicide probed', available at http://www.bbc.co.uk/news (accessed on 17/10/2008).

[110] For a text of the decision, see http://www.cps.gov.uk/news/nationalnews/death_by_suicide_of_daniel_james.html (accessed on 16/12/2008).

[111] It should be noted, however, that some clarification may emerge from debates on the Coroners and Justice Bill which is currently proceeding through the UK Parliament.

favour of a proper debate, and even of legalisation (subject, of course, to the usual caveats about opinion 'evidence').[112]

Conclusion

In all areas of life, the ability and the right to be self-determining are important characteristics of what it is to be a free, self-directing and autonomous person. The knowledge that our competent decisions will be respected helps us to realise our own goals, no matter how they are viewed by others, unless our choices will cause harm to third parties. The law is the vehicle by which our autonomy is said to be protected, and in medical decisions – as we have seen – this is commonly regarded as being the province of the law of consent. The presumption that a competent, autonomous decision should be respected specifically underpins medical law.

When the question at issue relates to treatment refusal, the single most important consideration is the legal competence of the decision-maker. What matters is that the individual has the legal capacity to make the decision; if so, then doctors are obliged to respect it. In other words, people who have treatment that could save their lives, or at least sustain them, can nonetheless choose to die. In this situation, the outcome is not at issue – rather the fact that death is generally seen as undesirable takes second place to respect for the autonomy of the decision-maker. No inquiry into the reasons for the decision is made. No account of the feelings of third parties is taken – simply there is an obligation to respect the individual's decision.

On the other hand, where people wish to make the same choice but require assistance to effectuate it, a number of additional hurdles are erected in their way. First, and arguably most importantly, is the purported distinction between acts and omissions. By categorising the withdrawing of treatment as an omission, the courts (and many doctors) can justify to themselves the conclusion that active assistance in dying is in a different category from treatment refusal. Yet, as I have argued, this is a distinction that does not stand up to scrutiny on logical grounds. Equally, it cannot be said to be supported by legal rules such as those of causality or causation.[113] For example, it has been said:

> Distinguishing physician-assisted suicide from the withdrawal of treatment on the basis of causation fails, because causation, in the right-to-die

---

[112] See editorial in *The Sunday Times*, 14 December 2008, under the heading 'The Public Wants a Say on Euthanasia'. In the same edition, see also Smith, D and Templeton, S-K, 'Public in strong backing for right to assisted suicide', referring to a YouGov survey of more than 2000 people, which notes that 85% of the people surveyed agreed with the decision not to prosecute Mr and Mrs James with 69% of respondents agreeing that the law should be changed.

[113] See, for example, Callahan, D, *The Troubled Dream of Life: In Search of a Peaceful Death*, Washington DC, Georgetown University Press, 2000.

context, depends on whether the physician owes a duty to the patient, which is itself a policy question. To say that the patient's illness, rather than the withdrawal of life-sustaining treatment 'causes' the patient's death simply means that a court will not hold the physician liable for the death. Legal causation is a question of policy, not mechanical connection.[114]

In other words, the differential categorisation of treatment refusal and assisted dying is a policy decision, taken, as we have seen, for reasons which are not about the individual nor about autonomy, but effectively about policy preferred by the law. Although it would be easy to change the law to take account of the express wishes of individuals to die with assistance – Brazier argues that all it requires is 'a means of obtaining unequivocal evidence of the individual's free and informed choice and that appropriate, human mechanisms exist to effect that choice'[115] – external considerations apply to assisted dying but not to treatment refusal. From the acts/omissions doctrine to the purported effects on others in society of permitting assisted dying, the individualistic account of autonomy is subsumed by legalism and a more relational position is adopted.

While not a sufficient argument for legal change, it is nonetheless interesting that the current law is sometimes ignored or its full rigour circumvented by judges and juries alike, suggesting that it may be at odds with what the public regards as an appropriate policy. Although Dr Nigel Cox was convicted of the manslaughter of his patient, he was not given a custodial sentence and was allowed to continue practising.[116] In 2000, a Dr Moor admitted to administering lethal doses of medicine to a number of patients, although he claimed he was primarily trying to relieve pain. He was acquitted.[117] It is, of course, not only doctors who may assist someone to die, and they too can expect to be treated leniently. In 2004, for example, an elderly man stabbed his nursing home-based wife to death, and was given a 12-month community rehabilitation order.[118] In 2005, a man who killed his terminally ill wife and then tried to kill himself was given a 9-month suspended sentence.[119] Finally, in the case of Daniel James, one of the considerations taken into account in the decision not to prosecute was the unlikelihood of a custodial sentence being imposed.

---

[114] 'Physician Assisted Suicide and the Right to Die with Assistance', *Harv L Rev*, 125, 2001: 2001–40, at p 2029.

[115] Brazier, M, 'Euthanasia and the law', *British Medical Bulletin*, 52(2), 1996: 317–25, at p 322.

[116] *R v Cox* (1992) 12 BMLR 38.

[117] 'Dr Moor: Landmark verdict', 28 November 2000, available at http://news.bbc.co.uk/hi/english/health/background_briefings/euthanasia/newsid_331000 (accessed on 29/4/2002).

[118] 'Wife killer, 100, spared prison', 8 July 2004, available at http://news.bbc.co.uk/1/hi/england/lancashire/3876615.stm (accessed on 9/7/2004).

[119] 'Suicide pact husband spared jail', 14 January 2005, available at http://news.bbc.co.uk/1/hi/eng;land/4174155.stm (accessed on 9/5/2005).

Were public policy truly opposed to legitimising assisted dying, one would expect that courts and juries would behave differently and/or that there would be a huge outcry about the leniency of the sentences imposed as compared with other cases of manslaughter. Yet, as Braithwaite notes, no such outrage followed these cases.[120] In fact, it seems that legal 'policy' may not in fact be the same as what the public wants or will tolerate. Further, although there are many who vociferously oppose legalisation of assisted suicide, convinced by faith, by fears of the slippery slope or by the Hippocratic tradition, this does not justify the imposition of their views on others who do not share them in the absence of more compelling arguments. While legalisation would allow those who wish to make an autonomous decision for death to do so, it would force nobody to make that decision. At present, the arguments of opponents operate as a brake on the right of others to make their own, self-determining decisions about their own death on grounds that seem spurious.

We have seen that there are a number of legal devices used to draw distinctions between treatment refusal and assisted dying and superimposed on these is a somewhat inconsistent approach to the idea of autonomy. If one – if not the – primary goal of the law of consent is to protect and vindicate individual self-determination, it might be expected that a coherent and principled picture would be visible in circumstances that are essentially the same. In fact, however, the application of the concept of autonomy in end of life decisions is inconsistent. Firmly based in the concept of decisional authority as the right of the individual, the right to refuse life-sustaining treatment is protected in law. On the other hand, a more relational account of autonomy seems evident from decisions about assisted dying, where the alleged interests of others – family, clinicians or other sectors of society – are often used to justify disrespecting individual choice. These external interests, in one way or another, are used to deny the validity of a choice for assisted dying.

Even if we were to accept that individual decisions for an assisted death should be constrained by the context in which they arise (and if we did, we would also have to reconsider treatment refusal cases) the evidence for the harm that is said to flow from respecting them is at best tenuous. As often as not the alleged harm consists of generalised, but untested, claims that society as a whole (or certain discrete parts of it) will suffer if people's autonomous decisions are given effect to. Somerville, for example, says that permitting an autonomous choice for an assisted death would 'damage important, foundational societal values and symbols that uphold respect for human life.'[121] But

[120] Braithwaite, M A, 'Taking the final step: changing the law on euthanasia and physican assisted suicide', *BMJ*, 331, 2005: 681–83, at p 682.
[121] Somerville, M, 'The Case Against Euthanasia and Physician-Assisted Suicide', *free enquiry*, 33–34, Spring 2003: 33, available at http://www.secularhumanism.org (accessed on 12/10/2008).

is this not true also of any decision to die, no matter how it is effectuated? In any case, Fraser and Walters argue that failing to allow patients full respect for their decisions at the end of life is 'arbitrary' given that 'autonomy is a highly valued principle … '.[122] In sum, they argue that, '[t]he criminalising of physician-assisted suicide is effectively a prohibition of suicide for many terminally ill patients.'[123]

Despite the intimate nature of the decision to die, when active assistance is needed the individualistic notion of autonomy is ditched in favour of a more relational account. The end result is that people seeking precisely the same outcome as those who reject life-sustaining treatment – that is, a death that is appropriate, even dignified, from their perspective – are denied the vindication of their competent, autonomous decisions. Warnock and Macdonald argue that 'when we think of euthanasia or even of assisted suicide, we see-saw between private and public morality … '.[124] If categorised as private, the individualistic account of autonomy triumphs; if public, the interests of others are given weight. In any case, it is not unreasonable to expect that the principles underpinning the law at the end of life are both clear and consistent. In the case of choosing death it would appear that they are not.

Safranek and Safranek argue that 'the concept of liberty must protect important personal decisions, such as the right to assisted suicide, from the tyranny of pluralism, for example, i.e., the majority vote of elected representatives of the people themselves.'[125] Price further argues that if we recognise that doctors already do play a role in assisting in the death of their patients, this 'might help facilitate constructive discussion of potential reforms by focusing attention on the central issues.'[126] Moreover, Jackson says that '[f]rom the patient's perspective, the line the law currently draws between lawful and unlawful life-shortening practices makes very little sense.'[127] Finally, Thomasma argues that:

> … once one adopts an autonomy-centered view of human life and the notion of personal ownership of one's body, then arguments in favour of suicide, assisted suicide, and euthanasia make eminent sense. They are furtherances of the rights of individuals over and against repressive social

---

[122] Fraser, S I, Walters, J W, 'Death – whose decision? Euthanasia and the Terminally Ill', *J Med Ethics*, 26, 2000: 121–25, at p 123.

[123] Ibid.

[124] Warnock, M, Macdonald, E, *Easeful Death: Is There a Case for Assisted Dying?*, Oxford University Press, 2008, at p 138.

[125] Safranek, J P, Safranek, S J, 'Assisted Suicide: The State versus The People', *Seattle University Law Review*, 21, 1997: 261–79, at p 265.

[126] Price, D P T, 'Assisted Suicide and Refusing Medical Treatment: Linguistics, Morals and Legal Contortions', *Medical Law Review*, 4, Autumn 1996: 270–99, at p 299.

[127] Jackson, E, 'Whose Death is it Anyway? Euthanasia and the Medical Profession', in Holder, J, O'Cinneide, C and Freeman, M (eds), *Current Legal Problems*, 57, 2004: 415–42, at p 433.

conventions and laws, not to mention ancient religious values incorporated in a culture that is increasingly pluralistic. A modern, secular Western state measures its progress through increasingly sophisticated protection of the privacy rights of its citizens.[128]

It must be concluded that the law's approach to end of life decision-making in terms of respect for autonomy is schizophrenic. On the one hand, the role of consent (or refusal) in respecting patient autonomy is trumpeted where a patient can achieve a chosen death by rejecting life-sustaining treatment. On the other, the autonomy of the individual is denied when that death requires active assistance. The reasons for this difference in approach do not, however, stand up to close scrutiny. As Fletcher says, '[w]hat it comes down to is that most people, including the courts, want the end – death – in certain tragic situations, but the taboo forbids the means.'[129] The result of this is an unhappy mix of two different accounts of autonomy; the individualistic, which allows for treatment refusal and the relational, which is in part responsible for denying that a choice for assisted death should be respected. Although, as we have seen, there are many who regard the relational account of autonomy as preferable to its individualistic counterpart, in end of life decisions it seems in practice to contribute to a somewhat perverse denial of self-determination. While I have argued that the differences between the two accounts are relatively small, when specific aspects of the relational model are extracted and prioritised then the *outcome* can be vastly different. Despite its appeal, the relational account when applied (without direct attribution) by courts and legislators can indeed widen the differences between the two and severely affect the right of people to make authentic and well-considered choices at the end of life.

[128] Thomasma, D C, 'An Analysis of Arguments For and Against Euthanasia and Assisted Suicide: Part One', *Cambridge Quarterly of Healthcare Ethics*, 5, 1996: 62–76, at p 73.

[129] Fletcher, J, 'The Courts and Euthanasia', *Law, Medicine & Health Care*, 15(4), Winter 1987/88: 223, at p 226.

Chapter 5

Autonomy and pregnancy

Like it or not, and however (in)effective in protecting autonomy it may seem to be, the doctrine of consent is the vehicle which offers patients a role in healthcare beyond the merely submissive or passive one which was seemingly historically expected. Achieving joint or shared decision-making, with the patient as ultimate arbiter, is the supposed ambition of the law of consent (and its corollary, the right to refuse). As we have seen, however, the way in which the law operates serves to distance the actual decision-maker from the decision, by focusing either on the standards adopted by the 'reasonable doctor' or the 'prudent patient'. In the routine medical case, the extent and quality of information that has to be provided to patients is set at a relatively low level, thereby casting doubt on the authenticity of any decision taken and allowing for subtle pressures to be brought to bear on patients to reach decisions that correspond to clinical recommendations. While apparently adopting a version of the individualistic model of autonomy, it has also been suggested that in some cases – like active assistance in dying – a more contextualised approach is sometimes used in law to reject the validity of an otherwise apparently autonomous choice.

From what has gone before, it seems that the individualistic approach is preferred except where there are ingrained 'policy' based reasons to move away from it. As became clear from the last chapter, this tends to occur when the issue under scrutiny is highly emotive. In this chapter, we will consider the law's approach to decisions made by pregnant women in managing their pregnancy and labour and test this against the so-called right to refuse treatment which – as we have seen in the last chapter – is supposed to be absolute for competent individuals.

Before considering the development of case law in this area, let me restate what I have said elsewhere.[1] Although cases in this area are sometimes referred to as examples of 'Maternal/Foetal Conflict', this language is inappropriate because it imports value-laden concepts that should not go unchallenged.

---

[1] McLean, S A M, 'Moral status: who or what counts?', in Bewley, S, Ward, R H (eds), *Ethics in Obstetrics and Gynaecology*, London, RCOG Press, 1994, at pp 26–33.

First, it represents the pregnant woman as 'mother', with all of the expectations that flow from this status. Second, the notion of a conflict implies some hostility or even threat. Since the foetus cannot will or intend anything, it casts the pregnant woman in the role of aggressor on her foetus. For these reasons, this language will not be used in this discussion, unless in quoting other commentators.

At the outset, it is helpful to consider the status of the human embryo/foetus, since 'whatever status we concede to the [embryo or] foetus is directly relevant to the status which we accord to the woman who is carrying it.'[2] In most Western countries, the embryo or foetus no matter its stage of development is accorded no legal standing. Even although once born it is possible to seek compensation for injuries sustained by the now born child pre-birth (and sometimes even pre-conception) this is a right that is applied retrospectively; that is, it accrues only on live birth.[3] While the moral status of the embryo or foetus may be subject to debate, the law is clear; the embryo/foetus is not a legal person (although there are some countries that are exceptions to this general rule[4]). Nor does the fact that abortion laws tend to become more restrictive as pregnancy progresses mean that embryos or foetuses are being accorded rights in law. Rather, in imposing limitations on the availability of abortion, the state is engaged in reflecting what it sees as legitimate social policy. Since this is essentially a policy issue, it is scarcely surprising that there is no universal agreement as to when, and what kind of, limitations are imposed.

While the law in many countries seems clear as to the non-legal standing of the embryo/foetus, moral status is arguably more complex, and resolving this to the satisfaction of everyone seems unlikely. As is often the case in biomedical ethics, there are polar extremes of opinion. For some, the human embryo in its earliest stages is little more than a collection of cells whereas for others it is equivalent to an actual (or sometimes potential) person. Those who hold to the former position would be unlikely – perhaps unable – to build a case for regulation of what can be done with or to the embryo, while those in the latter camp would accord it the full panoply of rights and interests held by a person already born.

However, arguably the most widely accepted view is that the embryo of the human species is more than a mere collection of cells, but less than a fully formed, born human being. It is, therefore, entitled to some respect; respect which grows as it develops towards birth.[5] It does not, however,

[2] McLean, S A M, *Old Law, New Medicine*, London, RiversOram/Pandora, 1999, at p 50.

[3] See, for example, *Hamilton v Fife Health Board* [1993] 4 Med LR 201; *De Martell v Merton and Sutton Health Authority* [1991] 2 Med LR 209; *B v Islington Health Authority* [1991] 2 Med LR 133; *Montreal Tramways v Leveille* [1933] 4 DLR 337; *Watt v Rama* (unreported, Supreme Court of Victoria, Australia, 1972); *X and Y v Pal and Others* [1992] 3 Med LR 195 (Court of Appeal, New South Wales).

[4] For example Ireland and Italy.

[5] See *Report of the Committee of Inquiry Into Human Fertilisation and Embryology* (Warnock Report), Cmnd 9314/1984.

possess, nor is it self-evidently able to claim to be a bearer of, rights. Indeed, it could be argued that any respect due to it stems not from its own characteristics, but rather from *our* interest in showing it respect.[6] The position adopted here will be that favoured in most Western countries and described by the Warnock Committee; namely, that 'the embryo of the human species ought to have a special status ... ',[7] and that 'although the human embryo is entitled to some added measure of respect beyond that accorded to other animal subjects, that respect cannot be absolute ... '.[8] Thus, on the face of it, the embryo is of importance but the born person is the holder of rights – in any 'competition' the rights of the born person should prevail.

While the embryo has no legal rights, the consequence of Warnock's gradualist approach is that the respect owed to it increases as it develops towards becoming a legal person; that is, when it becomes a foetus. This is generally reflected in abortion laws, which in the liberal tradition typically impose fewer limitations on the availability of pregnancy termination in the early stages, with constraints developing and strengthening as the embryo develops towards birth. However, countries that allow abortion do not make the critical judgement about its permissibility at the same stage in the pregnancy, and some impose reasonably strict criteria even in the earliest stages of pregnancy. There is therefore no universally agreed point at which moral status is attributed before birth. McCullogh and Chervenak see this as inevitable, saying:

> All accounts about whether or not the fetus possesses independent moral status commit a common error: they seek to find or reject some time, prior to or at delivery, during which the fetus possesses some intrinsic characteristic that in turn generates independent moral status. This matter is endlessly disputed because ... it is endlessly disputable.[9]

Thus, while 'the human embryo/foetus will always count as more morally relevant than even a fully grown animal', nonetheless 'it will not count as being as morally relevant as a human child or adult.'[10] Irrespective, developments in medicine, particularly in assisted reproduction and obstetrics, have potentially muddied the ethical and the legal waters, by (perhaps inadvertently) casting the relationship between the embryo/foetus and the pregnant woman as potentially adversarial. Advances in obstetrics mean that the embryo/

---

[6] Ibid at p 201.

[7] Cmnd 9314/1984, at p 63, para 11.17.

[8] Ibid., at p 62, para 11.15.

[9] McCullogh, L B, Chervenak, F A, *Ethics in Obstetrics and Gynecology*, Oxford University Press, 1994, at pp 100–1.

[10] McLean, S A M, *Old Law, New Medicine*, London, RiversOram/Pandora, 1999, at p 50.

foetus has become a visible entity; very often, the reality of pregnancy is concretised when the first scan pictures are available and proudly shown to friends and family. It is no longer necessary to wait until birth to see your potential child. Rapidly developing genetic (and other) knowledge also allows early diagnosis of problems in the embryo/foetus and may even permit foetal surgery. The result of this has been a tendency to treat the woman and the foetus as being two separate patients, with sometimes disparate needs that will on occasion conflict. As Mattingly notes:

> The biological maternal-fetal relationship has not changed ... but the medical model of that relationship has shifted emphasis from unity to duality. Clinicians no longer look to the maternal host for diagnostic data and a therapeutic medium; they look through her to the fetal organism and regard it as a distinct patient in its own right.[11]

If the embryo/foetus is seen as a separate patient, clinicians may feel professional obligations to it as well as to the pregnant woman, thereby posing dilemmas where women's decisions are inimical to its well-being. Consequently, the pressure on women to behave in certain ways during pregnancy and labour, irrespective of their own wishes or interests, has grown. Increasingly, this has led to the state becoming involved in enforcement of certain behaviour, or more accurately in bringing its weight to bear on those who resist clinical recommendations and interventions. Ikenotos says that '[t]he message used to justify state intervention is that a pregnant woman is a mother who should think and act first and foremost to protect the health of the fetus she carries ... '.[12] Further, Wells notes that clinical developments have generated a movement that 'seeks to subordinate the pregnant woman to the health and welfare of her foetus.'[13] As the potential of modern obstetrical medicine expands, and *in vivo* diagnostic and therapeutic interventions for the benefit of the embryo/foetus become more feasible, pregnant women are confronted with additional options – and pressures – in managing their pregnancy. While many will welcome this, not everyone will. Women are as likely to have an active interest in managing their own lives, including their pregnancy and delivery, as anyone else. Yet the combination of medical advance and increased scrutiny of embryonic and/or foetal development and environment exposes the possibility of conflict – this time a real one; not between women and the embryos/foetuses they are carrying, but rather between women and those providing their care. This can arise at two main stages –

---

[11] However, for further consideration, see McLean, S A M, *Assisted Dying: Reflections on the Need for Law Reform*, Routledge-Cavendish, 2007; Huxtable, R, *Euthanasia, Ethics and the Law: From Conflict to Compromise* Routledge-Cavendish, 2007.

[12] Ikenotos, L C, 'Code of Perfect Pregnancy', *Ohio State Law Journal*, 53, 1992: 1205–1306, at p 1235.

[13] Wells, C, 'Maternal Versus Foetal Rights', in Working Paper no 1, Feminist Legal Research Unit, University of Liverpool, 1992, transcript, at p 19.

during pregnancy and at the point of delivery. For the sake of logic, these will be considered in that order, but first we must explore the question from the women's perspective.

Women, pregnancy and the law

The presumption underpinning the law is that all citizens are equal – irrespective of age, race, sex or other personal characteristics. Thus, the competent adult is said, as we have seen, to be entitled to make decisions which are right *for them*. Of course, the idea of equality does not mean that everyone is the same, but they are entitled to equal respect. For women, this has, however, not always held true. Their sex, and importantly their reproductive capacities, have historically been factors in the development of, and even support for, societies in which women have been disenfranchised and disfavoured. Although some of these historical disadvantages have ostensibly been removed over time, the fact that women's biology makes them unique still singles them out for special attention, not always – or even very often – to their benefit.

Most particularly, women who are pregnant are generally expected to act in ways that help, or at least do not harm, the embryo or foetus they are carrying, in the same way as it is anticipated that they will behave responsibly, conscientiously and for the welfare of born children. It is, of course, not necessary to conceptualise the woman as being in some form of conflict with her foetus, and most women will do everything in their power to ensure that their future child has the best possible start in life. This holds true even if it means making personal sacrifices. For example, so many products in daily life are now known to be potentially harmful to the developing embryo that women will give them up; alcohol, cigarettes, even caffeine may all harm the embryo and are often willingly sacrificed by women when they become pregnant – sometimes even beforehand. Yet, on a liberal account, the woman is, and should be, entitled to make the opposite choice. While some commentators have proposed that once a woman decides to carry a pregnancy to term she must accept certain constraints on her personal freedom,[14] the liberal account would dispute this, arguing that what matters is that the individual woman is competent and making autonomous decisions; the consequences of these decisions are not relevant unless they harm others, a group to which non-persons arguably do not obviously belong.

It has already been suggested that the law generally pays lip service to an account of autonomy that is individualistic, although it has also become clear that this changes when doing so would lead to consequences which are seen (by some, including the courts) as undesirable. For example, in the case of

---

[14] See, for example, Brazier, M, 'Liberty, Maternity, Responsibility', *Current Legal Problems*, 52, 1999: 359–91.

the 'right' to assisted suicide, it has been shown that other factors are brought to bear that obscure the emphasis on individual autonomy. Public policy (whether or not it actually reflects what the public wants) intrudes to disrespect autonomous decisions. It has also been suggested that equality before the law should ensure that respect is given to people's personal choices without discrimination. Thus, the pregnant woman should be treated as a woman – a person – not as a mere vessel for foetal health and well-being. It is instructive, therefore, to consider whether or not this reflects what the law actually does.

Policing pregnancy

It is, of course, easier to create constraints on the choices of others – even intending parents – when the embryo is *ex vivo*. Restrictions can more readily be placed on what may be done to or with it, and although its genetic 'parents' may have interests that compete with what the law permits,[15] they are not physically affected in a direct way by these limitations (although they may be affected in other ways, for example if the law prohibits implantation of particular, desired embryos they may suffer psychologically).[16] On the other hand, when the embryo is *in vivo*, while others – such as doctors and potential fathers – may be able to see it using modern medical technology, it is primarily the pregnant woman who has direct control over it and its development.

It might be thought that there are few experiences in life more intimate and personal than pregnancy. The woman is in a unique position to experience new life in the making, and has a vital role in nurturing it and influencing its path towards birth. How she behaves – the care she takes of herself – will have a clear and direct effect on the embryo/foetus[17] as it develops. This is indisputable and women are increasingly aware of the impact of their life and lifestyle choices on their embryos/foetuses. As with all information, of course, women may choose to ignore it. Where women seek to make autonomous choices that are inimical to the welfare of the embryo/foetus it may be tempting to challenge them, but as Jackson says, ' … acknowledging the unparall[ell]ed intimacy of pregnancy does not necessarily render the concept of autonomy redundant or meaningless.'[18]

---

[15] For example, in the United Kingdom it is now prohibited to select an embryo for implantation which is known to carry a genetic or other defect involving a significant risk that a person with the abnormality will have or develop: (a) a serious physical or mental disability, (b) a serious illness, or (c) any other serious medical condition, where there are other 'normal' embryos available; see Human Fertilisation and Embryology Act 2008, s 14(4).

[16] See, for example, the case of *Evans v United Kingdom* (2007) 43 EHRR 21 in which a woman was not permitted to seek implantation of stored embryos following her partner's withdrawal of his consent.

[17] Except where logic dictates the contrary, references to embryos and foetuses can be taken to include both of them.

[18] Jackson, E, *Regulating Reproduction: Law, Technology and Autonomy*, Oxford, Hart Publishing, 2001, at p 3.

Disrespecting the autonomous decisions of pregnant women, however bene-ficent the motive for so doing, 'radically disvalues the pregnant woman and treats her like an inert incubator, or a culture medium for the foetus.'[19]

In the course of pregnancy, women may make a number of lifestyle choices that could either benefit or harm their embryo/foetus. As we have seen, even seemingly harmless activities like drinking coffee might have a negative effect on embryonic development. Equally, refusing medical interventions that could benefit the foetus may directly affect its ability to be born healthy (or at all). The courts have not stood by and passively observed this phenomenon. Rather, they have on occasion taken a fairly aggressive approach to intervening in women's decisions concerning their pregnancies. By and large, the majority of legal activity in this area has occurred in the United States, so it is from that country's jurisprudence that some examples will be drawn and examined.[20]

In a number of cases, most particularly (but not exclusively) where preg-nant women are using or addicted to legal or illegal substances, they have been subject to coercive legal interventions, even to the extent of depriving them of liberty or coercing them into unwanted behaviour, all in the pur-ported interests of their foetuses. The use of illicit drugs undoubtedly has negative consequences for individuals, families and societies, and obviously will potentially harm the unborn; so, too, of course, will the use of legal substances such as alcohol and tobacco. However, such behaviour is also relatively common; not every woman is willing or able to give up drugs, drinking or smoking. As long ago as 1990 Coutts reported that:

> According to one recent study as many as eleven percent of babies born in the U.S. (375,000 annually) are born to mothers who have used illicit drugs during their pregnancies ... Fetal alcohol syndrome, in which babies can suffer growth retardation, microcephaly, facial abnormalities and malformations of the limbs and organs appears once in every 1000 births in the U.S.[21]

In 1992, it was reported that around 167 women in the United States had been arrested 'because of their behavior during pregnancy or because they became pregnant while addicted to drugs.'[22] The same report highlighted

---

[19] Annas, G, 'Pregnant Women as Fetal Containers', *Hastings Center Report*, 16(6), 1986: 13–14, at p 14.

[20] The leading exception to this in the United Kingdom is the case of *Re F (in utero)* [1988] 2 All ER 193 in which a failed attempt was made to make a foetus a ward of court based on the pregnant woman's projected behaviour. The action failed on the basis that, *inter alia*, the foetus was not a person and could not therefore be made a ward of court.

[21] Coutts, M.C, 'Maternal-Fetal Conflict: Legal and Ethical Issues', ScopeNote 14, 1990, available at http://bioethics.georgetown.edu (accessed on 2/9/2008), at p 1.

[22] *Criminal Prosecutions against Pregnant Women National Update and Overview*, April 1992, compiled and written by Lynn M Paltrow, available at http://advocatesforpregnantwomen.org/file/1992%20State-by-State%20Case%20Summary.pdf (accessed on 16/9/2008) (hereafter referred to as National Update).

the case of *State v Pfannestiel*,[23] in which Wyoming officials brought criminal charges against a pregnant woman for drinking. The basis of the charges was that her behaviour amounted to child abuse since it endangered the foetus. Although the charges were dismissed, this was on technical rather than substantive grounds. In Missouri, Lisa Pindar was charged with second-degree assault and child endangerment after her son was born, allegedly with signs of fetal alcohol syndrome.[24] In what was to become one of the most (in) famous cases, Pamela Rae Stewart was arrested because she did not pay attention to her doctor's advice to take bed rest, stay off her feet, refrain from sexual intercourse and take medication to inhibit labour;[25] all of this entirely lawful behaviour, even if unwise in terms of the foetus.

Examples provided by the American Civil Liberties Union (ACLU) include the following:

- In Massachusetts, a lower court ordered a pregnant woman's cervix sewn up against her will to prevent a possible miscarriage. The woman was ultimately spared from undergoing the procedure by the Supreme Court of Massachusetts, which vacated the lower court's order because it had not adequately considered the woman's constitutional right to privacy (See *Taft v Taft*, 446 NE 2d 395, 396, 397 (Mass 1983)).
- In Wyoming, officials arrested a pregnant woman because of alcohol use and charged her with felony child abuse. She spent time in jail before a judge dismissed the charge.
- In Wisconsin, officials held a pregnant 16-year-old in secure detention for the sake of fetal development because the young woman tended 'to be on the run' and to 'lack motivation or ability to seek medical care'.
- In California, a deputy district attorney, concerned about a pregnant woman's mental state but lacking sufficient evidence to have her committed for psychiatric treatment, instead obtained a juvenile court order declaring her fetus a dependent child of the state and detaining the woman pending birth. An appellate court ultimately held that the district attorney had impermissibly manipulated the juvenile laws to detain the pregnant woman and released her when she was approximately 7 months pregnant (*In re Steven S*, 126 Cal App 3d 23, 27, 30–31 (Cal Ct App 1981)).[26]

---

[23] *Wyoming v Pfannenstiel*; No 1-90-8CR (Co Ct of Laramie, Wyoming, 1 February 1990).

[24] Ibid., at p 5.

[25] *People v Pamela Rae Stewart*, Declaration in Support of Arrest Warrant Case No M508 197 (28 August 1986).

[26] American Civil Liberties Union, 'Policing Pregnancy: *Ferguson v City of Charleston*, 1 November 2000, available at http://www.aclu.org/reproductiverights/lowincome/12511res20001101.html (accessed on 12/9/2008), at pp 5–6.

In 2006, Ehrich and Paltrow reported that women had been arrested in a number of states 'based on the claim that pregnant women can be considered child abusers even before they have given birth.'[27] Although it would seem that the majority of these women were addicted to drugs or alcohol, others were arrested for 'not getting to the hospital quickly enough on the day of delivery', or 'not following the doctor's advice concerning bed rest'![28]

There are many more examples, but these will suffice to show the willingness of law officers and judges to contemplate, if not always to carry through, the use of criminal sanctions against women because of their behaviour during pregnancy – not in the interests of the women, but rather in the purported interests of their foetuses.[29] And this may be the tip of a much bigger iceberg. Commentators have noted that, although very often women who are well-represented legally have been able to overturn the rulings against them, many others are poorly represented, advised to plead guilty and seldom raise an appeal.[30] The true number of women targeted in this way is, therefore, unknown.

Of course, it could be said that the state's interest in protecting potential life is strong and justifies coercive action; maybe even that the women arrested and/or incarcerated will themselves benefit from the intervention. On the former point, the landmark case of *Roe v Wade*[31] firmly declared the state's interest in the foetus, particularly from the point of viability. In a subsequent case concerning abortion, *Planned Parenthood v Casey*, the court further claimed that ' ... the State has a legitimate interest *from the outset of the pregnancy* in protecting the health of the woman and the life of the fetus that may become a child.' (emphasis added).[32] However, it must be moot whether or not this 'interest' in the developing embryo or foetus is sufficiently strong to negate the interest that women (and the state) also have in vindicating the right of citizens to equal protection under the constitution. In the case of these women, particularly when their behaviour is otherwise legal – for example, drinking alcohol – it is not in fact the behaviour that is the object of concern; rather, 'it is pregnancy and not the illegality of the substance that makes women vulnerable to state control and punishment.'[33] This defeats the equal protection purportedly offered to all US citizens and 'raises

---

[27] Ehrich, J B, Paltrow, L, 'Jailing Pregnant Women Raises Health Risks', *Women's eNews*, 20 September 2006, available at http://www.womensenews.org/article.cfm/dyn/aid/2894 (accessed on 12/9/2008), transcript, p 1.

[28] Ibid.

[29] For further and more extensive discussion, see Meredith, S, *Policing Pregnancy: The Law and Ethics of Obstetric Conflict*, Aldershot, Ashgate, 2005.

[30] For further information on this point, see National Update, n 22 above.

[31] 410 US 113 (1973).

[32] 505 US 833 (1992), at p 846.

[33] National Update, n 22 above, at p 1002.

the additional problem of essentially punishing for "status",[34] despite the fact that a woman 'is not assigned to a special 'class' when she becomes pregnant.'[35]

Additional concerns arise when the pregnant women in question are actually addicted to drugs (or alcohol). Addiction presents particular problems since it may reduce or even remove the woman's ability to make a choice not to cause harm to the embryo/foetus. While some may welcome legal intervention that gives them the opportunity to beat their addiction (for example by incarceration in a drug and alcohol free environment) others may well regard this as an unwarranted intrusion into their lives. While addiction to, or abuse of, licit and illicit substances is by no means confined to one socio-economic group, demographically the women who have been targeted by law enforcement on these grounds have been disproportionately representative of the lowest socio-economic groups, raising the very real spectre of discrimination within discrimination. Not only does their status as a pregnant woman seemingly invite coercive intervention in their life choices, if they are poor in addition to pregnant, they are more likely than others to be targeted. Paltrow, for example, discovered that:

> Most of the women arrested have been low-income women of color with untreated drug addictions. Thus, the arrests focus on those people and issues that are hardest to defend in the court of public opinion. Wrongly prejudged as irresponsible and uncaring, the public has expressed little support for them.[36]

The consequences have been an increased trend to use the force of law to coerce women into particular behaviours during pregnancy; a pattern that in 1997 took a particularly ominous turn in South Carolina (where, interestingly, many of these cases have arisen). In the case of *Whitney v State*,[37] the Supreme Court of South Carolina held viable foetuses to be persons, and, as Paltrow points out, this meant that 'the state's criminal child endangerment statute applied to a pregnant woman who used an illicit drug or engaged in any other behavior that might endanger the fetus. In so doing, the court took an unprecedented legal leap, apparently recognizing full legal personhood for viable fetuses.'[38] Since there is generally very little sympathy for women

---

[34] McGinnis, D M, 'Prosecution of Mothers of Drug-Exposed babies: Constitutional and Criminal Theory', *U Pa L Rev*, 139, 1990: 505–39, at p 517.

[35] McLean, S A M, Petersen, K, 'Patient Status: The Foetus And The Pregnant Woman', [1996] *AJHR* 6, available at http://www.austlii.edu.au/journals/AJHR/1996/6.html (accessed on 12/9/2008), transcript, p 2.

[36] Paltrow, L, 'Pregnant Drug Users, Fetal Persons, and the Threat to *Roe v Wade*', *Albany Law Review*, 62, 1999: 999–1054, at pp 1002–3.

[37] 492 SE 2d 777 (SC 1997), *cert denied* 1185 S Ct 1857 (1998).

[38] Paltrow, L, 'Pregnant Drug Users, Fetal Persons, and the threat to *Roe v Wade*', *Albany Law Review*, 62, 1999: 999–1054, at p 1005.

who have 'abused' their foetuses, the path was laid for continued exertions by the criminal law to protect embryos and foetuses even at the expense of the pregnant women. Paltrow further notes that from this date on, what had at first appeared to have been 'legal oddities or ... a collection of isolated incidents' soon became 'an increasing trend toward the recognition of fetal rights and women's subordination.'[39] The 'war on drugs' claimed one of its first and most significant casualties.

In addition to the concerns raised above about the possibility that women are prosecuted for 'status', and the over-representation of the poor and women of colour in the state's coercive activities, there is the additional problem that such efforts are unlikely to be successful. Were it the case that women would be helped by prosecution or other coercive behaviour, it might be possible to build a case in its support, perhaps especially if this also saved foetuses from further harm. However, the evidence to support the benefit of such interventions for women is not there. There are a number of reasons for this. One arises from the nature of addiction itself. McGinnis, for example, doubts that coercion of this sort will assist in deterring drug abuse or will in fact prevent addicted women from continuing to take drugs. Indeed '[i]f a woman becomes pregnant after she is addicted and when her drug use has become involuntary, it can be argued that drug-induced temporary insanity prevented her from recognizing or considering the likely ill effects of the drug on her fetus.'[40] In addition, Ehrich and Paltrow argue that '[m]edical knowledge about addiction and dependency treatment demonstrates that patients do not, and cannot, simply stop their drug use as a result of threats of arrest or other negative consequences.'[41] More is needed, yet more does not seem to be available. The bleak picture confronting these women is strikingly portrayed in Paltrow's excellent exposition of the problem, which is worth quoting at some length. She says:

> Numerous law review articles and amicus briefs submitted on behalf of public health groups have well-documented the multiple barriers pregnant women faced in seeking drug treatment and health care. For many years, pregnant women with drug problems were simply denied admission to drug treatment programs; today, many of the still-too-few programs that exist to meet their needs are in jeopardy, due to Medicaid, managed care, and other funding cuts. Many pregnant women who have substance abuse problems suffer enormous violence and abuse before turning to

[39] Ibid., at p 1009.

[40] McGinnis, D M, 'Prosecution of Mothers of Drug-Exposed babies: Constitutional and Criminal Theory', *U Pa L Rev*, 139, 1990: 505–39, at p 525.

[41] Ehrich, J B, Paltrow, L, 'Jailing Pregnant Women Raises Health Risks', *Women's enews*, 20 September 2006, available at http://www.womensenews.org/article.cfm/dyn/aid/2894 (accessed on 12/9/2008), transcript, p 1.

drugs. Once addicted, and then pregnant, they face numerous barriers to getting help. They learn that drug treatment programs do not exist, or categorically exclude them, or require them to give up custody of their children. If they seek help for the abuse in their lives they discover that most battered women's shelters do not accept women with drug problems. If they seek reproductive health services, they may find that abortion services are unavailable or unfunded, or that they cannot access prenatal care services without risking loss of custody of their children. Despite all of the obstacles, studies find, pregnant drug users do all that they can to take responsibility for their drug use and life circumstances, making efforts, for example, to stop or reduce their drug use and to improve their own health for the sake of the pregnancy.[42]

Faced with desperate circumstances, and with very limited help available, it is arguably merely a convenient legal shortcut around real and serious social problems to respond to these women's plight by the use of coercion rather than care; imprisonment rather than assistance. If weaning people off self-destructive behaviour is as difficult as it seems to be, we must ask whether the level and type of coercion used in the cases already referred to are proportionate. In fact, they smack more of a renewed attack on women's equality as citizens – defined, again, by their biology rather than their personhood – and of a clamp down on women's emerging reproductive liberty.

While, arguably, addicted women cannot make free choices, and deserve help not punishment, those who choose to drink alcohol in the course of a pregnancy are acting entirely legally and with free will, yet they too are condemned for their choices. While we might prefer that pregnant women do not behave in this way, and many will not, can it really be the role of the law to prevent them from doing so? Moreover, much of the harm done by ingesting alcohol and other possibly teratogenic substances occurs early in the pregnancy when women may not even know that they are pregnant. Must all sexually active women behave at all times as if they were pregnant in order to avoid condemnation and even potential prosecution? Quite apart from the ludicrous nature of such a proposal, no such limitation has ever been suggested in respect of their male partners whose behaviour may also affect the environment in which a pregnancy progresses, albeit usually not so profoundly.

Finally, it should be remembered that Anglo-American law does not recognise a duty to rescue. Placing limitations of this sort – and imposing punishment, including deprivation of liberty – on pregnant women is, at best, disproportionate. As Meredith says, ' ... any such attempts at third party interference in the course of pregnancy – which inevitably involve

---

[42] Paltrow, L, 'Pregnant Drug Users, Fetal Persons, and the threat to *Roe v Wade*', *Albany Law Review*, 62, 1999: 999–1054, at pp 1026–27.

compromising a woman's physical liberty, autonomy and bodily integrity – place pregnant women in a unique legal position.'[43] Arguably, one bright spot in this area came with the case of *City of Charleston v Ferguson*.[44] Commenting on this case, Weyrauch says that it is:

> ... the first Supreme Court case involving a maternal-fetal conflict in an addiction context, articulating that pregnant women cannot be 'searched' without probable cause under the Constitution. This may be the first of many cases in which the Supreme Court is asked to walk the fine line between what a woman does to her own body and what she does to her unborn child.[45]

Two additional cases also may mark a small, but potentially important, modification in the way the law deals with women in these circumstances. In 2006 the Maryland Court of Appeals decided that the state's child endangerment laws cannot be used to prosecute women who give birth to babies who have been exposed to drugs during pregnancy. In 2007, it was reported that the Supreme Court of New Mexico had overturned the conviction of Cynthia Martinez who had been convicted as a felony child abuser because of drug use in pregnancy.[46] These cases represent a growing trend,[47] but despite this apparent progress, women still remain vulnerable to criminalisation because of their behaviour during pregnancy. This is doubly of concern because, as Webb says '[m]ost commentators agree ... that subjecting women to criminal sanctions will not address the problem of children being exposed to alcohol [or other substances] *in utero*.'[48]

As Draper says, 'it is one thing to show what a woman ought to do in relation to her unborn child and quite another to say that this obligation ought to be enforced.'[49] While this situation has not directly arisen to the author's knowledge in the United Kingdom to date, in the United States it has in part emerged from a perceived drugs crisis and the ever more strident language of those opposed to abortion. These are both recognisable characteristics of the UK's modern society, so it would be unwise to be

---

[43] Meredith, S, *Policing Pregnancy: The Law and Ethics of Obstetric Conflict*, Aldershot, Ashgate, 2005, at p 28.

[44] 532 US 67, 67 (2001).

[45] Weyrauch, S, 'Inside the Womb: Interpreting the Ferguson Case', *Duke Journal of Gender Law & Policy*, 9, 2002: 81–90, at p 85.

[46] Available at http://www.advocatesforpregnantwomen.org (accessed on 16/9/2008).

[47] 'New Mexico joins more than 20 other states that have ruled on this issue and that have refused to judicially expand state criminal child abuse and related laws to reach the issues of pregnancy and addiction.', available at http://www.advocatesforpregnantwomen.org (accessed on 16/9/2008).

[48] Available at http://www.msd.govt.nz/documents/about-msd-and-our-work/publications-resources/journals-and-magazines/social-policy-journal/spj03/spj3-policing-pregnancy.doc (accessed 12/09/2008), at p 7.

[49] Draper, H, 'Women, Forced Caesareans and Antenatal Responsibilities', Working Paper no 1, Feminist Legal Research Unit, University of Liverpool, 1, 1992, at p 13.

complacent, although for the present, some reassurance can be taken from the judgement in *Re F (in utero)*[50] where it was said:

> If the law is to be extended … so as to impose control over the mother of an unborn child, where such control may be necessary for the benefit of that child, then under our system of parliamentary democracy it is for Parliament to decide whether such controls can be imposed and, if so, subject to what limitations or conditions.[51]

In one further UK case, pre-natal behaviour was taken into account in making an order in respect of a child after its birth, but this obviously did not involve the kind of coercion we have seen in the US cases that have been discussed.[52]

New developments in medicine may add another group of women to the addicted pregnant woman or those whose 'bad' behaviour might affect the embryo/foetus, meaning that they too may become vulnerable to forced interventions. When foetal therapy becomes more commonplace, the possibility of *in utero* treatment, even surgery, will allow women to enhance the possibility of healthy birth and many women will willingly undergo even invasive treatment to help their foetus to have a safe and healthy birth. However, others may not. More accurate pre-natal diagnosis may place women in the position of having to make decisions which, for some of them, will be problematic. The perception that doctors are now engaged with two patients rather than one, which was discussed briefly above, leads to the possibility that the interests of the pregnant woman may be sacrificed to the interests (or 'rights') of the foetus. This was attempted in the case of *Taft v Taft*.[53] Although the court eventually reversed an earlier court order compelling a pregnant woman to submit to a surgical procedure to prevent the likelihood of miscarriage, it would seem that the critical factor was that the foetus was pre-viable; in other words it could not have been saved in any event. This was not, it would seem, a decision based on concern for the woman, but rather one that focussed on the foetus. Had it been viable, it is not clear that the judgement would have been the same.

Zechmeister suggests that the ability to visualise the foetus in the womb means that 'the focus of surveillance will be less on the mother but increasingly on the foetus. For the profession it becomes "*their*" patient rather than the mother's baby.'[54] This, she continues, 'detaches and separates it from the

---

[50] [1988] 2 All ER 193.
[51] Ibid., at p 200.
[52] *D (a minor) v Berkshire County Council* [1987] 1 All ER 20.
[53] 446 NE 2d 395 (Mass 1983).
[54] Zechmeister, I, 'Foetal Images: The Power of Visual Technology in Antenatal Care and the Implications for Women's Reproductive Freedom', *Health Care Analysis*, 9, 2001: 387–400, at p 391.

mother's body. It conceals the relation of the foetus to the mother's body or even denies the existence of a relationship entirely.'[55] Where interventions into the woman's body are contemplated in the interests of the embryo/foetus the two-patient model is of particular concern as it seems to justify imposing on women an obligation to submit their bodies to interventions that would not be required were the child born.[56] In other words, a mother who could provide a compatible bone marrow transplant for her child might be reviled if she refuses to do so, but she certainly would not be legally forced to provide it. Yet, if she refuses to submit to therapy during pregnancy, attempts have been made to coerce her to do so using the full force of the law. Weyrauch is right to remind us that 'we must be careful not to use these medical advances as a weapon against pregnant women, who bring our society's children into the world.'[57] However, it is not merely during the course of the pregnancy that women find themselves the objects of legal scrutiny; this has also occurred at the point of delivery, in both the United States and the United Kingdom.

Non-consensual obstetrical interventions

Given that the law has concerned itself with the embryo or foetus as it develops – even before viability – it is unsurprising that it will also do so at the point of birth, when, if extruded from the womb, the foetus would become a child, with rights and interests which are usually seen as indisputable. Again, it should be borne in mind that most pregnancies will progress without incident and result in a healthy birth, so the cases we will examine are not typical of the average pregnancy and birth. Nonetheless, they are indicative of an attitude to women and foetuses which is disturbing for its apparent lack of concern for women's rights. As with the previous section, what follows is not intended to be a complete record of case law, but rather will use selected examples to highlight the problem.[58]

The United States

It is perhaps unexpected that a country which has a written constitution guaranteeing, amongst other things, the equality of all citizens, freedom of

---

55 Ibid., at p 392.

56 For example, Annas, G, *Judging Medicine*, Humana Press, 1988, at p 122, says 'No mother has ever been legally required to undergo surgery or general anaesthesia ... to save the life of her dying child. It would be ironic and unfair if she could be forced to submit to more invasive surgical procedures for the sake of her fetus than of her child.'

57 Weyrauch, S, 'Inside the Womb: Interpreting the Ferguson Case', *Duke Journal of Gender Law & Policy*, 9, 2002: 81–90, at p 90.

58 A full discussion of these cases can be found in Meredith, S, *Policing Pregnancy: The Law and Ethics of Obstetric Conflict*, Aldershot, Ashgate, 2005.

religion and privacy rights, which were clarified in cases such as *Roe v Wade*,[59] should have set such an egregious example of non-consensual interventions in pregnancy. It is probably not surprising, however, that the zeal with which the foetal rights or 'pro-life' movement has been pursued against pregnant women should continue to the point of birth.

The reality of childbirth for some US women is bleakly recounted in a chilling comment in *The Guardian* newspaper in 2004:

> In the name of foetal rights, women across the US have been dragged bleeding from hospitals into prison cells hours after giving birth, charged with homicide following stillbirths, pinned to hospital beds and forced to have Caesareans against their will, or had their babies removed at birth after a single positive test for alcohol or drugs. Since the mid-70s around 300 women have been arrested for these transgressions, and 30 states now have foetal homicide laws.[60]

Although not every case results in force at the point of delivery,[61] and while some courts have been prepared to hold that a woman has a right to refuse medical treatment 'derived from her rights to privacy, bodily integrity, and religious liberty, [that] is not diminished during pregnancy … ',[62] enough tragic cases exist to show how foetal 'rights' or interests can be used to trump the rights of women. As long ago as 1987, Kolder, Gallagher and Parsons identified a pattern that represented a shockingly casual approach to women's rights.[63] They were able to identify 11 states where court orders for caesarean sections had been granted, and discovered that in the 21 cases in which they were sought they were granted in 86% of them. Even more troubling is the fact that in 88% of these cases, the orders were issued within 6 hours of the request – scarcely, it might be thought, long enough to take serious account of the personal and constitutional issues at stake. Finally, in an eerie echo of the cases described earlier, 81% of the women involved were black, Asian or Hispanic and 24% did not have English as their first language. As with the policing pregnancy cases, the conclusion is inescapable – while all women may be at risk of coercion, the otherwise disadvantaged are disproportionately at risk. Those who are less able to defend themselves, or are unlikely to be adequately represented, are more likely to face intense and intrusive scrutiny of their behaviour and run the risk of coercive intervention.

---

[59] 410 US 113 (1973).

[60] Taylor, D, *The Guardian*, 23 April 2004, available at http://www.guardian.co.uk/society/2004/apr/23/health.genderissues (accessed on 12/9/2008).

[61] See, for example, *In Re Baby Doe*, 632 NE 2d 332 (Ill App Ct 1994).

[62] Ibid., at p 329.

[63] Kolder, V E, Gallagher, J, Parsons, M T, 'Court-ordered obstetrical interventions', *The New England Journal of Medicine*, 316, 1987: 1192–96.

While it is understandable that the state should have an interest in salvaging the life of foetuses at the point of birth, it is questionable whether or not this should be achieved over the protests of the pregnant woman. Bearing in mind that women have the right to refuse medical interventions, and that foetuses – even at this stage – have no rights, it would be reasonable to assume that the woman's decision, however reprehensible it might seem to others, would be respected. Nonetheless, this is not the pattern that has emerged. For example, in the cases of *Jefferson v Griffin Spaulding County Hospital Auth*[64] and in *In Re Madyyun*,[65] courts upheld forced caesarean sections. Perhaps the best known, and most poignant case, however, is that of a young woman named Angela Carder.[66] Mrs Carder had suffered from cancer on two previous occasions, but following treatment she had gone into remission. When she was about 26 weeks pregnant, it was discovered that her cancer had returned and that it had metastasised; her death was imminent. With the support of her husband, parents and hospital staff, a regime was agreed that it was hoped would keep her alive for another couple of weeks giving the foetus a better chance of survival. However, her condition continued to deteriorate and it was thought unlikely that she would survive long enough to achieve this.

Despite her best efforts, it seemed that both she and her foetus faced death. However, the administrators of the hospital in which she was a patient sought a judicial order to permit the carrying out of a caesarean section. She, her husband, her parents and obstetricians opposed the section, but an order was duly obtained. Mrs Carder further protested when she was told of the court's decision. As she was being prepared for surgery, her attorney tried to have the order blocked, but a three judge court of the D.C. Court of Appeals refused to issue such an order, and later issued an opinion upholding the original one. Neither she nor the baby survived; indeed the caesarean section was even listed as a contributing cause of her death.

The American Civil Liberties Union describes her situation as follows:

> In Washington, DC, a young pregnant woman, severely ill with cancer, several times mouthed the words 'I don't want it done' when told that a court had ordered her to undergo a cesarean and that she likely would not survive the operation. The cesarean was nonetheless performed; the baby died within a few hours of birth; and the woman died two days later.[67]

Although the case was successfully appealed,[68] this was, of course, too late for Angela Carder and her family. It is almost impossible to imagine Mrs

[64] 274 SE 2d 457 (Ga 1981).
[65] 114 Daily Wash L 2233 (DC Super Ct, 29 October 1986).
[66] *In re AC*, 533 A 2d 611 (DC 1987).
[67] Available at http://www.aclu.org/reproductiverights/gen/16529res19970930.html (accessed on 17/9/2008).
[68] *Re AC*, 573 A 2d 1235 (DC 1990).

Carder's feelings in this situation. For any person, being restrained and forced into unwanted surgery would be both terrifying and humiliating. How much worse for a young woman, coming to terms with her own imminent death? Powerful forces must be at stake for any court, or any hospital, even to contemplate such behaviour and the appeal court was scathing in its condemnation of the original judgement. Annas described the case in this way:

> They treated a live woman as though she were already dead, forced her to undergo an abortion, and then justified their brutal and unprincipled opinion on the basis that she was almost dead and her fetus's interests in life outweighed any interest she might have in her own life and health.[69]

The images generated by this tragic case should surely have been enough to discourage hospitals, law officers and courts from ever considering repeating it, but as we will see this was not the case. Indeed, even when women's refusals of caesarean sections *are* accepted, the law is not necessarily done with them. In 2004, a woman, Melissa Ann Rowland, who refused a caesarean section was subsequently charged with murder, but convicted of child endangerment, following the death of one of her twins. She was sentenced to 18 months' imprisonment and a fine, and was also required to enter into a drug treatment programme.[70] In fact, Rowland did agree to a section some 11 days after she first refused, at which time one child was discovered to have died; whether or not the death was directly related to the delay is not clear. What is clear is that women who dare to dispute their doctor's orders may still find themselves on the wrong end of the law.

The United Kingdom

Although British women seem to have escaped relatively unscathed from the pattern of intrusion into pregnancy that has emerged from the US cases discussed above, this has not been the case when it comes to obstetrical interventions at the point of birth. The first case to become public was that of *Re S*.[71] In this case, a woman declined for religious reasons to consent to a caesarean section even although she had been informed that her refusal could result in both her death and the death of her foetus. The health authority applied for a declaration that it would be lawful to proceed with the section even in the face of her refusal. The case was brought to the attention of court officials at 1.30 pm, the hearing began just before 2pm and judgement was delivered at 2.18pm. The judge, Sir Stephen Brown, while impressed by the

[69] Annas, G, 'She's Going to Die: The Case of Angela C', *Hastings Center Report*, 18(1), 1988: 23, at p 25.

[70] CBC News 'Woman who refused C-section sentenced to 18 months', 29 April 2004, available at http://www.cbc.ca/world/story/2004/04/29/csect040429.html (accessed on 12/9/2008).

[71] *Re S (adult: refusal of medical treatment)* (1992) 9 BMLR 69.

sincerity of the beliefs of S and her husband, nonetheless described the situation as 'desperate'.[72] In authorising the surgery, he said:

> He [the consultant] has done his best, as have other surgeons and doctors at the hospital, to persuade the mother that the only means of saving her life, and also, I emphasise, the life of her unborn child, is to carry out a Caesarian section operation. The consultant is emphatic. He says it is absolutely the case that the baby cannot be born alive if a Caesarian operation is not carried out.[73]

In these few sentences, and with S unrepresented by counsel, the judge swept aside the rights of a competent person to make her own healthcare decisions. In doing so, even respect for freedom of religion was overwhelmed by anxiety about the well-being of the foetus. While purportedly also concerned for the health of the woman, there can be little doubt that it was the risk to the foetus that persuaded the judge to ignore a general rule of law; namely that people have a right to reject medical treatment, a right which ' ... exists notwithstanding that the reasons for making the choice are rational, irrational, unknown or even non-existent.'[74] Interestingly, the judge also referred with approval to the US case of Angela Carder, which has already been discussed, but seemingly failed to note that it had already been reversed.

The general rule about the right to refuse medical treatment was re-phrased by Lord Donaldson in the same year.[75] While agreeing that '[a]n adult patient who ... suffers from no mental incapacity has an absolute right to choose whether to consent to medical treatment, to refuse it or to choose one rather than another of the treatments being offered ... ', interestingly he entered the caveat that '[t]he only possible qualification is a case in which the choice may lead to the death of a viable foetus.'[76] Quite where this interpretation of the law comes from is less than clear, but it was arguably to pave the way for a series of subsequent cases of forced obstetrical interventions in the United Kingdom.

In some cases, the argument has been couched in terms of women's competence, rather than overtly in terms of foetal rights. For example, in the case of *Tameside and Glossop Acute Services Trust v CH*,[77] the patient was diagnosed as schizophrenic. She apparently wanted her child to survive but was not deemed capable of comprehending the need for the intervention. In *Norfolk and Norwich Healthcare (NHS) Trust v W*,[78] a woman arrived at hospital,

---

[72] Ibid., at p 70.
[73] Ibid.
[74] *Re T (adult: refusal of medical treatment)* [1992] 4 All ER 649, at p 653.
[75] Ibid.
[76] Ibid., at pp 652–53.
[77] (1996) 31 BMLR 93.
[78] (1996) 34 BMLR 16.

obviously in labour but refusing to accept that she was even pregnant. She did not appear to be suffering from a mental disorder, but in light of her strange refusal to admit to being pregnant, the court declared her not to be competent, and agreed that, if necessary, surgical intervention could proceed.

It might be said that these cases are considerably less troubling than cases like *Re S* and Angela Carder. In *Tameside* and *Norfolk and Norwich Healthcare*, the patients in question were of dubious competence. As Butler-Sloss was to say in a later case, it might therefore not be wrong to assume that '[i]t must be in the best interests of a woman carrying a full-term child whom she wants to be born alive and healthy that such a result should if possible be achieved.'[79] Although attempts to coerce women were to continue, a change of direction became evident in English law.[80]

As long ago as 1978 it was said that, '[t]he foetus cannot, in English law, in my view have any right of its own at least until it is born and has a separate existence from its mother.'[81] If this did in fact reflect UK law, as it purportedly did, then the decision in *Re S* should have been different. If the law supports the rights of individuals to reject even life-sustaining treatment, as it manifestly does, *Re S* should have been decided differently. Despite this, a number of women did find themselves forced into major surgical interventions until a case decided in 1997 clarified the legal position, to the benefit of women. In *Re MB*,[82] Butler-Sloss declared that:

> The fetus up to the moment of birth does not have any separate interests capable of being taken into account when a court has to consider an application for a declaration in respect of a caesarean section operation. The court does not have the jurisdiction to declare that such medical intervention is lawful to protect the interests of the unborn child even at the point of birth.[83]

In a landmark decision, she laid down a set of guidelines, which are paraphrased below:

1. Every person is presumed to have the competence to consent to or to refuse medical treatment unless and until that presumption is rebutted.
2. A competent woman who has the capacity to decide may for religious reasons, other reasons, for rational or irrational reasons or for no reason at all, choose not to have medical intervention, even though the consequences may be the death or serious handicap of the child she bears, or

---

[79] *Re MB* [1997] 8 Med LR 217.
[80] No cases have been heard in the courts of any of the other UK jurisdictions.
[81] *Paton v Trustees of BPAS* [1978] 2 All ER 987, at p 989.
[82] (1997) 38 BMLR 175.
[83] Ibid., at p 227.

her own death. In that event the courts do not have the jurisdiction to declare medical intervention lawful and the question of her own best interests objectively considered, does not arise.

3. Irrationality is here used to connote a decision which is so outrageous in its defiance of logic or of accepted moral standards that no sensible person who had applied his mind to the question to be decided could have arrived at it.[84]

It would seem, therefore, that women in the United Kingdom are protected by these guidelines. However, the judge did introduce one important caveat, which is at first sight difficult to explain. She indicated that the principles contained in the guidelines 'are not intended to be determinative in every case, for the decision must inevitably depend on the particular facts before the court.'[85] It was perhaps this apparent concession that saw the emergence of the final case for consideration in this section; *St George's Healthcare NHS Trust v S*.[86] In this case, the woman was adamant that she did not agree to a caesarean, and seemed to meet the terms of the guidelines in that she was deemed to be competent. Rather than accepting her decision, however, she was sectioned under the Mental Health legislation, although this was later expressly disapproved of by the Court of Appeal. The point remains that even after *Re MB* efforts were still being made to force women to 'manage' their delivery in ways which both comply with medical instructions and are likely to preserve the foetus, even at the expense of the woman's competent choice and fundamental right to make her own decisions.

This is arguably somewhat surprising, given what the law says about the right of competent people to make autonomous choices about healthcare. For example, as we have seen, in a number of cases it has been made clear that the competent adult person has a free hand in making healthcare decisions even if these are to refuse treatment. Indeed, in the case of *Re MB* it was said that '[a] mentally competent patient has an absolute right to refuse to consent to medical treatment for any reason, rational or irrational, or for no reason at all, even where that decision may lead to his or her own death ... '[87] In the case of *Airedale NHS Trust v Bland*,[88] Lord Mustill said that [a] doctor has no right to proceed in the face of objection, even if it is plain to all, including the patient, that adverse consequences and even death will or may ensue.[89]

Perhaps surprisingly, neither the existence of a Bill of Rights nor a written Constitution has, it would seem, served to protect American women from

---

[84] Ibid., at p 224.
[85] Ibid., at p 223.
[86] [1998] 3 All ER 673; (1998) 44 BMLR 160.
[87] Ibid., at p 182.
[88] (1993) 12 BMLR 64.
[89] Ibid., at p 136.

the (mis)application of the law. Happily, it seems likely that the situation in the United Kingdom now is, and presumably will continue to be, different. The adoption of the European Convention on Human Rights into UK law by the Human Rights Act 1998 seems likely to strengthen the legal protection women might reasonably expect. The status to be accorded to the foetus has been somewhat clarified in the European Court of Human Rights, specifically in the case of *Paton v UK*.[90] In this case, the Court was invited to consider whether existing abortion law in England and Wales violated Articles 2 and 8 of the Convention. The first important question was whether a foetus was owed a right to life under Article 2. Although the Court did not deliver a definitive account of foetal rights, it did deny that Article 2 conferred on the foetus a 'strong' right to life. The remaining options outlined by the Court would have meant either that Article 2 did not apply to the foetus at all, or that in early pregnancy any right to life the foetus may have was defeated by the woman's rights. In the more recent case of *Vo v France*,[91] although again the Court did not take a position on when the right to life begins, it nonetheless declared that the foetus is not a person for the purposes of Article 2 of the Convention, and that even if it were to be so considered the interests of the mother would nonetheless predominate.[92] From the woman's perspective the decision in *X v Austria* might also bring some comfort.[93] In this case, in consideration of article 8 of the Convention – the right to private and family life – it was said that 'a compulsory medical intervention ... must be considered as an interference with this right.'[94] This was also effectively the judgement in the case of *Herczegfalvy v Austria*.[95] Referring to this case, Hale LJ in a later case said that 'the decision to impose treatment without consent upon a protesting patient is a potential invasion of his rights under article 3 or article 8.'[96]

Article 3 of the Convention unequivocally prohibits the use of torture, inhuman or degrading treatment. While forced caesarean sections might not qualify as torture (although given what the women must have gone through it must come pretty close) it is certainly plausible that they could amount to inhuman or degrading treatment. In *Denmark, Norway, Sweden and the Netherlands v Greece*,[97] the European Court of Human Rights (ECHR) stated that 'treatment or punishment of an individual may be said to be degrading if it grossly humiliates him before others or drives him to act against his will or

---

[90] (1980) 3 EHRR 408; discussed by Garwood-Gowers, A, Tingle, J, Lewis, T, in *Healthcare Law: The Impact of The Human Rights Act 1998*, London, Cavendish, 2001, at pp 261–2.
[91] (2005) 40 EHRR 12.
[92] Ibid., at para 80.
[93] (1980) 18 DR 154.
[94] Ibid., at p 156.
[95] (1992) 15 EHRR 437.
[96] *R (on the application of W) v Broadmoor Hospital* [2001] EWCA 1545, at para 79.
[97] (1969) 12 YB 1, at p 186.

conscience.'[98] It is hard to imagine anything more degrading or humiliating than forced obstetrical interventions.

Although UK courts have not considered a case in point since the 1998 Act became law, one part of the judgement in *Herczegfalvy* has some resonance in this area. In this passage, the Court stated that while '[m]easures taken out of therapeutic necessity cannot be regarded as inhuman or degrading treatment ... ' nonetheless 'the court must satisfy itself based upon the evidence that the medical necessity has been convincingly shown to exist.'[99] Since all patients are entitled to reject even life-sustaining or life-saving treatment, the 'therapeutic necessity' of operating on an unwilling woman clearly would be hard to defend, and since the foetus is not a 'person', even if there were thought to be a 'therapeutic necessity' to save it, this is legally irrelevant. In *R (on the application of W) v Broadmoor Hospital*[100] a UK court considered the issue of forced treatment and declared that:

> Article 3 is perhaps more obviously in play because the forcible injection of an unwilling patient must constitute at the very least degrading treatment and, if the appellant is properly to be regarded as capacitated, it clearly violates his fundamental rights to autonomy and bodily inviolability. Even if article 3 is not breached, runs the argument, article 8 is, there being no sufficient justification under article 8.2 for so fundamental an invasion of the appellant's autonomy and inviolability, basic ingredients of his right to privacy.[101]

Arguably, therefore, taking the default position that the foetus is not a person with rights guaranteed by the Convention, women might well find themselves with a strong case to argue that their rights under Article 3 or Article 8 would be breached by forced caesarean sections. Thus, the loophole seemingly left open by the *Re MB* judgement will have likely have little, if any, impact.

Conclusion

It has been suggested throughout this discussion that the concept of autonomy is problematic, as it can be conceptualised in a variety of ways some of which have been described in Chapter 1. On an individualistic account of autonomy, women should be as free as anyone else to make their own healthcare and/or personal decisions irrespective of outcome. However, when it comes to the protection of embryos and foetuses, additional considerations

---

[98] Ibid.
[99] (1992) 15 EHRR 437, at paras 779–84.
[100] [2001] EWCA Civ 1545.
[101] Ibid., at para 14.

have been used to temper the apparent commitment to this model of autonomy. Lew suggests that this, in part, is a result of the fact that '[c]onflicts between a woman's needs and those of her fetus are vexing because they pit powerful cultural norms against one another; the ideal of autonomy and the ideal of maternal self-sacrifice.'[102] We expect mothers (including it would seem pregnant women) to behave in the interests of their children (or foetuses), and it is not unreasonable to do so. However, the question remains whether or not this expectation should be translated into law. As has been said, '[s]elf sacrifice is a gift.'[103] An individualistic account of autonomy could not coerce self-sacrifice, however minimal that sacrifice might be.

On the other hand, a more relational account of autonomy would see the pregnant women as intimately linked to her social network, perhaps especially to her embryo/foetus. Bennett notes that '[t]he relationship of pregnancy does not fit easily into the liberal conceptualizations of individuality and separateness ... While pregnancy is about connectedness, the language of rights and autonomy is about separation.'[104] Unlike Purdy, who asserts that '[r]espect for our right, as moral agents, to control our bodies, is a keystone of liberal society',[105] she argues that:

> Autonomy is not simply about the rights and ability of an individual to assert his or her interests against the rest of the world. Rather, it is more nuanced, more relational. It is about the ways that our desires, dreams and interests may be expressed within the rich, complex and unruly tangle of relationships that are part of life in modern society. Without this understanding, autonomy remains just an empty shell.[106]

However, I have already argued that an individualistic account of autonomy does not necessarily imply selfishness or disconnectedness and that it can share characteristics with the relational account. Indeed, it is difficult to see how one could reach a decision which is totally unaffected by who we are, where we came from and where we are now. One plausible consequence, however, of adopting a more contextual (relational) account of autonomy in the situations discussed in this chapter is that doing so might make it possible to build a case that women should always and at all times act for the benefit of their foetuses, since relational autonomy requires her to consider the context of her decisions and the consequences for others, beyond her own self-regarding interests. Jackson counters that ' ... by effectively conflating

---

[102] Lew, J B, 'Terminally Ill and Pregnant: State Denial of a Woman's Right to Refuse a Caesarean Section', *Buffalo Law Review*, 38, 1990: 619–46, at pp 621–22.

[103] Ibid.

[104] Bennett, B, *Health Law's Kaleidoscope: Health Law Rights in a Global Age,* Aldershot, Ashgate, 2008, at p 105.

[105] Purdy, L M, 'Are Pregnant Women Fetal Containers?', *Bioethics*, 4(4), 1990: 273–91, at p 273.

[106] Ibid., at p 111.

being female with being a fertile, heterosexual and sexually active woman, the critique of autonomy which is grounded in its inability to accurately describe women's lives may itself be fundamentally flawed.'[107] It might seem strange that the relational account of autonomy, which for some commentators is more appealing than the purely individualistic one, may result in the deprivation of fundamental freedoms, just as appears to be the consequence when it is applied in the debate on assisted dying. If women are to be treated as equal citizens, they need equal rights: in this case, the right not to have treatment (or punishment) imposed upon them in the purported interests of their embryos/foetuses. Defending women's freedom in this situation seems to require adherence to the individualistic model; anything else arguably opens the door to coercion. As was seen in the case of assisted dying, the law's ingenuity in simultaneously proclaiming adherence to individual autonomy yet using a more relational account to reject its application in hard cases knows no bounds. This was clearly recognised in the case of *St George's Healthcare NHS Trust v S*,[108] where the judge said:

> When a human life is at stake the pressure to provide an affirmative answer authorising unwanted medical intervention is very powerful. Nevertheless, the autonomy of each individual requires continuing protections even, perhaps particularly, when the motive for interfering with it is readily understandable, and indeed to many would appear commendable.[109]

Thus, even although the outcome (for the embryo or foetus) of forced interventions in pregnancy or at the point of birth may be beneficial (that is, enhancing the possibility of a healthy future life or even existence itself), we need to be cautious in too readily assuming that this is what should form the basis of the law's approach in this situation. The beneficence and contextual analysis that motivate the desire to intervene without the woman's consent disguise a version of autonomy that effectively discounts individual self-determination.

The freedom to make important life choices is valued by everyone – unsurprisingly, also by pregnant women. Yet from what has gone before, it seems clear that courts have not always respected it on their behalf, preferring rather to compel behaviour that favours the embryo/foetus rather than the woman. Moreover, this has been taken to extremes. While we might well disapprove of women who do not do what they can to protect and preserve their embryo/foetus, courts in some jurisdictions have gone one step further in *imposing* that disfavour by coercing women into making certain decisions or depriving them of liberty in the course of their pregnancy. It is

---

[107] Jackson, E, *Regulating Reproduction: Law, Technology and Autonomy*, Oxford, Hart Publishing, 2001, at p 3.
[108] [1998] 3 All ER 673.
[109] Ibid., at p 688.

interesting to note that, although in the United States some of these decisions are legislatively mandated,[110] many coercive decisions are taken by law
enforcement officers and judges. The reality is that ' ... in their efforts to
secure the healthiest possible live birth of the foetus, doctors and the law
have on occasion seemingly ignored the respective status of women and foetuses.'[111] Indeed, some women's lives have been effectively ruined by the
law's failure to hold to the autonomy rights of individuals. This may well be
the direct result of the changing face of pregnancy – the ability to visualise
the foetus and to envisage it as a separate patient, entitled to available
resources and therapies. In addition, our understanding of foetal development
has meant that 'researchers have begun to offer scientific data that conclusively links maternal action during pregnancy with the health outcome
for newborns.'[112] The impetus for intervention is, then, both scientific and,
some might argue, moral. Fortunately, in the United Kingdom, more recent
judgements have disputed the legitimacy of this kind of treatment and
British women seem to be safer than their American counterparts when it
comes to respect for decisions that are right *for them*.

Protecting the foetus at the expense of the woman has been said to be 'a
monumental misunderstanding of the concept of respect and a perverse
interpretation of the value of human rights.'[113] That the law and professional
guidelines[114] in the United Kingdom seem finally to have accepted the
individualistic concept of autonomy in this area is to be welcomed, even
although it sits at odds with an intuitive concern for embryos and foetuses.
Quite simply, however, the consequences of the alternative are too grave to
contemplate. With due respect to those who prefer the more relational
approach, applying it in these cases could well result in the kind of situation
still current in the United States where women continue to be subject to
harsh and sometimes counter-productive intrusions into their liberties. The
lesser evil, I would argue, is that some women will make 'bad' choices in the
course of their pregnancies or at the moment of birth but that these will
have to be respected. Requiring the sacrifice of important personal liberties
in the interest of others might satisfy some versions of autonomy, but it
threatens important freedoms of action and belief. Yet again, however, we

---

[110] For further discussion, see Cave, E, 'Drink and Drugs in Pregnancy: Can the Law Prevent Avoidable
Harm to the Future Child?', *Medical Law International*, 8(2), 2007: 165–88.

[111] McLean, S A M, Ramsey, J, 'Human Rights, Reproductive Freedom, Medicine and the Law', *Medical
Law International*, 5, 2002: 239–58, at p 244.

[112] Webb, M B, http://www.msd.govt.nz/documents/about-msd-and-our-work/publications-resources/
journals-and-magazines/social-policy-journal/spj03/spj3-policing-pregnancy.doc (accessed 12/09/2008),
transcript, p 1.

[113] McLean, S A M, *Old Law, New Medicine*, London, Pandora, 1999, at p 69.

[114] See, for example, Royal College of Obstetricians and Gynaecologists, *Law and Ethics in Relation to
Court-Authorised Obstetric Interventions*, Ethics Committee Guideline No 1, September 2006, available at
http://www.rcog.org.uk/index.asp?PageID=1044 (accessed on 4/2/2009).

can conclude that the law's approach has not been based in one consistent approach to autonomy, nor does it even seem to have consistently applied the principles of consent law. If so, then it is again difficult to accept the claim that the law on consent is in fact the legal embodiment of the ethical principle of personal autonomy. When it suits policy (or even just the intuitions of judges) autonomy has on too many occasions become of secondary concern. In the face of this, the debate around autonomy seems somewhat sterile, and the law is complicit in rendering the principles said to inform the law of consent essentially impotent.

Chapter 6

Autonomy and genetic information

The so-called genetics revolution poses many challenges for both individuals and society. The potential benefits and possible drawbacks of the generation and use of genetic information are significant and may well challenge the law's commitment to privacy[1] and confidentiality, because of the familial nature of genetic information. Although medical information is generally regarded as falling into the sphere of privacy, protected by both data protection laws and the professional obligation of confidentiality, in part this is because it usually concerns no one but the patient him- or herself. Some exceptions to the general obligation of confidentiality do exist, but they are either based on the individual patient's consent or welfare or on the wider public interest.[2] By and large, then, people anticipate that health related information will, save in relatively rare circumstances, be maintained in confidence.

Advances in genetics, however, are seen by some as likely to challenge this assumption in ways previously unconsidered. For example, the world-wide development of biobanks raises issues about security of information and the involvement of (ideally) large sections of the population in clinical research for the benefit of others.[3] Also, the increased availability of tests may mean that people are increasingly curious about their genetic status and may accumulate information that they would prefer not to be disclosed to others without their consent. Why is this so important in the case of genetic information? The answer is twofold. First, although it is important not to overestimate what genetic information can tell us – since it often more about

---

[1] It should be noted that the existence of a law on privacy was only directly acknowledged in the United Kingdom in the case of *Douglas and Others v Hello! Ltd* [2001] 2 All ER 289. For an excellent discussion of genetic privacy, see Laurie, G, *Genetic Privacy: A Challenge to Medico-Legal Norms*, Cambridge University Press, 2002.

[2] For an excellent discussion of confidentiality see Mason, J K, Laurie, G T, *Mason and McCall Smith's Law and Medical Ethics* (7th edn), Oxford University Press, 2006, at Chapter 8.

[3] For a discussion of some of these issues in the UK context, see Webster, A, *et al*, *Public attitudes to third party access and benefit sharing: their application to UK Biobank*, June 2008, available at http://www. egcukbiobank.org.uk/assets/wtx052208.pdf (accessed on 6/1/2009).

possibilities than probabilities – it is clear that predictive health information could be of interest to third parties. For example, insurance companies or employers might be tempted to use this information to weight premiums or make hiring decisions. Indeed, in some jurisdictions legislation specifically designed to offer additional protection to genetic information has been either proposed or put in place. While this might seem sensible, some commentators object to what they call 'genetic exceptionalism', arguing that genetic information is not inherently different from other medical information and should not be treated as such.[4] Although these are important issues, they will not be further dealt with in this chapter as they raise questions different from those under consideration in this narrative.

Second, genetic information *is* different from other medical data in that it has consequences for families. Two problems arise from this. First, the decision to seek genetic information may have consequences that go beyond those normally associated with obtaining knowledge about health status. Second, control of the information may be more problematic because of the interests that others may have in sharing it. The challenge for the individual is to manage the knowledge that genetics can provide. The challenge for society is to formulate a principled basis from which to engage appropriately with the ethical and legal issues that arise from genetic science and the information derived from it.

For our purposes, the important questions for consideration concern the use and control of genetic information, as these pose challenges both for the tested individual and the healthcare professional involved. For the individual, the decision as to whether or not to share their genetic information with others may be more complex than, for example, telling relatives that you have high blood pressure. As we will see, even if an individual feels an obligation to inform relatives of their genetic status, it is not always the case that this will be welcomed. On the other hand, Petrila argues that '*access* to such information may prove useful as well, particularly to people who may be at genetic risk for particular diseases.'[5] Tensions, then, may arise between competing interests in learning about genetic information. In addition, healthcare professionals may feel themselves to have an obligation to ensure that relatives are informed in some cases, even when the patient protests.

It is plausible that the individual who seeks genetic information already has reason to believe that there may be problems within the family. This, however, does not necessarily mean that they regard whatever they find out as being any less personal or confidential than any other health related

[4] See, for example, Wolf, S A, 'Beyond "Genetic Discrimination": Towards the Broader Harm of Geneticism', *Journal of Law, Medicine and Ethics*, 23, 1995: 345–53; Hellman, D, 'What Makes Genetic Discrimination Exceptional?', *American Journal of Law and Medicine*, 29, 2003: 77–116.

[5] Petrila, J, 'Genetic Risk: The New Frontier for the Duty to Warn', *Behav Sci Law* 19, 2001: 405–21, at p 406.

information. However, the mere possession of genetic knowledge places them in a potentially uncomfortable position. Given the familial nature of genetics, it must be asked what moral obligations do we have here? Additionally, what is the proper approach of the professionals who hold this information? Resolving these questions has become increasingly urgent as the volume of genetic information being gathered increases exponentially. Indeed, the knowledge gained from the science of genetics will likely take on increasing importance in direct proportion to the availability of genetic tests and the emergence of links between genes and health. Glasner and Rothman say that:

> It has been acknowledged for some time that 'knowledge' is the most important global factor in determining standards of living in today's world, and the new genetics is becoming a major contributor in the twenty-first century ... [6]

Moreover, the genetics revolution is changing, and will continue to change, people's attitudes to themselves and their community. Callahan, for example, has argued that medical progress, which obviously will include advances in genetic knowledge, 'reshapes our notions of what it is to have a life ... '.[7] It is in the nature of medical advance to depend on the accumulation and interpretation of information and in the nature of medical encounters that they generate yet further information. It is very much in the interest of societies and individuals that we learn what we can about disease states, their genesis and their treatment. Although the promise of therapies and cures that was held out at the beginning of the genetics era has not yet been fully realised, progress *is* being made. More and more disease states can now be shown to have a genetic basis, meaning that testing of individuals can reveal information about their susceptibility to particular conditions, and in some cases allow them to take avoiding action; for example by modifying lifestyle. The more we know about the contribution of genes to (ill) health, the more we have come to realise just how many people may be affected. A significant percentage of the population will carry genes which will predispose them to potential health problems, and understanding this may help them to avoid the onset of these conditions. In other cases, where no intervention is possible, knowledge of their genetic status may at least allow them to come to terms with their future.[8]

---

[6] Glasner, P, Rothman, H, 'New genetics, new ethics? Globalisation and its discontents', *Health, Risk & Society*, 3(3), 2001: 245–59, at pp 247–48.

[7] Callahan, D, *What Kind of Life: The Limits of Medical Progress*, New York, Simon and Schuster, 1990, at p 25.

[8] For a discussion of this, see British Medical Association, *Our Genetic Future: The Science and Ethics of Genetic Technology*, Oxford University Press, 1992, at p 1.

It is clear, therefore, that genetic information has real significance for individuals and societies, and indeed other organisations, such as industry.[9] Testing individuals for genetic markers which may predict future health status is a powerful political, economic and social tool, as well as a matter of personal interest. As Black notes, '[t]esting is … not simply a neutral technique and a private issue; it has significant social consequences.'[10]

However, as is often the case, arguably science 'can outstrip the ability of its lines of social, ethical and regulatory support to keep up.'[11] Or, as Mannion puts it, science sometimes 'roars ahead',[12] before the ethics and law have been adequately considered. Thus, he argues, ' … we should strive to consider our reactions to such developments long *before* the scientific and legislative agendas have left ethics behind.'[13]

For modern medicine, advances in genetic knowledge hold out tantalising possibilities for diagnostic, and ultimately therapeutic, interventions. It seems likely, then, that the more we know about the relevance of genetics for health status, the more pressure there will be to test people for genetic predisposition. In this way, it may be hoped, genetic predispositions and conditions can be identified and perhaps treated earlier than was previously possible. This, Hepburn says, 'is almost an article of faith in medicine … ',[14] since 'the ascendancy of science has engendered a growing desire to exert control over events and to reduce uncertainty.'[15] The consequence of this, it has been said, is that '[h]uman beings will be genetically laid bare and vulnerable as never before.'[16]

Of course, this may be entirely unproblematic. Genetic information can be seen as merely one additional piece of medical information, albeit a potentially very important one. If we already have in place adequate legal and ethical guidance on how to manage other medical information, why would this not be sufficient to manage genetic information? Although, as we have seen, some commentators object to the creation of laws specifically to deal

---

[9] Salter, B, Jones, M, 'Regulating human genetics: the changing politics of biotechnology governance in the European Union', *Health, Risk & Society*, 4(3), 2002: 325–40.

[10] Black, J, 'Regulation as Facilitation: Negotiating the Genetic Revolution', in Brownsword, R, Cornish, W, and Llewelyn, M (eds), *Law and Human Genetics: Regulating a Revolution*, Oxford, Hart Publishing, 1998, 29, at p 45.

[11] Salter, B, Jones, M, 'Regulating human genetics: the changing politics of biotechnology governance in the European Union', *Health, Risk & Society*, 4(3), 2002: 325–40, at p 327.

[12] Mannion, G, 'Genetics and the Ethics of Community', *HeyJ*, XLVII, 2006: 226–56, at p 233.

[13] Ibid., at p 247.

[14] Hepburn, E R, 'Genetic testing and early diagnosis and intervention: boon or burden?', *Journal of Medical Ethics*, 22, 1996: 105, at p 105.

[15] Ibid., at p 107.

[16] Fletcher, J C and Wertz, D C, 'An International Code of Ethics in Medical Genetics Before the Human Genome is Mapped', in Bankowski, Z and Capron, A (eds), *Genetics, Ethics and Human Values: Human Genome Mapping, Genetic Screening and Therapy*, xxiv CIOMS Round Table Conference, 1991, at p 97.

with genetic knowledge[17] – for example anti-discrimination laws which are specific to genetics – in the family context, which will be the focus of this chapter, troubling issues do arise. Testing one person reveals information about relatives, and this will obviously have implications for the exercise of autonomy as one person's decision may affect the ability of others to make autonomous choices. This makes genetic information different from most other medical knowledge on two counts; first, because it is not only information about the individual and second because it may also affect reproductive decisions.[18]

The primary difference, therefore, between genetic information and other medical information is that what we discover about an individual is also information about relatives, close or distant, and is also relevant for future children. Questions inevitably arise about the extent to which (if at all) there is a duty on individuals to ensure that relatives are informed of the results of genetic tests. Further, this raises questions about what physicians can or perhaps should do with information gleaned from one person that will likely affect others. As a consequence, while 'the confidentiality of diagnostic information is usually jealously preserved by doctors, tensions may emerge when the traditional principles of medical ethics are tested in genetic disorder cases.'[19]

Before considering these problems and the ethical and legal issues raised by them, it is helpful to explore the range of situations in which testing might be conducted in order to illuminate the breadth and depth of the questions that may arise and the interests at stake. This discussion relates to people who are *prima facie* assumed to be autonomous, but it must not be forgotten that the interests of these people are not confined to themselves. For example, when making reproductive decisions people may wish to ensure that genetic problems are not present in their offspring. Using *in vitro* fertilisation (IVF) coupled with pre-implantation genetic diagnosis (PGD) intending parents may choose to select against certain embryos. Equally, pre-natal tests are available to all pregnant women in the United Kingdom and elsewhere that may result in a decision not to continue with an established pregnancy. However, although testing is now available at these stages, this will not be taken any further here as arguably the issues raised are different from those that are central to this discussion. Nonetheless, autonomy issues do arise in respect of testing before birth, and they should not be entirely

---

[17] See, for example, Wolf, S A, 'Beyond "Genetic Discrimination": Toward the Broader Harm of Geneticism', *Journal of Law, Medicine & Ethics*, 23, 1995: 345–53; Hellman, D, 'What Makes Genetic Discrimination Exceptional?', *American Journal of Law and Medicine*, 29, 2003: 77–116.

[18] Nuffield Council on Bioethics, *Genetic Screening: a Supplement to the 1993 Report by the Nuffield Council on Bioethics*, London, 2006, at p 28, para 5.1.

[19] McLean, S A M, 'Genetic Screening of Children: The UK Position', *The Journal of Contemporary Health Law and Policy*, 12, 1995: 113–30, at p 117.

overlooked; not least the matter of when the state can properly intervene in people's choices about what kind of children to have.[20]

More relevant for this discussion are decisions that are taken within the context of an existing family. People may seek tests on their own behalf, of which more later, but they may also decide to have their children tested. Given the concerns already highlighted about autonomy and privacy, permitting such decisions is arguably more value laden than the usual responsibilities that parents take for their children. Not only can the information obtained from genetic tests affect the individual child, now and in the future, they will also have implications for the rest of the family – not just the nuclear one, but also the extended one. Questions arise here, then, concerning control and dissemination of information.

Testing children

It is generally accepted that parents have both the right and the responsibility to act in the best interests of their children, and this may include gathering the most accurate information available about their current and future health. The development of more and more genetic tests, and the increased ability to link genes and health, might encourage parents to seek information about their children. Tests may seek to identify genetic conditions which manifest at birth, during childhood or later in life. As each of these potentially raises different issues, they will be dealt with sequentially.

Testing children for genetic conditions could be seen as essentially no different from any other diagnostic medical intervention. Indeed, it could be argued to be the act of responsible parents, particularly where the test result leads to the possibility of treatment that can cure or palliate the condition identified. For example, the test for Phenylketonuria (PKU) – a rare inherited condition – is offered to parents of all newborns in the United Kingdom. Crucially, the test is minimally invasive and the condition is treatable. Despite the manifest benefits to a child of diagnosing and treating PKU, and arguably society's interest in avoiding needless suffering, parental autonomy has been taken as paramount here. In the Irish case of *North Western Health Board v W (H)*,[21] for example, the court declined to grant a declaration that parental refusal to accept the test was inimical to the rights of their son and that it would be lawful to proceed without their consent. Laurie notes that the legal test to be applied was agreed by all of the judges to be the best interests of the child, and that 'the majority considered that the presumption is that the welfare of the child is to be found in a determination of those interests by the family exercising its authority as such, and that this can only

---

[20] For further discussion, see McLean, S A M, *Modern Dilemmas: Choosing Children*, Edinburgh, Capercaillie Books, 2006.
[21] [2001] IESC 70, 8 November 2001.

be rebutted by countervailing constitutional considerations such as an immediate threat to life.'[22] In the United Kingdom too, it has been said that screening or testing has moved from 'a "public health" model', to one which requires and embraces individual choice.[23] Thus, even if children's lives could be radically improved by insisting on testing, the law will not force this on unwilling parents. Newson welcomes this, saying that the law 'should not enter to mandate newborn screening when parents decline. Intrusion into private life is improper, save for extreme circumstances such as a risk of death or extreme welfare risk such as child abuse.'[24] However, although the sphere of private life is worthy of respect, it seems somewhat odd that parents should be given so much latitude to make decisions that are potentially immensely damaging for their children. This must be particularly true when the condition being tested for is entirely treatable and the consequences so grave. It would seem that the law protects a highly individualistic approach to parental autonomy in such cases, arguably disregarding the interests of the child.

Tests are also available for conditions that are either not treatable, or where the genetic component is of uncertain impact. Terrenoire says that '[a]dvances in genetic research have put modern medicine in the uncomfortable position of being able to foresee future conditions that it cannot treat.'[25] Kerruish and Robertson further point out that because of developments in molecular genetic diagnostics, 'it is feasible to test whole populations of newborns for genetic susceptibility to common disorders, such as diabetes and asthma.'[26] However, they also note that the consequences of these advances could be problematic since the information gained 'contains a much greater component of uncertainty.'[27] Thus, they say, we may grow a legion of the 'worried well' thereby 'creating psychological morbidity and straining medical resources.'[28] Where no therapy is available, it must be asked why parents would seek out the information in the first place.

Of course, while learning that your child will suffer from a childhood onset genetic condition which is not treatable is highly distressing, it may serve other purposes which are not directly concerned with the child. Any benefits that accrue might be for the parents (and perhaps existing siblings), since it may enable them to come to terms with the reality of their child's

[22] Laurie, G, 'Better to hesitate at the threshold of compulsion: PKU testing and the concept of family autonomy in Eire', *J Med Ethics*, 28, 2002: 136–38, at p 136.

[23] Newson, A, 'Should Parental Refusals of Newborn Screening Be Respected?', *Cambridge Quarterly of Healthcare Ethics*, 15, 2006: 135–46, at p 137.

[24] Ibid., at p 142.

[25] Terrenoire, Gwen, 'Huntington's Disease and the ethics of genetic prediction', *J Med Ethics*, 18, 1992: 79–85, at p 79.

[26] Kerruish, N J, Robertson, S P, 'Newborn screening; new developments, new dilemmas', *J Med Ethics*, 31, 2005: 393–98, at p 394.

[27] Ibid., at p 395.

[28] Ibid.

likely (albeit not always inevitable) future illness and even provoke them into having their own genetic status checked. If parental autonomy is the predominant value in this matter, then it would be entirely within their right to find out the information. Knowing that their child has a propensity to (or the certainty of developing) a particular condition can help them to cope, may assist them in relating to the rest of the family and might inform future reproductive decisions.

For the child, however, the benefits of genetic knowledge are less obvious. For the very young child, this obviously is not an option, but should s/he survive early childhood, questions arise about what rights they have vis a vis knowledge about their own genetic make-up. Clearly, they can no longer claim a right to privacy as the information is already in the family domain. Equally, there are concerns about how young people would handle the information that they have an untreatable medical condition, even if it is not life-threatening. While some argue that children are entitled to receive information relevant to their future health and prospects, others argue that they should be spared the burden of having to live with this knowledge. Whatever position is correct, most policies 'strongly advise against testing children for a disease in which surveillance, pre-emptive, or definitive medical treatment is not available in childhood.'[29] The dilemmas of disclosure are obviated by not obtaining the information in the first place. However, if parental authority takes pride of place in respect of their children's health, should they not be entitled both to seek the information and then decide how to handle it? Differences of opinion on this exist even within the clinical community. For example, The Working Party of the (UK) Clinical Genetics Society published a report on screening children some years ago.[30] One of their more interesting findings was that '[g]eneticists and coworkers were less likely to view parental wishes alone as sufficient to justify testing than were paediatricians and others.'[31] This finding may be the result of a difference in both attitude and expertise between these groups, with paediatricians routinely used to accepting parental authority and geneticists being more alert to the possible down-side of genetic testing. Where the condition tested for is not treatable, Clarke identifies a number of matters that should be taken into consideration when contemplating childhood testing:

(i)   the 'right' of parents to arrange genetic testing on their child (Do such rights exist? Or is it more helpful to consider the responsibility of parents and society to act in the best interests of the child?);

---

[29] Kerruish, N.J., Robertson, S.P., 'Newborn screening; new developments, new dilemmas', *J Med Ethics*, 31, 2005: 393–98, at p 396.

[30] Working Party of the (UK) Clinical Genetics Society, 'The Genetic Testing of Children', *Med Genetics*, 21, 1994: 785–97.

[31] Ibid., at p 787.

(ii) the judgement as to whether the child is sufficiently mature and of sufficient understanding to make their own decision, or to participate in a collective decision process;

(iii) the abrogation of the child's future capacity to make their own informed, autonomous decision as an adult;

(iv) the likely loss of confidentiality concerning the child's genetic status, which would be protected if they were not tested until older; and

(v) the possibility of negative emotional consequences for the child resulting from discrimination, stigmatization or altered parental expectations associated with the genetic test results.[32]

On the other hand, he argues that '[w]here there is a clear medical benefit from genetic, or any other type, of diagnostic testing then it is ethically unexceptionable.'[33] In this case, he views genetic testing as little different from other diagnostic tests, although – as will be discussed in what follows – it is arguable that even where treatment is available, the implications of the information are different from those that attach to other medical information and this may create an addition layer of complexity. Of course, many children who survive to be old enough to make their own decisions may not be unhappy to have the knowledge about their genetic status and may be positively pleased where that information has been used to benefit other members of the family, physically or psychologically. The problem is that this is unpredictable. When mature, young people might prefer not to know their genetic status and feel that the invasion of their privacy as a consequence of the sharing of information is a harm that should have been prevented. Again, we cannot know which children would feel this way, suggesting that the commitment to parental autonomy which has been shown to exist in this, as in other,[34] healthcare situations may be more problematic than it is taken to be.

Before leaving the subject of testing children, one further situation remains to be considered; namely, testing for so-called 'late onset' conditions, such as Huntington's Disease which will commonly not begin to affect people until they are in their 30s or even older. For the moment Huntington's is untreatable and unless people die of an unrelated cause it will be fatal. Any benefits that families may claim to derive from knowing about other non-treatable conditions could equally be said to apply here, but the question must be, at what cost to the child? The Clinical Genetics Society's Working Party Report was concerned that such testing holds out the

---

[32] Clarke, A, 'Introduction', in Clarke, A (ed), *The Genetic Testing of Children*, Oxford, Bios Scientific Publishers, 1998, 1–16, at p 6.

[33] Ibid., at p 6.

[34] For further discussion, see Elliston, S, *The Best Interests of the Child in Healthcare*, London, Routledge-Cavendish, 2007.

potential for discrimination, as well as the possibility that it may affect the child's self esteem, change the way in which the child is treated within the family and prevent a future exercise of autonomy. Kopelman says that not testing for untreatable late onset conditions represents the 'professional consensus'.[35] Those holding an opposite opinion would, however, argue that 'policy should reflect what is best for children … [and] testing young children is often useful and affirms parental authority to decide what is best for their own children.'[36] Of course, even without being told, children as they mature may well 'unofficially' become aware that a particular condition is present in their family and for that reason Malpas has argued that children are entitled to be told about their genetic status. The logic of this, he concludes, means that '[t]he reasons given for defending disclosure of genetic conditions in the family are also important reasons for cautiously defending predictive genetic testing of children for adult-onset diseases.'[37] Yet again, however, we cannot know whether or not a child or young person would have preferred not to live their life in the knowledge that they may (in some cases will) suffer from a non-treatable illness that may well be fatal. It is too late to worry about this once the cat is out of the bag.

Whereas it may seem easy to agree that parents should have the authority to seek and agree to testing their children for conditions which can be treated or ameliorated as a result of the knowledge gained, where no treatment is available and/or the condition is late onset it is tempting to challenge this. If, as the PKU example suggests, parental autonomy is paramount, this would entitle parents to make decisions on behalf of their children even if they have detrimental consequences for the child as s/he grows and becomes aware. Parents, Dickens argues, may not have a positive duty to do good; rather, their function can be defined 'by reference to the negative standard of protecting children from harm.'[38] Whether this encompasses the liberty to find out information that may help them, yet where there is the possibility of it causing psychological or other problems for their children, is not clear. On the other hand, parental authority over children (at least until they are old enough to make their own decisions) is generally regarded as a private matter. In line with common law and the terms of Article 8 of the European Convention on Human Rights, '[t]he law … stops at the door of our houses, most of the time … ',[39] and this is the case even if ' … the threshold for

[35] Kopelman, L M, 'Using the Best Interests Standard to Decide Whether to Test Children for Untreatable, Late-Onset Genetic Diseases', *Journal of Medicine and Philosophy*, 32, 2007: 375–94, at p 376.

[36] Ibid., at p 377.

[37] Malpas, P J, 'Why tell asymptomatic children of the risk of an adult-onset disease in the family but not test them for it?', *J Med Ethics*, 32, 2006: 639–42, at p 642.

[38] Dickens, B M, 'The Modern Function and Limits of Parental Rights' (1981) 97 *LQR* 462, at p 464.

[39] Newson, A, 'Should Parental Refusals of Newborn Screening Be Respected?', *Cambridge Quarterly of Healthcare Ethics*, 15, 2006: 135–46, at p 142.

state intervention in parental decisions made on behalf of children remains poorly defined.'[40]

There are many reasons why parents may seek genetic tests on their children – perhaps to prepare themselves and friends or relatives for the likely onset of a debilitating condition, or to identify whether or not a particular inherited disorder is in the family's gene pool. Manifestly, however, deciding to test a child poses a number of problems which are different from those which would be encountered were an adult to seek such a test. Where the condition has childhood onset and is treatable, respect for parental autonomy in seeking genetic information is arguably unproblematic, as the child will be likely to suffer its effects before the age at which he or she could legally make personal decisions and the information is needed to offer therapy. In this situation, it might be said to be in his/her best interests that the test is undertaken, perhaps so that parents can help prepare the child for what will come next or so that action can be taken to avoid or minimise the impact of the condition.[41] This would hold even if there were also benefits derived by the parents themselves and/or other family members as the child's interests and those of his or her family are not mutually exclusive. Where the condition is late onset, however, a sound balancing of benefits and burdens may be less easy to make. Ross differentiates the two situations in this way:

> Predictive genetic testing for childhood onset conditions differs from predictive genetic testing for late-onset conditions because it does not involve concerns regarding the child's right, as an adult, to make the decisions for him- or herself, nor the right to confidentiality with regard to the decision and the information. These concerns are not raised in predictive testing for childhood onset disorders because the diseases most likely will manifest themselves before the children have the autonomy to decide for themselves whether to undergo testing and while the parents still have health care decision-making authority.[42]

Manifestly, matters of confidentiality, privacy and decision-making authority differ when the disease will not manifest itself until later in life. It seems self-evident therefore that parents may struggle 'to balance the interests of one person with those of other family members.'[43] In this respect, Ross asks

---

[40] Ibid, at p 140.

[41] The use of the best interests test is explicitly endorsed in the guidelines developed by the General Medical Council; see Seeking patients' consent: the ethical considerations, November 1998, General Medical Council, available at http://www.gmc-uk.org/guidance/current/library/consent.asp (accessed on 25/10/2006), transcript, p 6, para 23.

[42] Ross, L F, 'Predictive Genetic Testing for Conditions that Present in Childhood', *Kennedy Institute of Ethics Journal*, 12(3), 2002: 225–44, at p 226.

[43] Kopelman, L M, 'Using the Best Interests Standard to Decide Whether to Test Children for Untreatable, Late-Onset Genetic Diseases', *Journal of Medicine and Philosophy*, 32, 2007: 375–94, at p 376.

'whether parents must focus on the children's best medical interest or whether they can make decisions that balance the children's interests and needs with the needs and interests of other family members.'[44] Attaining this balance pervades discussion of all genetic testing, and will be considered in more depth in the following section.

Currently, in the United Kingdom, tests are not routinely undertaken in childhood except in respect of conditions which are serious and for which there is a known treatment. No matter what other benefits may flow from the obtained information for others, it is generally the case that societies seek to protect children from interventions which have no, or few, benefits for them. Until therapeutic and diagnostic capacities are closer together than they currently are, this pattern seems likely to continue. Nonetheless, the 'availability of more and more genetic tests will create unique dilemmas for parents, their children, and their health care providers.'[45] If parental autonomy trumps the actual or potential interests of children, however, resolution of these dilemmas may occur without direct reference to the interests of the tested child, particularly when they are at the most vulnerable stage of their lives.

Genetics, autonomy and the adult

Since genetic information is also family information, its mere existence can pose dilemmas for the tested individual. One important issue relates to what is or should be done with the information. Is it truly private like other health related information or is there a moral obligation to share it with others in the family who may also be at risk? While sometimes this will present no problems, in other cases personal and other considerations could result in an internal struggle – a debate between one's own individualistic autonomy on the one hand and the contextual or relational approach that would encourage disclosure on the other.

Sharing information

Adults may, of course, decide that they wish to obtain genetic testing for and about themselves for a number of reasons – altruistic or otherwise. Their reasons will likely have an effect on how they then deal with the results. For example, if a person is just curious about their genetic inheritance, their motivation could be entirely selfish. While they might nonetheless accept moral responsibilities to their family, and choose to share the information,

---

[44] Ross, L F, 'Predictive Genetic Testing for Conditions that Present in Childhood', *Kennedy Institute of Ethics Journal*, 12(3), 2002: 225–44, at p 226.

[45] Hoffman, D E and Wulfsberg, E A, 'Testing Children for Genetic Predispositions: Is it in Their BEST Interest?', *Journal of Law, Medicine & Ethics*, 23, 1995: 331, at p 341.

they may also feel that this information is private to them. Indeed, if the tests show up a problem, there are potential concerns that the risks of disclosing are greater than those associated with non-sharing of the information. This also raises questions about professional obligations, which will be returned to later.

On the other hand, some people may seek out genetic information precisely and specifically for the benefit of others. Hallowell *et al* offer one example of this. They conducted a study of 30 women who had a previous diagnosis of breast cancer and had subsequently undergone *BRCA1/2* mutation searching. If they were found to have this mutation, there was a possibility that so too would some of their female relatives. Identifying the genetic mutation would allow these women to inform their at risk relatives, who could then choose to be tested themselves and – if positive – even undergo prophylactic mastectomy. In their study, all of the women indicated that they wanted the genetic information for others, and 90% indicated that the most important, or the sole, reason for having the test was to obtain the information for their relatives. In other words, '[m]utation searching was ... perceived as enabling one to demonstrably care for others – to act as a moral agent and fulfil one's obligations to care for other family members.'[46]

In these cases, the clear intention was to disseminate the information to appropriate third parties, and medical confidentiality or privacy is not an issue since patients can in any situation waive their right to the expectation of confidentiality. This is not, however, to say that the outcome was unproblematic for the women concerned. Although the intention was to help others, many of the sample felt that the result of gaining the information meant that they 'perceived themselves as potentially forced into a situation in which they would be responsible for causing others harm.'[47] Of course, they are not causing the genetic problem, but they clearly felt that telling a sister or daughter about their risks would cause them distress – a burden that they felt keenly. Interestingly, however, Hallowell *et al* discovered that the dilemma presented by the possession of the information was not the one most commonly discussed – that is *whether* or not to tell relatives – but rather *how* to tell them. They conclude that this example suggests that 'we need to ground consent upon an ethic that takes into account the social nature of human beings.'[48] They favour, therefore, what could be classified as a relational model, with decisions being grounded in and informed by relationship rather than individualism. Indeed, the nature of genetics makes a relational approach seem *prima facie* not only preferable, but perhaps even

---

[46] Hallowell, N, Foster, C, Eeles, R, Ardern-Jones, A, Murday, V, Watson, M, 'Balancing autonomy and responsibility: the ethics of generating and disclosing genetic information', *J Med Ethics*, 29, 2003: 74–83, at p 75.

[47] Ibid., at p 77.

[48] Ibid., at p 78.

mandatory. As emerged from our earlier discussion, however, the development of an ethic specific to genetic information misses the point that the differences between the individualistic and the relational account are sometimes exaggerated. Indeed, in a commentary on Hallowell's article, Clarke makes the point that:

> Social obligations do not prevent those who experience them from making real choices – from exercising their autonomy. Rather these obligations, sometimes mutually incompatible, provide the framework within which (difficult) choices have to be made.[49]

Of course, the sample studied by Hallowell *et al* could be seen as atypical in that the decision to undertake genetic testing was entirely altruistic. Nonetheless support for their experience comes from other research. In a study of people who were tested for risk of breast/ovarian cancer (36 in the study – 31 women and five men), d'Agincourt-Canning found that 'all individuals who underwent genetic testing for breast/ovarian cancer took on the responsibility for sharing this information with others ... Participants frequently expressed the view that not only was it their responsibility to inform family members of their genetic risk but that their relatives had a right to know this information.'[50] Further, Kent reports that:

> Work undertaken by the Genetic Interest Group indicates that among those living in families where there is a diagnosis of a substantial risk of genetic disease, there is a strongly held view that such information should not be seen as the private property of the individual. Rather it should be seen as family information held in common by all those to whom it applies.[51]

In these families, there is clearly an incentive to act altruistically and to share information. Perhaps sadly, however, this will not always be the case even though '[a] particular feature of genetic information is that information about one person may be obtained through information about another.'[52] Not everyone is willing to accept the familial responsibilities that may be expected to flow from that fact.

---

[49]   Clarke, A, 'Commentary', in Hallowell, N, Foster, C, Eeles, R, Ardern-Jones, A, Murday, V, Watson, M, 'Balancing autonomy and responsibility: the ethics of generating and disclosing genetic information', *J Med Ethics*, 29, 2003: 74–83, 80–82, at p 82.

[50]   d'Agincourt-Canning, L, 'Experience of Genetic Risk: Disclosure and the Gendering of Responsibility', *Bioethics*, 15(3), 2001: 231–47, at p 237–38.

[51]   Kent, A, 'Consent and confidentiality in genetics: whose information is it anyway?', *J Med Ethics*, 29, 2003: 16–18, at p 17.

[52]   Human Genetics Commission, *Inside Information*, London, 2002, at p 69, para 4.1.

Confidentiality, privacy and disclosing genetic information

Some people who have undergone a genetic test might regard it as reasonable to assume that, just like other medical information, the results will be subject to the usual duty of confidentiality, which Laurie describes as 'characterized by a relationship involving two or more individuals, one or more of whom has undertaken, explicitly or implicitly, not to reveal to third parties information concerning the other individual in the relationship.'[53] At first sight, then, since doctors have made such an undertaking, they have corresponding duties to maintain confidentiality. However, while individuals generally believe that they have a right to confidentiality, it is seldom absolute. Indeed, it is commonly accepted that breach of confidentiality may be permissible where it is necessary to prevent harm occurring to a third party. The (UK) Human Genetics Commission notes, however, that any breach of confidentiality by a doctor in this situation should occur only after s/he has tried to persuade the individual to agree and only where 'on balance, the harm caused by non-disclosure is thought to outweigh the harm caused to the patient by breaching confidentiality.'[54] This is also the view preferred by the General Medical Council in the United Kingdom, and appears in the guidelines of a number of other organisations. For example, The American Society of Human Genetics Social Issues Subcommittee on Familial Disclosure says:

> Disclosure should be permissible where attempts to encourage disclosure on the part of the patient have failed; where the harm is highly likely to occur and is serious and foreseeable; where the at-risk relative(s) is identifiable; and where either the disease is preventable/treatable or medically accepted standards indicate that early monitoring will reduce the genetic risk.[55]

Additionally, they agree that, '[t]he harm that may result from failure to disclose should outweigh the harm that may result from disclosure ... ',[56] and that '[a]t a minimum, health-care professionals should be obliged to inform patients about the implications of their genetic test results and about the potential risks to their family members.'[57] Finally, the Joint Committee on Medical Genetics says that '[i]n special circumstances it may be justified to break confidence where the aversion of harm by the disclosure substantially

[53] Laurie, G T, 'Challenging Medical-Legal Norms: The Role of Autonomy, Confidentiality and Familial Group Rights in Genetic Information', *Journal of Legal Medicine*, 22, 2001: 1–54, at p 15.

[54] Human Genetics Commission, *Whose hands on your genes?*, London, 2000, at p 17, para 6.3.

[55] The American Society of Human Genetics Social Issues Subcommittee on Familial Disclosure, 'Professional Disclosure of Familial Genetic Information', *Am J Hum Genet*, 62, 1998: 474–83, at p 474.

[56] Ibid.

[57] Ibid.

outweighs the patient's claim to confidentiality.'[58] The Joint Committee also reiterates the need to try to 'persuade the patient in question to consent to disclosure ... ', and repeats that 'the benefit to those at risk should be so considerable as to outweigh any distress which disclosure would cause the patient ... '[59]

The meat of these exceptions to the general rule of confidentiality is the underpinning principle that disclosure should be made only when doing so can reasonably be expected to result in the avoidance of harm to the third party who is to be given the information. While this seems eminently reasonable, from the perspective of UK law it is arguably unusual for a number of reasons. First, it is widely accepted that there is no duty to rescue in UK law. In other words, I may stand aside (literally or metaphorically) and take no action to save others even if their lives are at stake. If my legitimate expectation of confidentiality can be breached to avoid harm to third parties, are we *de facto* creating a professional duty to rescue, when no similar obligation would be imposed on the test subject him or her self? While the law does permit breaches of confidentiality to protect others in some cases, these are justified either because not telling third parties puts them *and possibly others* at avoidable risk (for example from HIV/AIDS), or the individual is in an already vulnerable state and unable to protect themselves (for example in the case of children). The problem with unconsented-to disclosure of genetic information is that it is not the *acquisition* of the information that puts the third party at risk; the genetic problem exists whether or not someone is tested for it and whether or not they are aware of their risk status. On the other hand, the interest that individuals have in maintaining their medical information in confidence is strong and equates to what Laurie describes as 'informational privacy', which 'concerns the interest of the patient in maintaining such information in a state of nonaccess and preventing unauthorized use or disclosure of the information to third parties.'[60] In the absence of a duty to rescue, this interest in informational privacy is worthy of respect, whether or not the information is genetic.

In addition, the individual's right to privacy (or confidentiality) is protected by the terms of Article 8 of the European Convention on Human Rights which was incorporated directly into UK law by the Human Rights Act 1998. Article 8 holds that, '[e]veryone has the right to respect for his private and family life, his home and his correspondence.' There can be few things more personal or private than medical information, genetic or not. As

---

[58] Joint Committee on Medical Genetics, *Consent and confidentiality in genetic practice. Guidance on genetic testing and sharing genetic information*, London, Royal College of Physicians of London, 2006, at p 14, para 2.5.3.

[59] Ibid., at p 14, para 2.5.3.

[60] Laurie, G T, 'Challenging Medical-Legal Norms: The Role of Autonomy, Confidentiality and Familial Group Rights in Genetic Information', *Journal of Legal Medicine*, 22, 2001: 1–54 at pp 29–30.

with most Convention rights, however, there are permissible derogations which in this case are as follows:

> There shall be no interference by a public authority with the exercise of this right except such as is in accordance with the law and is necessary in a democratic society in the interests of national security, public safety or the economic well-being of the country, for the prevention of disorder or crime, for the protection of health or morals, or for the protection of the rights and freedoms of others.[61]

It must be moot whether or not any of these derogations would be satisfied were an individual's genetic information disclosed to family members. Where no treatment is available, it would seem in fact that none of them is engaged, as no change in the genetic status of any other family member is possible. Even where some therapy may be available, it must be asked whether it is 'necessary in a democratic society' that individuals' confidentiality is breached, particularly when the third party could themselves seek the information made available by the foresight of their relative in seeking a genetic test. This position seems to be in line with the views of the United Nations Economic, Social and Cultural Organisation (UNESCO) which says:

> In order to protect human rights and fundamental freedoms, limitations to the principles of consent and confidentiality may only be prescribed by law, for compelling reasons within the bounds of public international law and the international law of human rights.[62]

In the United States, however, it would appear that a different approach has sometimes been taken. In the case of *Schroeder v Perkel*,[63] for example, a New Jersey court had held that a doctor's duty 'may extend beyond the interests of a patient to members of the immediate family of the patient who may be adversely affected by a breach of that duty.'[64] Some years later, at the beginning of the genetics 'revolution' courts in both Florida and New Jersey made extremely important decisions in respect of the obligations of physicians when dealing with genetic information. In *Pate v Threkel*,[65] the highest court in Florida unanimously held that a physician has a duty to warn a third party about a genetically inherited disease. The plaintiff was being treated for medullary thyroid carcinoma, and sued the doctors who had previously treated her mother for the same condition. She claimed that the doctors should have told her mother about the possibility of genetic transmission of

---

[61] Article 8(2).
[62] Universal Declaration on the Human Genome and Human Rights, UNESCO, 1997, Article 9.
[63] 432 A 2d 834 (NJ) (1981).
[64] Ibid., at p 839.
[65] 661 So2d 278 (Fla 1995).

the condition. Although accepting that there was a duty to warn, this court held that this was satisfied by alerting the patient to the genetic ramifications of the disease, and that doctors could not be expected to find and warn every member of the family. However, in *Safer v Pack*,[66] the court held that the physician's obligation extended to warning immediate family of the risk of avoidable harm from a genetically transmissible condition.

While these two cases paved the way for further development of a professional duty to warn, they did differ somewhat in their conclusions. While the Florida court concerned itself with the obligation to warn the patient about the possibility that their condition was heritable, the New Jersey court went further, and also acknowledged that 'a case could arise in the future in which a court would have to choose between the physician's responsibility to adhere to the request of the patient to not breach confidentiality and the physician's duty to minimize risks … '.[67] As has been pointed out, '[t]he fact that the first two courts to examine the issue provided support to the notion of a duty to warn creates a foundation for plaintiffs' lawyers who wish to pursue similar claims in the future.'[68]

Later, in *Molloy v Meier*,[69] the parents sued a number of paediatricians. Their claim was that the failure to test for specific genetic abnormalities resulted in the birth of a child suffering from the undiagnosed condition. Although the doctor had ordered some genetic tests on request of the mother, he failed to order Fragile X testing which was a common test where children showed developmental delay. The court found in favour of the families, leading The Minnesota Medical Association, The Minnesota Hospital Association, The Minnesota Medical Group Management Association and The American Medical Association to say in their *amicus* brief:

> Unless the opinion … is reversed, Minnesota physicians will face liability to persons with whom they had no professional relationship – in fact, to persons whom they have never met or even heard of – for failure to diagnose genetic disorders.[70]

Burke and Rosenbaum, however, argue that the decision is by no means so radical as this suggests, claiming only that 'the ruling is consistent with a classic common law doctrine known as the "duty to warn".'[71] On the other

---

[66] 677 A2d 1188, cert den'd, 683 A2d 1163 (NJ 1996).

[67] Petrila, J, 'Genetic Risk: The New Frontier for the Duty to Warn', *Behav Sci Law* 19, 2001: 405–21, at p 410.

[68] Ibid., at p 411.

[69] Nos C9-02-1821, C9-02-1837 (Minn 2004).

[70] Amicus Brief, available at http://www.ama-assn.org/ama1/pub/upload/mm/395/molloy_v_meier.pdf (accessed on 23/9/2008), transcript, p 3.

[71] Burke, T, Rosenbaum, S, '*Molloy v Meier* and the Expanding Standard of Medical Care: Implications for Public Health Policy and Practice', *Public Health Reports*, 120, March/April 2005: 209–10, at p 209.

hand, in *Olson v Children's Home Security of California*[72] it was held that there is no duty on an adoption agency to disclose the existence of a genetic condition.

The 'duty to warn' is obviously more thoroughly developed in the United States than in the United Kingdom, and is generally recognised as deriving from the case of *Tarasoff v Regents of the University of California*.[73] In this case, a patient told his psychotherapist that he intended to kill a woman, which he subsequently did. Her parents sued the psychotherapist, claiming that he should have warned them or their daughter about the threat. The psychotherapist, on the other hand, claimed that since the woman was not his patient, he did not owe her a duty of care. The Supreme Court of California disagreed, indicating that he did indeed owe a duty to exercise reasonable care to protect a potential victim if he was satisfied that his patient posed a serious threat. Although it is possible in at least some US states that failure to warn relatives of a risk discovered through the genetic testing of an individual may be actionable, it would seem that this is not required by UK law, and may even be regarded as unacceptable. However, the situation remains relatively unclear, and is arguably not completely clarified by the adoption of any one particular ethical position on autonomy rights. In these circumstances, the individualistic model seems inherently selfish, especially if there is a possibility of alleviation or cure following disclosure of the information. On the other hand, the relational model seems somewhat simplistically to discount the very real importance of confidentiality or privacy, even when disclosure would serve little purpose.

While in the United Kingdom disclosure may be justified, it is not required – as yet. Nonetheless there are some indications that something approaching a duty to warn is being developed. For example, although professional guidelines do not directly refer to a *duty* to breach confidentiality, they do permit such breaches in certain circumstances. In reported cases, breaches of confidentiality have been condoned in cases where risk to third parties was present and clear. For example, in the case of *R v Crozier*,[74] it was declared to be legitimate that a psychiatrist disclosed his report on an accused to counsel for the Crown. The court held that the public interest in the information being made available was greater than the interest of the accused in confidentiality. In *W v Edgell*,[75] the anticipation of real risk to the public was held sufficient to justify breaching confidentiality. As Mason and Laurie say, the court was nonetheless concerned to reiterate that '[o]nly the most compelling circumstances could justify a doctor acting contrary to the patient's perceived interests in the absence of consent.'[76] This position

---

[72] 204 Cal App 3d 1362 (1988).

[73] 17 Cal 3d 425 [1976].

[74] (1990) 8 BMLR 128.

[75] [1990] 1 All ER 835.

[76] Mason, J K, Laurie, G T, *Mason and McCall Smith's Law and Medical Ethics* (7th edn), Oxford University Press, 2006, at p 262.

arguably falls considerably short of the US position with its roots in the *Tarasoff* judgement mentioned earlier. As has already been pointed out, however, genetic information arguably differs from the information held by the psychotherapist in cases such as *Tarasoff*. Failing to tell family members about genetic risk does not generally have the same implications as failing to inform of a direct threat of violence. While violence can be prevented, genetic status cannot, and even if disclosing the risk might allow for the possibility of avoiding or alleviating symptoms it is less directly related to the disclosure than is the link between credible threats and ultimate violence.

Confidentiality acts as a brake on the unauthorised disclosure of medical information, but since it is generally not regarded as absolute this does not imply that the individual owns the information about their health status or can control it entirely. What it does mean is that there is an expectation of privacy, which has been described as 'a right to maintain a certain level of control over the inner spheres of personal information.'[77] Nonetheless, The Declaration of Inuyama seems entirely clear on the need to respect the confidentiality/privacy of genetic information, and states that:

> The central objective of genetic screening and diagnosis should always be to safeguard the welfare of the person tested: test results must always be protected against unconsented disclosure, *confidentiality must be ensured at all costs* ... (emphasis added)[78]

This, however, is not universally accepted. While the individualistic account of autonomy would entitle the person to hold the information privately, there are, as we have seen, other ways of viewing autonomy. Rabino points again to the fact that information gleaned from genetic testing ' ... pertains also to others to whom the patient is linked by kinship and affects those linked by marriage (when reproductive choices are involved).'[79] The potential consequences of failure to share genetic information can therefore transcend generations and have an impact on an extensive range of choices. The problem is, as Weiss says, that the nature of genetic information generates 'a conflict between the duty to protect confidentiality and the duty to warn.'[80] If a more relational model of autonomy were adopted, it could be argued

---

[77] Moore, A D, 'Owning Genetic Information and Gene Enhancement Techniques: Why Privacy and Property Rights May Undermine Social Control of the Human Genome', *Bioethics*, 14(2), 2000: 97–119, at p 104.

[78] Declaration of Inuyama (Council for International Organizations of Medical Sciences, 22–17 July 1990), Human Genome Mapping, Genetic Screening and Gene Therapy, Article IV.

[79] Rabino, I, 'Genetic Testing and Its Implications: Human Genetics Researchers Grapple with Ethical Issues', *Science, Technology & Human Values*, 28(3), Summer 2003: 365–402, at p 385.

[80] Weiss, M J, 'Should Genetic Information Be Protected? An Ethical and Legal Dilemma', *BC Itell Prop & Tech F*, 1999, available at http://www.bc.edu/bc_org/avp/law/st_org/iptf/commentary/content/1999060509.html (accessed on 3/9/2008), transcript, p 2.

that the interest of an individual in maintaining genetic information in confidence is relatively weaker than in circumstances where health related information does not impart information about relatives. On this basis, it becomes plausible to argue against the confidentiality/privacy model that is traditional in the doctor/patient relationship. Indeed, Wertz and Fletcher say that the nature of genetic information is such that it 'cuts against the grain of a rights-based approach. An approach that values the relationships of persons, rather than individual rights, may provide a richer understanding and source of guidance for such complex problems.'[81] They conclude, therefore, that rather than 'seeing atomistic individuals in conflict and competing for space ... ' we should instead use an approach that accepted that the '"patient" is a family, or rather several social and biological families.'[82] Donchin agrees, arguing that genetic information 'brings clearly into focus underlying tensions between prevailing accounts of personal autonomy dominant in bioethics ... and the interpersonal dependencies so prevalent in families with inherited genetic disorders.'[83] Moreover, she says, a further down-side of the individualistic account of autonomy is that it 'hampers effective medical decision making, gives insufficient attention to the impact of decisions on family members, undermines the agency of those who are excluded from the decision-making process, and often imposes unjust burdens on those affected by others' decisions.'[84] Eckenwiler too claims that '[w]ith advances in genetics, we have reached the point where there is no denying the significance of our relations to others and the larger society.'[85] She also notes that ' ... the individualistic formulation of informed consent has rendered many researchers and health professionals ill-equipped to negotiate certain challenges – including those posed by genetics – involving decisions, hence consents, that affect others.'[86]

This approach to information sharing also emerged from a canvass of the views of members of the American Society of Human Genetics where it was found that virtually all of them – 94% of those who participated – believed that patients should inform their relatives of test results where they were relevant to their health or reproductive decisions. Nonetheless, around half of them also indicated that they would respect patient confidentiality.[87] Interestingly,

---

[81] Wertz, D D, Fletcher, J C, 'Privacy and Disclosure in Medical Genetics Examined in an Ethics of Care', *Bioethics*, 5(3), 1991: 212–32, at p 212.

[82] Ibid., at p 213.

[83] Donchin, A, 'Autonomy and Interdependence: Quandaries in Genetic Decision Making', in Mackenzie, C, Stoljar, N (eds), *Relational Autonomy: Feminist Perspectives on Autonomy, Agency, and the Social Self*, Oxford University Press, 2000, 236–58, at p 241.

[84] Ibid., at p 252.

[85] Eckenwiler, Lisa A, 'Genetics Research and Third Parties: Implications for Education in the Health Professions', *The Journal of Continuing Education in the Health Professions*, 21, 2001: 278–84, at p 279.

[86] Ibid., at p 280.

[87] Rabino, I, 'Genetic Testing and Its Implications: Human Genetics Researchers Grapple with Ethical Issues', *Science, Technology & Human Values*, 28(3), Summer 2003: 365–402, at p 389.

between 26 and 32% said that they would pass on this information without the patient's consent, but only if relatives asked for it.[88]

There are therefore two main approaches to the disclosure of genetic information. The first, Skene calls the 'legal' approach, which prioritises the individual's right to privacy.[89] The second approach, she says, 'is based primarily on what many doctors consider to be the best in caring for an inquirer and the inquirer's family. It envisages that genetic information (and also tissue that is tested) should be shared among blood relatives and that individuals should not be permitted invariably to prevent this.'[90] These models can also be said to reflect the philosophical differences between the individualistic or 'liberal' account and the relational/communitarian one. While the former holds autonomy to be 'the highest moral value ... ', the latter would mean that '[i]f there are multiple people at risk, they should be informed.'[91] As Gilbar explains, the latter approach has the additional benefit of recognising that the individual has an 'interest in maintaining familial relationships and in living in a community with which he or she can identify.'[92]

Genetics may seem to be the most obvious area in which a relational approach to autonomy is appropriate. There can be few examples that more clearly exemplify the embeddedness of the individual in a community, and as we have seen, many people will willingly disclose information that they appreciate is important to family members. However, the reality is that many commentators and respected organisations find the decision as to what is appropriate more difficult and nuanced than straightforward adoption of a relational account of autonomy would imply. For example, the Joint Committee on Medical Genetics (UK), while noting that the rule of confidentiality is not absolute, nonetheless does not recommend breaching it unless 'special circumstances' exist: circumstances which are related to cases 'where the aversion of harm by the disclosure substantially outweighs the patient's claim to confidentiality.'[93] Like the other organisations referred to above, the Committee reinforces this by insisting that an effort should have been made to persuade the individual to make the disclosure him- or herself, before confidentiality can be breached, and even then breach is permissible only where it can be agreed that the risk to the third party is 'so considerable as

---

[88] Ibid.

[89] Skene, L, 'Patients' Rights or Family Responsibilities? Two Approaches to Genetic Testing', *Medical Law Review*, 6, Spring 1998: 1–41, at p 11.

[90] Ibid., at p 24.

[91] Fulda, K G, Lykens, K, 'Ethical issues in predictive genetic testing: a public health perspective', *J Med Ethics*; 32, 2006: 143–47, at p 145.

[92] Gilbar, R, 'Communicating genetic information in the family: the familial relationship as the forgotten factor', *J Med Ethics*, 33, 2007: 390–93, at p 390.

[93] Joint Committee on Medical Genetics, *Consent and confidentiality in genetic practice. Guidance on genetic testing and sharing genetic information*, London, Royal College of Physicians of London, 2006, at p 14, para 2.5.3.

to outweigh any distress which disclosure would cause the patient ... '.[94] In addition the committee proposes that, even if non-consensual disclosure is made, the information should be 'anonymised and restricted as far as possible to that which is strictly necessary for the communication of risk.'[95]

UNESCO's Universal Declaration on the Human Genome and Human Rights,[96] attempts a resolution of the problems associated with the disclosure of genetic information by on the one hand re-asserting the value of confidentiality while on the other passing to the law the responsibility for generating acceptable derogations, which, as we have already seen, should be careful not to run foul of Article 8 of the Human Rights Act 1998. In other words, they should be able to satisfy the exceptions described in Article 8(2) of the European Convention on Human Rights. Since these seem to be concerned with 'public' rather than 'private' health, it is arguably unlikely that this article would support breaches of confidentiality in this area. While it would clearly authorise breaches when, for example, an infectious disease threatens the public, the genetic risk for the relative exists irrespective of disclosure, and the withholding of information is likely to have serious consequences primarily in those situations where the genetic risk poses a serious threat to health or life which cannot be averted. On the other hand, lesser risks, say from multi-factorial conditions, might be preventable, yet these may fail to meet the seriousness requirement needed to justify disclosure.

The picture for healthcare professionals, therefore, is somewhat murky and will require them to exercise careful judgement in deciding whether or not to breach the confidentiality of their patient. From the tested individual's perspective, no similar legal duties arise. While they may have emotional ties to relatives, they do not owe them a duty of care similar to that owed by doctors. The value that we attribute to privacy in healthcare might well override our emotional ties to family. People may feel themselves to be diminished by the knowledge learned from genetic tests and prefer that others do not know of test results. While this may appear selfish, it is incontrovertibly a legitimate, autonomous choice. While a more relational concept of autonomy would support the sharing of information within families, the individualistic account permits its withholding. In the case of the tested individual, the law's preference seems to lie with the individualistic model of autonomy, whereas in the case of the physician a more relational approach seems to be taken.

It must, however, also be borne in mind that save in certain single-gene conditions, as Hubbard and Wald say, '[g]enetic predictions ... are based on

---

[94] Ibid., at p 14, para 2.5.3.

[95] Ibid., at p 14, para 2.5.3.

[96] UNESCO, 1997, Article 9 says: 'In order to protect human rights and fundamental freedoms, limitations to the principles of consent and confidentiality may only be prescribed by law, for compelling reasons within the bounds of public international law and the international law of human rights.'

the assumption that there is a relatively straightforward relationship between genes and traits.'[97] However, as they point out, 'genetic conditions involve a largely unpredictable interplay of many factors and processes.'[98] That being the case, the rationale for insisting on disclosure would become weaker, since – except in a small number of cases – it is not clear whether it is solely the gene rather than the environment, or a combination of both, that predicts future health. The obligation which we are said by some commentators to owe to our relatives is arguably lessened by this conclusion, especially if the relative is him or her self an adult and could find the information out for themselves should they wish to have it.

This leads to one final consideration. If we assume that there may be some obligations attached to genetic information that do not apply in the case of other medical information, how are these to be fulfilled in a manner that benefits rather than harms? One possible harm resulting from disclosure might be that the person receiving the information did not in fact want to have it. Being given the information might in itself cause distress and anxiety that they would rather have avoided.

A right not to know?

According to UNESCO, '[t]he right of every individual to decide whether or not to be informed of the results of genetic examination and the resulting consequences should be respected.'[99] Nonetheless, there are many who believe that the individual does not have a right not to know about their genetic inheritance, because, 'genetic ignorance implies *harm to others*.'[100] Harris and Keywood argue that ' … the claim that competent individuals are the best interpreters of their own best interests is powerful, but this does not amount to an unassailable right nor to an entitlement to be ignorant of one's health status.'[101] Andorno, on the other hand, claims that 'people should be free to make their own choices with respect to information. If we understand autonomy in this wider sense, then the decision not to know should be, at least in principle, as fully respected as the decision to know.'[102] While our earlier discussion focussed on the relationship question as potentially imposing some kind of duty to share genetic information, this leaves

[97] Hubbard, R, Wald, E, *Exploding the Gene Myth*, Boston, Beacon Press, 1993, at p 36.

[98] Ibid.

[99] UNESCO Universal Declaration on the Human Genome and Human Rights (11 November 1997, Paris), Article 5 c).

[100] Wilson, J, 'To Know Or Not To Know? Genetic Ignorance, Autonomy and Paternalism', *Bioethics*, 19 (5-5), 2005: 492–504, at p 495.

[101] Harris, J, Keywood, K, 'Ignorance, Information and Autonomy', *Theoretical Medicine*, 22, 2001: 415–36, at p 417.

[102] Andorno, R, 'The right not to know: an autonomy based approach', *J Med Ethics*, 30, 2004: 435–40, at p 436.

unanswered the question of balancing the totality of harms and benefits resulting from accepting an ethical obligation to inform relatives. Genetic information can cause distress to the person who has discovered their genetic status; this must be equally true of relatives or partners. If an obligation to disclose information were to exist, it should surely be tempered by the fact that mere awareness of genetic information can cause harm. As Laurie says, '[w]e must ... recognize the possibility that family members might be surprised, or even loath, to learn of a relative's predisposition to a particular genetic condition, given the likelihood that they carry a similar risk.'[103]

The so-called 'right not to know' has been widely canvassed and debated. Fulda and Lykens, for example declare that, just as the individual may choose not to know about genetic information, '[f]or family members, there is also a right not to know.'[104] Malek and Kopelman seem to agree, arguing that 'relatives could suffer psychological harms or could be discriminated against if their genetic information exists and is made available to them or to others'.[105] However, they also acknowledge that, on the other hand, relatives might *benefit* from this knowledge because 'they could be made better able to prevent or prepare for what is to come ... '.[106] The problem is that we do not know what the result of disclosure will be, and since in many cases genetic information raises possibilities rather than probabilities, any distress that may result from its disclosure could be unnecessary. Further, if relatives have both a right to know and a right not to know, how is the tested person or the physician to know what is the better option? As Laurie succinctly points out, ' ... it is difficult to see how one can exercise meaningfully a choice not to know unless one has a certain degree of knowledge that there is something to know.'[107]

Although some commentators object to treating genetic information differently from other medical information, it seems unarguable that in fact it is. There are some conditions which will have potentially negative effects on those close to us, for example where a transmissible disease has been diagnosed, sharing that knowledge can prevent harm. On the other hand, sharing genetic information may prevent nothing and avoid no harm. What calculus can the individual who holds the information be expected to use in making the decision whether or not to disclose? While the individualistic model of autonomy has the benefit of clarity, the relational model does not since it is

---

[103] Laurie, G T, 'Challenging Medical-Legal Norms: The Role of Autonomy, Confidentiality and Familial Group Rights in Genetic Information', *Journal of Legal Medicine*, 22, 2001: 1–54, at p 9.

[104] Fulda, K G, Lykens, K, 'Ethical issues in predictive genetic testing: a public health perspective', *J Med Ethics*; 32, 2006: 143–47, at p 145.

[105] Malek, J, Kopelman, L M, 'The Well-being of Subjects and Other Parties in Genetic Research and Testing', *Journal of Medicine and Philosophy*, 32, 2007: 311–19, at p 315.

[106] Ibid.

[107] Laurie, G T, 'Challenging Medical-Legal Norms: The Role of Autonomy, Confidentiality and Familial Group Rights in Genetic Information', *Journal of Legal Medicine*, 22, 2001: 1–54, at p 21.

not clear whether disclosing information will assist or harm others and the justification for sharing therefore is less obvious. However this conundrum is presented, it 'places health professionals in a dilemma',[108] and also, self-evidently, tests the character and ethics of the tested individual.

Conclusion

Whatever the academic debate about the role of autonomy in genetics, the legal position seems relatively straightforward. While there has been legislative activity in countries such as the United States to make special provision for the privacy of genetic information, it has tended to focus on issues arising in areas such as insurance and employment, rather than on any obligations that might exist between family members. Courts have also become involved in this debate in the United States, but not so far in the United Kingdom. However, what is clear is that the tradition of confidentiality and privacy is potentially threatened by genetic information. After all, what distinguishes genetic information from other clinical information is the fact that we share it with those we (usually) love. What is the 'right' thing to do with this information is, however, not clear and resort will usually have to be made to both professional and legal standards for guidance. The professional is placed in what could be described as a uniquely difficult position and risks may arise. As has been said:

> Physicians should make every effort to inform patients of the relevance of the information to relatives, persuade the patient of the need for intrafamilial disclosure and offer to inform relatives on behalf of patients. If patients refuse to have information disclosed, non-consensual disclosure is not legally compelled and may in fact be punishable.[109]

It is, of course, not just for the healthcare professional that quandaries can result from the holding of genetic information. The individual too has to reconcile their own interest in privacy with the potential interest of family members in being alerted to the possibility of genetic compromise. In considering this, Bell and Bennett doubt that there is any obligation to disclose, arguing that although there may be 'strong reasons for eschewing a thoroughly 'individualistic' approach to genetic information ... ',[110] adopting the communitarian, or relational model, 'involves a significant departure

---

[108] Harris, J, Keywood, K, 'Ignorance, Information and Autonomy', *Theoretical Medicine*, 22, 2001: 415–36, at p 421.

[109] Lacroix, M, Nycum, G, Godard, B, Knoppers, B M, 'Should physicians warn patients' relatives of genetic risks?', *CMAJ*, 178(5), 26 February 2008: 593–95, at p 595.

[110] Bell, D, Bennett, B, 'Genetic Secrets and the Family', *Medical Law Review*, 9, 2001: 130–61, at p 132.

from the basic presumption or starting point that individuals who are the source of information of a medical nature are entitled to have that information kept secret, even from close relatives.'[111] They conclude:

> There may be very good reasons for treating families differently from other social units or associations, but those reasons must at the very least be articulated and justifiable. The communitarian approach postulates only genetic connection as the basis of difference. Accordingly, not only does it risk participating in an ideology which views the families as essentialistic, but it may conjoin this discourse with one which privileges biological, and specifically *genetic*, connections between people – what has been called an ideology of Geneticism.[112]

This critique reflects a number of the concerns raised in this chapter. It tackles the notion that familial obligations can be defined by genetics, as well as explicating the need to question whether or not the existence of family relationships raises different expectations as to what is moral or ethical behaviour. At least, Bell and Bennett ask for clarification as to *why* families should be treated differently.

In trying to find a way to deal with genetics, it would seem that the law has predominantly adopted an individualistic approach for the individual, but – as seems especially clear in parts at least of the United States – it prefers a more relational account when professional decisions are taken. It is probable, however, that more legal activity will be needed to understand the picture fully. Even in the United States, however, the duty to warn is not yet as extensive as a relational account of autonomy would seem to require. Oddly, while individual confidentiality and privacy are regarded as significant in this as in other areas, the relational model seems particularly attractive in the case of genetics. While in other cases, such as assisted dying, the arguments for adopting a relational approach seem relatively weak, in this case it could be said to make sense to *begin* a discussion of the uses of genetic information from this perspective. Yet this law, in the United Kingdom at least, has so far been reluctant to do in the case of the individual tested, despite the fact that this is arguably the one person who has the most clear obligations to others; doctors' duties are arguably more complex and they function at one step removed from the family, yet they seem more likely than the tested individual to be expected to make disclosure.

The situation seems to be that genetic information is regarded as so relevant or important to relatives that attempts should be made to promote its disclosure by the tested individual; on the other hand, disclosure will not be compelled. Further, the current legal position provides no guidance on what

---

[111] Ibid., at pp 132–33.
[112] Ibid., at p 160.

kind of genetic information should be disclosed, and whether or not there are, or should be, limitations on this depending on its consequences. As I have said elsewhere, '[t]he traditions of privacy and confidentiality in health care are ... threatened by the advances currently being made by geneticists, precisely because there is, as yet, no serious effort being made by the law to underscore the values which inform civilised societies.'[113] Arguably, this situation cannot be maintained in the face of likely developments in genetics. While research suggests that individuals by and large do act (or at least say they will) with concern for others, whether or not the law can or should expect or require this of them is moot. Downgrading the values embedded in respect for confidentiality and privacy may be too large a sacrifice for the unknown benefits that might result. Yet again, the law's approach seems somewhat schizophrenic. Where healthcare professionals are concerned, the presumption seems to lie – however tenuously – in favour of them taking account of the interests and needs of others, but in the case of the tested individual the opposite is the case. This seems once more to reflect a policy based approach – where it is socially acceptable to intervene (as is the case where professional obligations arise) the law may do so; where the rights of the individual are concerned, intrusion into private decisions is generally eschewed, even when the decision makers are parents rather that the tested individual him- or herself. No single account of autonomy seems to take precedence in this area, resulting in confusion as to what are the underlying values of the law in this area, and defeating efforts at bringing consistency and certainty to the law.

---

[113] McLean, S A M, *Old Law, New Medicine*, London, RiversOram/Pandora, 1999, at p 177.

Chapter 7

Autonomy and organ transplantation

Organ transplantation is widely agreed to be one of medicine's most effective therapeutic tools, at least in the developed world. In the relatively short time since the tentative early stages of transplantation programmes, more and more organs (or parts of them) can be used to save lives – and to do so for increasingly long periods of time. In 2003, the World Health Organisation noted that:

> The transplantation of organs, cells and tissues has become the treatment of choice for a wide range of both fatal and non-fatal diseases, resulting in high levels of demand for transplantation services, particularly in high- and middle-income countries.[1]

However, worldwide, transplantation programmes have been bedevilled by the disparity between supply and demand. As Teo says, 'a major obstacle to more transplant procedures is the persistent shortage of transplantable human organs.'[2] As of January 2009, 16,004,940 people – 26% of the population of the United Kingdom – have signed up to the Organ Donor Register, indicating their willingness to donate organs after their death.[3] Since 1 April 2008, UK Transplant says that 751 people have donated organs, an additional 1,466 people have donated corneas, 2,127 people have received transplants, yet 7,901 people are still waiting for transplants.[4] In light of these figures – and similar ones in other countries – it is unsurprising that how to make up the shortfall between those needing an organ (or organs) and the number of organs available for transplantation has been the

---

[1] World Health Organisation, Human Organ and Tissue Transplantation, EB113/14, 27 November 2003, available at http://www.who.int/gb/ebwha/pdf_files/EB113/eeb11314.pdf (accessed on 13/10/2008), transcript, p 1, para 2.

[2] Teo, B, 'Is the Adoption of More Efficient Strategies of Organ Procurement the Answer to Persistent Organ Shortage in Transplantation?', *Bioethics*, 6(2), 1992: 113–29, at p 113.

[3] This information is available at http://www.uktransplant.org.uk/ukt/default.jsp (accessed on 28/1/2009).

[4] Ibid.

subject of considerable interest and debate. The undoubted success of transplantation has driven this discussion urgently; the number of lives lost because of the unavailability of transplantable organs is often described as a major scandal. In addition, while the figures above point to the importance of securing more organs for transplantation, even they do not offer a complete picture of the tragedy that results from the shortage of available organs. The numbers officially on waiting lists do not paint the whole picture; there is an unknown number of people who are no longer likely to benefit from a transplant because of deterioration in their condition, or perhaps their age, and who are not therefore even listed for surgery. Moreover, the more that transplantation success rates improve, and the more conditions for which it is an appropriate treatment, the more it is likely that supply and demand will increasingly lose sight of each other unless some way round this problem is found.

There are two main sources of organs, each of which will be considered in turn, before considering some of the proposed alternative regimes whose aim is to increase the numbers of available organs. Traditionally, organs were harvested from the deceased. Programmes depended, in the early stages of transplantation, on the ability to rescue organs – a process that became more successful as the definition of death was changed from irreversible cessation of respiration to the so-called Harvard definition, which accepted brain stem death as the legal definition of death.[5] The major benefit of this redefinition of death for transplantation programmes is that once brain stem death has been diagnosed, respiration can be maintained thereby ensuring the viability of the organs.

However, as we will see later, the legislative regime that governs transplantation will also have a profound impact on whether or not organs can be, and are, salvaged. What follows is not intended as a comprehensive review of specific laws – although these may sometimes be referred to – but rather of the *approach* to transplantation and its impact on the availability of organs, specifically within the context of autonomy. Before considering cadaveric donation, however, it is important to discuss an increasingly important form of transplantation – that is, donation between living individuals.

Living donation

By 2003, the number of live organ donations was showing a marked increase. The World Health Organisation in that year reported that '[g]lobally, just over half the kidneys transplanted each year are obtained from living donors, while in most developing countries almost all kidneys come

---

[5] For a discussion of this, see Capron, A M, 'Legal Definition of Death', *Annals of the New York Academy of Sciences*, 315(1), 'Brain Death', 1978: 349–62.

from living donors.'[6] In the United Kingdom, UK Transplant reports that the number of living donors is increasing, from 589 in 2005–6, to 690 in 2006–7 and 829 in 2007–8, representing 'more than one in three of all kidney transplants.'[7] In the United States, Ross says that '[t]he year 2001 was a watershed year: it was the first time in which there were more living than deceased kidney donors … ',[8] even though she also believes that ' … living donors should be donors of last resort. We should be sobered by the trend that more donors are living than deceased because of the risks to which living donors are exposed.'[9] While there are risks to the donor, the decision to donate is one which is fully covered by the principle of self-determination, although there are, of course, limitations on the kinds of organs that can be removed from people when alive. Most commonly, donation will be of kidneys (since people can survive with only one kidney) although lobes of liver can also be transplanted and will grow *in situ*. Although 'altruistic' donation – that is donation between strangers – is technically possible, often donations will come from family members; indeed, in the United Kingdom in the past it was necessary to scrutinise any intending non-related donation.[10] In part, this may have been because of suspicion about the motivation of non-related donors, although it is also the case that when donor and recipient are related, donations are more likely to be successful. Motivation for donation is obviously important, and it is sometimes assumed that stranger donations are suspect, while families will, of course, want to help a loved one by acting altruistically in coming to their rescue.

The World Health Association argues, however, that '[a] genetic relationship between the donor and the recipient increases, but does not guarantee, the likelihood of altruistic motivation; nor does it preclude coercion or financial incentives.'[11] If so, and voluntariness is at the heart of organ transplantation programmes, how can we identify and take account of the internal pressures generated by the nature of family relationships? How, for example, could parents ever refuse to donate to their children or siblings to their brother or sister? Is the relationship coercive in situations like this? In other words, can intra-family donations actually be truly autonomous? Relationally speaking, of course, they could be, but a more individualistic

[6] World Health Organisation, Human Organ and Tissue Transplantation, EB113/14, 27 November 2003, available at http://www.who.int/gb/ebwha/pdf_files/EB113/eeb11314.pdf (accessed on 13/10/2008), transcript, p 2.

[7] See http://www.uktransplant.org.uk/ukt/default.jsp (accessed on 28/1/2009).

[8] Ross, L F, 'The Ethical Limits in Expanding Living Donor Transplantation', *Kennedy Institute of Ethics Journal*, 16(2), 2006: 151–72, at p 151.

[9] Ibid., at p 167.

[10] Human Organs Transplant Act 1989 (now replaced by the Human Tissue Act 2004).

[11] World Health Organisation, Human Organ and Tissue Transplantation, EB113/14, 27 November 2003, available at http://www.who.int/gb/ebwha/pdf_files/EB113/eeb11314.pdf (accessed on 13/10/2008), transcript, p 8.

approach might cast doubt on this conclusion. Crouch and Elliott, however, argue that:

> If we are ever to get straight about the nature of voluntariness, we must recognize that moral and emotional commitments are not exceptional, are not constraints of freedom, but are rather a part of ordinary human life. More specifically, they are a part of ordinary *family* that we must take seriously if we want to understand how family members can make free choices about organ donation.[12]

Live donations, therefore, could arguably satisfy the interests of both relational and individualistic autonomy, particularly since, as I have suggested, these two accounts are not so fundamentally different. However, live donation is obviously limited since certain organs cannot be removed without killing the donor, and there are legal limits on the extent to which people are allowed to inflict harm on themselves.[13] Inevitably, therefore, recourse to cadaveric donation will be necessary, and this will take up the majority of what follows, not least because it is here that alternative strategies that directly involve the question of autonomy have most commonly been proposed.

Cadaveric donation

Many countries adhere strictly to the vision of transplantation as a 'gift' or 'donation'. These so-called 'opting in' systems depend on 'an appeal to altruism.'[14] The idea that removal of organs for transplantation purposes should hinge on the decision of the individual (now deceased) is reinforced by the World Medical Association, which says:

> The voluntariness of tissue donation must be ensured. The informed and non-coerced consent of the donor or his/her family members is required for any use of human tissue for transplantation. Free and informed decision-making is a process requiring the exchange and understanding of information and the absence of coercion.[15]

As Veatch puts it, '[i]n a liberal society, it is the individual who is deemed to have the first priority for making decisions about his or her body.'[16]

---

[12] Crouch, R A, Elliott, C, 'Moral Agency and the Family: The Case of Living Related Organ Transplantation', *Cambridge Quarterly of Healthcare Ethics*, 8, 1999: 275–87, at p 278.

[13] *R v Brown* [1994] 1 AC 212.

[14] Gerrand, N, 'The Notion of Gift-Giving and Organ Donation', *Bioethics*, 8(2), 1994: 127–50, at p 127.

[15] *World Medical Association Statement on Human Tissue for Transplantation*, Adopted by the WMA General Assembly, Copenhagen, Denmark, October 2007, at para 3.

[16] Veatch, R M, 'Why Liberals Should Accept Financial Incentives for Organ Procurement', *Kennedy Institute of Ethics Journal*, 12(1), 2003: 19–36, at p 25.

Recent scandals concerning the unauthorised removal and retention of organs from (primarily but not exclusively) children in the United Kingdom served to reinforce the idea that dispositional control should vest either in the individual or, in the case of children, in their parents.[17] Authority, therefore, lies with the individual, and not the state. The legislation which followed the inquiries into these events, resulted – predictably enough – in a strengthening of the opting in system for organ donation.[18] While this will obviously satisfy those who suffered under the old regime, and those who hold altruism and voluntariness to be the most important considerations in organ transplantation, Scheper-Hughes argues that:

> The language of organ donation, which stresses altruism and bene-
> volence, both obscures and contributes to the social inequalities of the
> larger medical system … Under traditional cadaver donation, the 'gift'
> of life simultaneously demands a 'gift of death'. It demands that griev-
> ing family members readily accept 'brain death' as the end of the life of
> a loved one.[19]

Notwithstanding this, it is plausible that not only might potential donors prefer a system that retains the concept of control – of autonomy, even after death – so too might potential recipients. Indeed, there is some evidence that '[m]any transplant recipients add that a donated organ is more easily accep-ted because they know it has been positively given by the deceased whereas presuming consent would turn donation into an action by default.'[20] A recent report from the UK Organ Donation Taskforce also found evidence to support this contention. As the report says:

> The working group considering clinical implications also heard powerful
> evidence from recipients of organs who stressed their need to know that
> organs had been freely given by donors and their families, and from
> donor families who often find great comfort in being an active part of
> the decision to donate.[21]

---

[17] *Learning from Bristol: The Report of the Public Inquiry into children's heart surgery at the Bristol Royal Infirmary*, Cm 5207(1), 2001; *The Royal Liverpool Children's Inquiry*, London, HMSO, 2001; *Report of the Independent Review Group on the Removal and Retention of Organs at Post-Mortem*, Edinburgh, The Stationery Office, 2001.

[18] Human Tissue Act 2004; Human Tissue (Scotland) Act 2006.

[19] Scheper-Hughes, N, 'The Ends of the Body: Commodity Fetishism and the Global Traffic in Organs', *SAIS Review*, XXII(1), (Winter-Spring), 2002: 61–80, at p 74.

[20] Available at http://www.uktransplant.org.uk/ukt/newsroom/statements_and_stances/statements/opt_in_or_out.jsp (accessed on 9/10/2008), transcript, p 3.

[21] *The Potential Impact of an Opt Out System for Organ Donation in the UK. An independent report from the Organ Donation Taskforce*, 17 November 2008, available at http://www.dh.gov.uk/en/Healthcare/Secondarycare/Transplantation/Organdonation/index.htm (accessed on 8/12/2008), at p 4, para 1.20 (hereafter UK Organ Donation Taskforce).

Given the value routinely attributed to autonomy in healthcare, '[t]he major goals of organ procurement policy have been to respect individual and/or family autonomy while maximising the supply of available organs in an ethically acceptable way ... '.[22] However, where people have not 'opted in' to the system, it is the consent of relatives rather than the individual that will be required to justify donation legally. Thus, although the UK public – as many as 90% of it if polls are to be believed – supports organ donation,[23] 'the actual donation rate in the UK remains inadequate, and in part this is a consequence of the 40% of relatives who refuse to give consent for donation.'[24] As Spital notes, '[g]iven the high rates of family refusal, it is clear that respecting autonomy in this situation clashes with maximising organ recovery.'[25] However, the refusal rate when people have signed up to the Organ Donor Register is considerably lower. The Organ Donation Taskforce found that where a loved one has registered their willingness to donate the refusal rate is only 10%.[26] The fact that so many people die while awaiting an organ has generated enthusiasm for finding alternative strategies to improve the availability of organs. Much contemporary discourse on cadaveric organ transplantation has therefore focused on a variety of ways in which this problem might be averted, or at least minimised; the gift metaphor, it would seem, has been unsuccessful. Some of the major alternatives to the 'opting in' scheme will be considered in what follows.

Required request

Although not yet tested in the United Kingdom, in the United States laws have been formulated which aim to increase the number of available organs using a device known as required request. These laws 'require that hospitals develop and implement policies to ensure that healthcare providers ... approach all families of donor-eligible patients about organ donation once brain death is determined.'[27] Although this scheme at face value has the potential to increase the number of organs available for transplantation, it also could be argued to lack sensitivity by routinising something that is otherwise left to the discretion of the healthcare professionals caring for the brain dead patient. It might also engender fears that clinicians are making

[22] Spital, A, 'Conscription of Cadaveric Organs for Transplantation: Neglected Again', *Kennedy Institute of Ethics Journal*, 13(2), 2003: 169–74, at p 170.

[23] *Organs for Transplants: A report from the Organ Donation Taskforce*, London, Department of Health, January 2008, at p 5, para 1.11.

[24] Ibid.

[25] Spital, A, 'Conscription of Cadaveric Organs for Transplantation: Neglected Again', *Kennedy Institute of Ethics Journal*, 13(2), 2003: 169–74, at p 170.

[26] UK Organ Donation Taskforce, n 21 above, at p 5, para 1.15.

[27] Siminoff, L A, Mercer, M B, 'Public Policy, Public Opinion, and Consent for Organ Donation', *Cambridge Quarterly of Healthcare Ethics*, 10, 2001: 377–86, at p 378.

decisions about death in the interests of the potential organ recipient rather than the person under their care. However, assuming that those approaching relatives are separate from the team caring for the patient, this latter concern can be minimised. In fact, of course, the worry that decisions about death are taken for reasons that are about third parties may unfortunately arise irrespective of the system in place, especially for those families who do not trust the definition of brain stem death. For this reason, it is arguably unavoidable in any system for procuring organs.

That said, required request laws have turned out to be something of a disappointment. Teo notes that ' ... a survey of a number of states where "required request" laws are instituted showed only a marginal improvement in the availability of donated organs and in the organ donor pool ... ',[28] although Childress speculates that they may have 'perhaps prevented a decline in donations.'[29] The reality, of course, is that required request laws are only a supplement to direct consent, replacing it when necessary with surrogate or proxy consent. This means that it is perfectly possible that a similar number of relatives will refuse to donate in this system as do so under the 'opting in' scheme. In other words, improving supply is still likely to require that individuals' initial views are either recorded or have been discussed with those likely to be approached for surrogate consent. Consent from the deceased individual will remain an important predictor of organ availability. Perhaps it is for this reason that required request laws have not been as successful as was originally hoped.

Mandated choice

At first sight, the option of so-called mandated or required choice seems more likely to improve the numbers of organs available for transplantation. If, as we are often told, the majority of people support organ donation but simply fail, perhaps through inertia, to register their support then one might anticipate that establishing a system whereby they are – at some point in their life – put in a position to express that support formally and without effort could make a dramatic difference. In addition, it would mean that the individual him or her self would clearly be the decision-maker 'thus eliminating the need for surrogate family decisionmakers at the time of death.'[30] However, some object to this option as it could 'require individuals to state their preferences regarding organ donations in conjunction with some other state-mandated task, such as renewing a driver's licence or filing income tax

---

[28] Teo, B, 'Is the Adoption of More Efficient Strategies of Organ Procurement the Answer to Persistent Organ Shortage in Transplantation?', *Bioethics*, 6(2), 1992: 113–29, at p 113.

[29] Childress, J F, 'The Failure to Give: Reducing Barriers to Organ Donation', *Kennedy Institute of Ethics Journal*, 11(1), 2001: 1–16, at p 9.

[30] Siminoff, L A, Mercer, M B, 'Public Policy, Public Opinion, and Consent for Organ Donation', *Cambridge Quarterly of Healthcare Ethics*, 10, 2001: 377–86, at p 380.

forms ... '.[31] Childress argues that it is therefore 'excessively individualistic, rationalistic, and legalistic.'[32]

Quite why this is problematic is not entirely clear, however. It could, for example, be argued that getting individuals to make choices *for themselves* is precisely what the law should seek to achieve. Why should this opportunity not be offered to individuals at the same time as they are undertaking another task? Facilitating individual choice is said to be central to the law, and if this makes the process 'legalistic' this is surely not a problem. If it were the case that mandated or required choice *in fact* increased the pool of organ donors, Childress's concern might be regarded as nitpicking since organ donation and saving lives are generally regarded as 'good' things. There is, however, one further possible objection to this option. Sadly, it may be that introducing the request for consent into circumstances as mundane as, for example, renewing a driving licence could result in the individual actually paying less attention to their real wishes than they might do when it is necessary to make a conscious decision to opt in. In other words, it may not facilitate a real choice. While this may be no problem for those who support organ transplantation but have simply failed to register their willingness to donate – and indeed it may encourage their registration – it may also 'lead many who resent being forced to make a decision to refuse consent.'[33]

Selling organs

Although much of the debate about a market in organs is concerned with the living donor, it is considered because it would be equally possible to develop one in cadaver organs with any reward being used to benefit remaining family members or others. While it is a mantra of most common law systems that the body cannot be subject of property, the law which established the non-property rule is potentially out of step with modern recognition that the human body (and its parts) may indeed have some commercial value to its 'possessor'. In the modern world, where cell lines can be generated from human tissue and transplantation of tissue and organs between individuals (to name but a few examples) is not uncommon, it is simply counter-intuitive to deny that the body (or its parts) has financial value. Indeed, it is common in some countries that payment is made for sperm or blood – why, it might be asked, should the same not apply to organs or parts of them? A few examples will suffice to demonstrate the potential value of body parts in the modern world.

---

[31] Childress, J F, 'The Failure to Give: Reducing Barriers to Organ Donation', *Kennedy Institute of Ethics Journal*, 11(1), 2001: 1–16, at p 13.

[32] Ibid.

[33] Etzioni, A, 'Organ Donation: A Communitarian Approach', *Kennedy Institute of Ethics Journal*, 13(1), 2003: 1–18, at p 3.

Consider first the case of Henrietta Lacks.[34] Mrs Lacks was a young black woman diagnosed with cervical cancer in February 1951 at the Johns Hopkins Hospital and dead from the disease a mere 8 months later. However, as one commentary puts it, '[n]ot all of Henrietta Lacks died that October morning ... '.[35] While in the care of the hospital, researchers took a portion of her tumour, cut it into small pieces, treated it with nutrients and incubated it. What they observed thereafter changed medical science forever. The cells, called 'HeLa' cells after Mrs Lacks, multiplied incredibly rapidly – so much so that they were ultimately passed around many laboratories, and continued to grow. They have since been used in research into cancer, AIDS and many other areas of research. Nobody in Henrietta's family knew of this until 1975, some 5 years after the death of the head of the laboratory where the cells had been isolated. Henrietta's daughter has expressed the family's concerns, not least about the fact that Johns Hopkins did very well out of the HeLa cells in terms of money and repute, while the family – too poor to hire a lawyer – received nothing financially, and feel that Henrietta's contribution to science has gone virtually unrespected.

Many years later, a man named John Moore challenged the Regents of the University of California.[36] Mr Moore suffered from hairy cell leukaemia, which was confirmed by a Dr Golde at the UCLA Medical Centre in 1976. In October 1976, Dr Golde advised Mr Moore that it was necessary to remove his spleen to slow down the progress of the disease; Mr Moore gave his consent, and the surgery was duly carried out. On several subsequent visits, and in the belief that this was necessary for his treatment, Mr Moore allowed blood, blood serum, skin, bone marrow aspirate and semen samples to be taken. Unknown to Mr Moore, Dr Golde and others were using his samples for research purposes and hoped to benefit financially from this research. Some years later, a cell line was established from Mr Moore's T-lymphocytes and a few years after that the Regents of the University applied for a patent for the cell line, which was issued in 1984. Moore sued both the Regents of the University and Dr Golde. Although many of his claims were dismissed outright, the court did spend some time on one issue – that of the tort of conversion, which they described as a 'novel claim to own the biological materials at issue in this case', and also as being 'problematic'.[37]

While these cases seem to reinforce the position that there are no property rights in the body or its parts, in the *Moore* case at least this conclusion rested both on both technical and non-technical considerations. The technical

[34] For a discussion of this case, see http://www.citypaper.com/news/story.asp?id=3426 (accessed 15/10/2008).

[35] Transcript, p 1.

[36] *Moore v Regents of the University of California*, 51 Cal 3d 120 (9 July 1990). Transcript available at http://en.wikipedia.org/wiki/John_Moore_v._the_Regents_of_the_University_of_California (accessed on 15/10/2008).

[37] Ibid., transcript, p 13.

ground related essentially to patent law, and is therefore worth only brief consideration here. Things (like cells) can become patentable (subject to property rights) when – amongst other things – they show an element of invention. In other words, it was not the cells themselves that were the object of property, but rather what they became after Dr Golde and his colleagues worked on them. As the court in Moore said ' ... the patented cell line and the products derived from it – cannot be Moore's property. This is because the patented cell line is both factually and legally distinct from the cells taken from Moore's body.'[38]

A second consideration was whether or not, in the absence of a remedy based in intellectual property rights, there were any common law grounds on which to support his claim, for example using the legal device of conversion – a strict liability tort involving a voluntary act by one person which is not consistent with the ownership rights of someone else. The court declared that there were three reasons why it was disinclined to extend the theory of conversion to cover Mr Moore's claim:

> First, a fair balancing of the relevant policy considerations counsels against extending the tort. Second, problems in this area are better suited to legislative intervention. Third, the tort of conversion is not necessary to protect patients' rights.[39]

Important for this discussion is the extent to which arguably extraneous or non-technical considerations – such as the likely effect on medical research – were also used to justify the court's judgement. Arabian, J, for example, while concurring in the majority decision, felt it necessary to issue a separate judgement in order to address what he called 'the moral issue', and spoke of the 'conflicting moral, philosophical and even religious values at stake.'[40] He further described the anxiety – which, while not proven nonetheless existed – that a market in human body parts would have a negative impact on medical research and was concerned about the potential for tort liability of researchers.

Ownership of human tissue was also considered in the case of *Greenberg v Miami Children's Hospital Research Institute Inc.*[41] The plaintiffs were parents of children afflicted with Canavan Disease and a group of non-profit organisations that provided funding to the defendant's research into the genetic basis of the disease. They also contacted other sufferers' families who donated various samples – blood, urine, etc – as well as offering financial support and assistance in identifying families internationally. Sample collection began in

---

[38] Ibid., transcript, p 12.
[39] Ibid., transcript, p 13.
[40] Ibid., transcript, p 20.
[41] 264 F Supp 2d 1064 (SD Fla 2003).

the 1980s and the plaintiffs alleged that they had believed that the samples would be used to research Canavan disease and that any carrier and prenatal tests developed would be made available at an affordable price. Importantly they had also believed that the research would be in the public domain and available to benefit other families. In 1993 the research team successfully isolated the gene while the families continued to supply samples to assist in finding out more about the disease and the gene itself. In 1994, without the plaintiffs' knowledge, the researchers applied for a patent for the genetic sequence they had discovered. This was granted in 1997, and allowed them to restrict activity relating to the gene and the tests associated with it. The plaintiffs claimed that they did not learn about this until 1998, and sought a permanent injunction against the defendants to prevent them from enforcing their patent rights.

Their argument was based on a number of legal grounds. First, they argued that they should have been told about the intention to patent; in other words, they alleged that they had not given an informed consent. This was rejected on the basis of the arguments in *Moore*. Second, they alleged that there had been a breach of fiduciary duty by the researcher, but again this was dismissed on the basis that no such relationship arises automatically when a researcher accepts medical donations. A third argument was based in unjust enrichment, which the court found had indeed been established. Although other arguments were put forward, the final most important one was, as in Mr Moore's case, based on the tort of conversion. The plaintiffs alleged that they had a property interest in both their bodily tissue and the genetic information generated by it. However, based on the *Moore* case, and other Florida cases such as *State v Powell*,[42] the court was not inclined to support this claim. Indeed, it noted that even where property rights have been recognised over body tissue, these cases were not relevant as they did not involve voluntary donations for medical research. In an echo of the *Moore* case, the court also argued that medical research would be 'crippled' if this case were to succeed.

The final case for consideration is *The Washington University v Catalona, et al* (2007).[43] In this appeal case, the issue before the court was to determine the ownership of biological materials contributed by individuals for genetic cancer research and held by the University of Washington (WU). WU sought to establish its ownership of the materials, while Dr Catalona sought a declaration that the donors could transfer their biological materials to him. At the first hearing, the district court had held that WU owned the biological materials which had been placed in a Biorepository developed by Dr Catalona, and that neither he nor the donors had any ownership or

---

[42] 497 So 2d 1188 (Fla 1986).

[43] 20 June 2007, available at http://prostatecure.wustl.edu/pdf/8thCircuitOpinion.pdf (accessed on 7/1/2009).

proprietary rights in the materials. Dr Catalona had worked with prostate cancer at WU and began collecting samples in the 1980s, as one of his major research interests was the genetic basis of prostate cancer. Each donor signed a consent form which usually included a waiver of any rights to the donated tissue. In 2003, Dr Catalona left WU for another position and requested that the materials he had gathered were transferred to his new place of employment, as he wanted to continue his research. He wrote to his patients and their relatives telling them that he was leaving and requesting that they agree to the transfer of the materials. The Appeals Court affirmed the decision of the district court, and held that when people donate tissue for medical research they have no property rights in it and therefore they cannot authorise its transfer.

Cases like these raise hard questions; can a law which was developed in a particular social context and for arguably outmoded reasons genuinely be relevant in today's world? It seems evident that parts of the bodies of Mr Moore, Mrs Lacks and the rest undoubtedly did have commercial value, yet they and their families were unable to benefit financially from this, nor were they able to control the uses to which they were put.

Given contemporary recognition of the possible financial value of human tissue – including whole organs – it is scarcely surprising that some commentators have tried to build a case in favour of a market. Their arguments are not based only (or sometimes at all) on the idea that people should have general property rights in their body parts, but rather that they should have ultimate authority over their bodies (as theoretically they do) using a property rather than a consent model which could entail some compensation or reward when their organs or tissue become financially productive. Additionally, a market in organs might not only respect that authority, it could also increase the number of organs available for transplantation. After all, not everyone is motivated by altruism – or at least, not solely by altruism – and a nudge, by way of incentive, might push us over the line from apathy to consent. On the other hand, for some, the idea that people should be able to profit financially from selling their organs is anathema. Alta Charo, for example, concludes that:

> Although treating our bodies and tissues as property would offer an avenue toward strong protection of personal autonomy, it is not the only way to accomplish this goal. Nor is it without costs, in terms of possible losses to the collective interest in research ... [44]

Those who fundamentally disagree that a market in organs is acceptable appeal to concepts such as human dignity as well as expressing concerns that

---

[44] Alta Charo, R, 'Body of Research – Ownership and Use of Human Tissue', *NEJM*, 12 October 2006: 1517–19, at p 1519.

a market system would disproportionately target the poor, who would be unduly influenced to make a decision to undertake serious surgery most commonly for the benefit of the rich – that is, those who can afford to purchase an organ. Even if the organs are to be sold on death, perhaps to benefit family left behind, a similar objection applies. A decision to sell an organ is not, therefore, on this account an autonomous one, but rather a coerced one. There is, therefore no autonomous decision to respect in this case and public policy can and should step in to prevent such transactions in the interests both of human dignity and the prevention of exploitation or discrimination.

While human dignity is a notoriously slippery concept, it has common currency and is referred to in virtually every human rights treaty. Therefore, while we may be unable to define it precisely, we have a sense of what it means. Those opposed to the sale of organs would claim that:

> Public resistance to the sale of human body parts, no matter how voluntary or well-informed it may be, is grounded in the conviction that such a practice would diminish our human dignity and common humanity. It derives from the belief that if people were to turn themselves into commodities, not only their humanity but that of everyone would be degraded.[45]

On this argument, even if people believe themselves to be making a free and autonomous decision, they should nonetheless be prohibited from effectuating it because it offends the dignity of all of us by turning us into commodities. Fear of commodification is rife in many areas – such as surrogacy arrangements – although the link between the ability to sell services (or products, even of the body) and commodification is, in my view, somewhat opaque. Scheper-Hughes, however, sees the link as perfectly clear arguing that markets 'reduce everything – including human beings, their labor, and their reproductive capacity – to the to the status of commodities that can be bought, sold, traded, and stolen. Nowhere is this more dramatically illustrated than in the market for human organs and tissues.'[46] A major problem with this analysis, however, is that people already do sell their labour – indeed, it is generally expected of them. It is not clear that this turns them into commodities. Equally, were I permitted to sell one of my organs, or to benefit from the sale of any of my tissues, I would not feel myself any less worthy of being classified amongst those who deserve respect for their human dignity. I would not regard myself as a commodity (any more than I do when I accept a salary for doing my job), nor would there be any reason for

---

[45] Cohen, C B, 'Public Policy and the Sale of Human Organs', *Kennedy Institute of Ethics Journal*, 12(1), 2002: 47–64, at p 59.

[46] Scheper-Hughes, N, 'The Ends of the Body: Commodity Fetishism and the Global Traffic in Organs', *SAIS Review*, XXII(1), (Winter-Spring), 2002: 61–80, at p 62.

others to so regard me. The argument from diminution of respect for human dignity seems, therefore, less than convincing. However, if the ability to sell organs were coupled with a discriminatory and disproportionately negative impact on certain groups (such as the poor), we might have a stronger reason to object to it.

The World Medical Association, without further explanation, decries a market in organs, saying:

> Financial incentives such as direct payments for donating tissue for transplantation are to be rejected – in the same way that they are in connection with organ transplants. All other steps, such as the procurement, testing, processing, conservation, storage and allocation of tissue transplants, should likewise not be commercialised.[47]

So too does the Council of Europe's Convention for the Protection of Human Rights and Dignity of the Human Being with regard to the Application of Biology and Medicine: Convention on Human Rights and Biomedicine.[48] Section 21 of this Convention says that '[t]he human body and its parts shall not, as such, give rise to financial gain.'[49] Although no overt explanation is given, presumably, at least in part, it is to be found in the alleged potential for exploitation. It has, for example, been said that a 'major ethical objection against legalizing a commercial market for organs is its great potential for abuse and its tendency to foster unfair access to organ resources and exploitation of the poor.'[50] Equally, a commercial market might 'dissolve communal bonds and relationships based on goodwill and altruism.'[51] However, Clark suggests that '[p]rohibiting low income people from receiving financial incentives for donating their organs for fear of abuses doesn't really help them, it just leaves them poor.'[52] Of course, there may be deep and inherent flaws in the market approach, and Etzioni acknowledges this. He concludes, however, that although 'we, as a society, should *first* try an approach that does not involve commodification of organs, and hence does not risk the public costs that commodification entails ... ', nonetheless 'if non-commercial approaches continue to fail, some form of financial incentives might be

---

[47] *World Medical Association Statement on Human Tissue for Transplantation*, adopted by the WMA General Assembly, Copenhagen, Denmark, October 2007, at para 4.

[48] Oviedo, 4.IV.1997 The text is available at http://conventions.coe.int/Treaty/EN/Treaties/Html/164. htm (accessed on 12/1/2009).

[49] It should be noted that the United Kingdom has not ratified this Convention.

[50] Teo, B, 'Is the Adoption of More Efficient Strategies of Organ Procurement the Answer to Persistent Organ Shortage in Transplantation?', *Bioethics*, 6(2), 1992: 113–29, at p 124.

[51] Ibid., at p 125.

[52] Clark, P A, 'Financial Incentives For Cadaveric Organ Donation: An Ethical Analysis', *The Internet Journal of Law, Healthcare and Ethics*, 4(1), available at http://www.ispub.com/ostia/index.php?xmlFilePath= journals/ijlhe/vol4n1/organ.xml (accessed on 6/1/2009).

justified in order to save lives and reap the other benefits of increased organ supplies.'[53] This still, of course, does not answer the question of potential discriminatory consequences for the poor and disadvantaged.

Veatch builds an interesting argument here, noting that '[v]irtually any financial transaction would seem to have effects that differentiate based on income level.'[54] If so, he argues, then this might not be what is actually at the root of objections to a market in organs. Rather, he suggests, it might be that the third concern identified above – namely that a decision to sell an organ may not be truly autonomous – is what should be taken seriously. Thus, he argues, if an offer made by the wealthy to the poor, to 'people who are destitute, who desperately need food, clothing or medical care for themselves or members of their family ... ',[55] is attractive it could actually be categorised as coercive rather than discriminatory. However, even if what he calls 'irresistibly attractive' offers are made, 'the morally critical issue is whether the one making the offer has the option of addressing the desperate need in some other way.'[56] He concludes that in countries such as the United States, which have failed repeatedly to take action to lift people out of poverty or to provide universal healthcare, there is no alternative option; this, he says could potentially justify a market in organs.

Gill and Sade suggest that we could usefully consider an analogy. They use the example of paying people to participate in potentially dangerous drug trials to show that commercial activity is not always outlawed in healthcare, so long as certain standards apply and are observed.[57] In addition, in a return to consideration of autonomy, Teo argues that:

> ... legalizing a commercial market would truly respect individual autonomy and freedom, while giving individuals opportunities to exercise personal generosity. As owners of their bodies and as consenting moral agents, justice demands that the state refrain from restricting individuals in their right to determine the fate of their bodies so long as no harm comes to others.[58]

Moreover, Gill and Sade note the somewhat paradoxical position that '[t]he only component of the organ procurement process not currently paid is the

[53] Etzioni, A, 'Organ Donation: A Communitarian Approach', *Kennedy Institute of Ethics Journal*, 13(1), 2003: 1–18, at p 4.

[54] Veatch, R M, 'Why Liberals Should Accept Financial Incentives for Organ Procurement', *Kennedy Institute of Ethics Journal*, 12(1), 2003: 19–36, at p 27.

[55] Ibid., at p 27.

[56] Ibid., at p 28.

[57] Gill, M B, Sade, R M, 'Paying for Kidneys: The Case against Prohibition', *Kennedy Institute of Ethics Journal*, 12(1), 2002: 17–45.

[58] Teo, B, 'Is the Adoption of More Efficient Strategies of Organ Procurement the Answer to Persistent Organ Shortage in Transplantation?', *Bioethics*, 6(2), 1992: 113–29, at pp 123–24.

most critical component, the possessor of the kidney, who is *sine qua non* for organ availability.'[59] This does seem unfair, and certainly does not respect the individual's autonomy or contribution (arguably just what occurred in the cases of Mr Moore and Mrs Lacks). And, although financial incentives might be the most appealing for those in need of money, Veatch suggests that, if this is a problem, we should perhaps consider non-financial incentives which might be less likely to be coercive.[60] Of course, if we believe that incentives negate autonomy, non-financial ones could have the same effect and would, on these grounds, be no more acceptable.

None of this discussion is designed to support a black market in organ sales, nor to argue for an entirely *laissez faire* approach to any market established. Rather, as Gill and Sade have proposed, 'the buyers of kidneys [should] be the agencies in charge of kidney procurement or transplantation; that is, we propose that such agencies should be allowed to use financial incentives to acquire kidneys ... kidneys will not be traded in an unregulated market.'[61] Above all, it is argued that before dismissing this option we must take account of the entirety of the situation requiring us to 'frame in our mind an image of these sick people, as well as of their families and friends, that is just as vivid as our image of the healthy kidney sellers.'[62]

Despite the potential arguments in favour of organ sales (again, obviously excluding those that would result in the death of, or serious harm to, the donor) Cohen argues that 'publicly accepted foundational values ... ' might nonetheless justify rejecting it, even at the expense of 'limiting individual liberty.'[63] Ross agrees, saying that ' ... strangers have obligations not to harm each other, but they have no positive obligation to expose themselves to grave risk in order to help another. To prohibit a market in kidneys restricts autonomy, but it may be within the purview of the state to do so.'[64] There may, however, be social goods which can come from *not* rejecting this option. Clark, for example, points to potential societal benefits and asks why nothing has yet been done to harness them, saying:

> If so much good can come from organ donation, not only saving lives but saving government money on health care which benefits society,

[59] Gill, M B, Sade, R M, 'Paying for Kidneys: The Case against Prohibition', *Kennedy Institute of Ethics Journal*, 12(1), 2002: 17–45, at p 19.

[60] Veatch, R M, 'Why Liberals Should Accept Financial Incentives for Organ Procurement', *Kennedy Institute of Ethics Journal*, 12(1), 2003: 19–36, at p 26.

[61] Gill, M B, Sade, R M, 'Paying for Kidneys: The Case against Prohibition', *Kennedy Institute of Ethics Journal*, 12(1), 2002: 17–45, at p 19.

[62] Ibid., at p 39.

[63] Cohen, C B, 'Public Policy and the Sale of Human Organs', *Kennedy Institute of Ethics Journal*, 12(1), 2002: 47–64, at p 48.

[64] Ross, L F, 'The Ethical Limits in Expanding Living Donor Transplantation', *Kennedy Institute of Ethics Journal*, 16(2), 2006: 151–72, at p 155.

then why are new incentives not being explored? If one of the basic tenets of economics is that incentives matter, then it follows that positive incentives, like money, would not only increase the number of donations but would overcome other costs and disincentives. If financial incentives would be good for all concerned, donors/families, recipients and society as a whole, then why not institute such a program?[65]

While some want to argue that the provision of incentives actually diminishes or denies the altruism that many regard as vital in this area, Clark claims that '[t]rue altruism, which is an unselfish regard for the welfare of others, should not be deterred by financial incentives that can help donors and donor families.'[66] In the long run, while there may be anxieties about the consequences of a market in human organs, if it is appropriately regulated, and not subject simply to the vagaries of the free market, it could serve as a way of increasing the availability of organs, while at the same time arguably being as much a reflection of individual autonomy as is the altruistic gift of organs for transplantation.

Opting out

Possibly the most popular alternative to the 'opting in' system is what is sometimes called a system of 'presumed consent'. In what follows, unless in a direct quotation, I will not use this language, preferring instead the terminology of 'opting out'. Primarily, this is because – in an age when consent is so important – it is, in my view, dangerous to presume its presence. We should, rather, robustly defend the need for the individual to demonstrate their wishes – not just assume what they might choose.

While the possibility of moving to an opting out system is, as we will see, gathering considerable support in some quarters in the United Kingdom, it has been effectively discounted in the United States:

> A Subcommittee of the UNOS Ethics Committee that was mandated to study this issued rejected it for three reasons: First, presumed consent offers inadequate safeguards for protecting the individual autonomy of prospective donors. Second, the Subcommittee was unimpressed with mechanisms in place in countries which employ presumed consent to protect the rights of objectors to donation. Third, the Subcommittee felt that the alternative of 'required response' (all individuals would be required by public authorities to express their preferences regarding organ donation)

[65] Clark, P A, 'Financial Incentives For Cadaveric Organ Donation: An Ethical Analysis', *The Internet Journal of Law, Healthcare and Ethics*, 4(1), available at http://www.ispub.com/ostia/index.php?xmlFilePath= journals/ijlhe/vol4n1/organ.xml (accessed on 6/1/2009).

[66] Ibid.

had a more positive response as a viable alternative. Presumed consent could be viewed as an exploitation of human weakness.[67]

The critical distinction between opting in and opting out systems is that the former requires a positive act on the part of the potential donor to record his or her *willingness* to be a donor, while an opting out system requires a positive decision to register *unwillingness* to donate. Essentially, failure to opt out would mean that – at least on a strict version of this system – 'the body of the individual goes to the state after death and any rights of the family or respect associated with the cadaver end with the individual's death.'[68] In the United Kingdom support for an opting out system has been expressed by senior politicians, and – perhaps more importantly – by the British Medical Association (BMA). A staunch opponent of opting out for very many years, the BMA has now changed its position, favouring what it calls a 'soft' opting out system, which would still entail a role for relatives, albeit a limited one. Under this system, relatives would still have a role to play but their views would be canvassed primarily to ascertain whether or not they knew of an unregistered objection or to find out whether or not taking organs would cause them 'major distress'.[69]

Interestingly, however, the BMA also tries to claim that opting out is as protective of autonomy as is the opting in system, claiming that 'genuine choice over organ donation can be facilitated through a soft system of presumed consent whereby adults can choose to opt-out of organ donation during their lifetime, rather than having to opt into donation, as is the status quo.'[70] This somewhat counter-intuitive argument is based, says the BMA, 'on what most people claim to support.'[71] The BMA produces the following 'evidence' of apparent support for opting out to bolster this claim:

> There has been a marked public shift in support of presumed consent over the past nine years. In May 1999 the Department of Health commissioned a survey of public opinion on preferences between the status quo and a change to a system of presumed consent. In that survey, 50% expressed a preference for the current system, 28% supported a shift to presumed consent and 22% expressed no preference. Since then, however, there has been more publicity about the shortage of donors and

---

[67] Ibid.

[68] Shannon, T A, 'The Kindness of Strangers: Organ Transplantation in a Capitalist Age', *Kennedy Institute of Ethics Journal*, 11(3), 2001: 285–303, at p 301.

[69] British Medical Association, 'Presumed Consent for Organ Donation', July 2008, available at http://www.bma.org.uk/ap.nsf/Content/PresumedconsentfororgandonationJuly08 (accessed on 13/10/2008), transcript, p 2.

[70] Ibid., transcript, p 1.

[71] Ibid.

about presumed consent and a number of more recent surveys have shown increasing support for such a shift.

In October 2007 a YouGov survey commissioned by the BMA showed that 64% of respondents would support a soft system of presumed consent.

In July 2000, an Omnibus survey of 2,000 people carried out on behalf of the National Kidney Research Fund found that 57% of those questioned would support a system of presumed consent.

In February 2001, a telephone poll conducted by Watchdog Healthcheck attracted nearly 52,000 people and found that 78% of those who responded supported a shift to presumed consent.

A survey of MPs carried out in March 2001 by the National Kidney Research Fund found that 59% of the 163 MPs who completed the questionnaire supported a soft system of presumed consent.

BBC 4's 'Today' programme before Christmas 2003 asked listeners to vote on suggested Private Members' Bills. The second most popular bill in the poll was to allow all organs to be used for transplant after death unless an individual had opted out.

In May 2005, a representative sample of 2,067 people over 16 years of age were interviewed on behalf of the BBC and 6/10 respondents supported a shift to presumed consent.[72]

I report this 'evidence' in full here, in order to show that it is, in fact, essentially anecdotal (and occasionally rather ambivalent). Moreover, we have no way of truly evaluating the *quality* of the research referred to, and should – as with all opinion 'evidence' – be careful in how we interpret and use it. 'Evidence' that the majority of the public support organ donation, even though only around 26% have formally registered their wishes should be subject to careful scrutiny. If people do not actually record their wish to donate when it is extremely easy to do so, how seriously should we take their purported desires when questioned by pollsters and the like? This is, in fact, a vitally important question, since it is central to the argument that supports a change to an opting out system. It is often, for example, said that by not moving to an opting out system, those who support transplantation but do not record their wish to donate will be disrespected after death if their organs are not used. This would be fair enough if we *knew* that these people actually, as opposed to when they are asked a question for an opinion poll, would wish to donate. But we do not know this. In any case, if we move to an opting out system, it could just as easily be argued that a significant number of people will find that their failure to register is taken as equivalent to 'consent' even if it only results from apathy about opting out. They too would find their true wishes disrespected. The UK Organ

[72] Ibid., transcript, p 3.

Donation Taskforce says that an opting out system is 'often described as consent for the disorganised ... '.[73] However, it also notes that there is reason to be concerned that 'a proportion of the 10% to 35% of the population who would not have wished to donate their organs, but never got round to registering an objection, could mistakenly be considered as willing donors under an opt out system.'[74] Conceding for the moment that there is some support – perhaps even majority support – for a shift to opting out, it is nonetheless disingenuous to suggest (as the BMA does) that an opting out system actually means that people will become more proactive about registering their wishes during life. There is frankly no evidence to support this assertion, but it does highlight the extent to which the BMA believes that it is necessary to justify the scheme used to harvest organs on the basis of autonomy.

There are, of course, other arguments against opting out. Siminoff and Mercer, explain some of them in this way:

> Presumed Consent assumes that the general public is well informed on the issue of organ donation and furthermore assumes that individuals will be proactive in documenting their refusal. Of greater concern is the possibility that presumed consent may increase a sense of distrust in the medical profession and, ultimately, persuade people who were originally in favor of donation to document their refusal. It is also of concern that the economically disadvantaged and ethnic minorities precisely the people most likely to object to organ donation – will not be able to adequately avail themselves of an 'opt-out' system.[75]

Picking up on this last point, Fisher argues that it would be necessary to ensure that the public was aware of the alteration to the system and also that opting out is made simple. If this can be achieved, Fisher says, 'an opt-out or presumed consent donation policy is ethically acceptable.'[76] Maybe so, but it must be remembered that the opting in system is widely known about and easy to subscribe to, yet the majority of people still do not sign up. It is not clear, in the face of the other objections to the opting out system, that ease of access, or widespread awareness, makes any difference to its ethical standing. Moreover, this still begs the important question whether 'our social, organizational, and bureaucratic conditions allow silence to be so meaningful as to signify agreement, so that we can honestly speak about presumptions of

---

[73] UK Organ Donation Taskforce, n 21 above, at p 8, para 4.3.

[74] Ibid.

[75] Siminoff, L A, Mercer, M B, 'Public Policy, Public Opinion, and Consent for Organ Donation', *Cambridge Quarterly of Healthcare Ethics*, 10, 2001: 377–86, at p 381.

[76] Fisher, J, 'An expedient *and* ethical alternative to xenotransplantation', *Medicine, Health Care and Philosophy*, 2, 1999: 31–39, at p 38.

deliberate undertakings?'[77] It is certainly not common in law that failure to act, in the absence of a pre-existing arrangement, is taken to imply agreement. If silence equals consent, then many medical interactions which currently need firm authorisation could presumably proceed – the right of the individual patient would be reduced to a right to object.

Jacob has further problems with opting out, arguing that it 'may negatively alter the very meaning of the act of donating organs. What used to be an altruistic act could now become routine procedure ... Organ procurement could, thus, lose its solidarity component, since it would have no 'donation' ethics.'[78] The UK Organ Donation Taskforce agrees, saying that opting out would 'challenge commonplace assumptions about consent and individual decision making at a time of greater expectation of individual autonomy among the public.'[79] While seeming to agree with the BMA that an opting out system can protect autonomy, Etzioni nonetheless concludes that it is 'still quite coercive, or at least high-handed. It becomes an individual's responsibility to guarantee that the government does not procure his or her body upon death.'[80]

Of course, we might be prepared to overlook the concerns about opting out were it clear that this system actually does increase the availability of organs for transplantation. This, however, is not necessarily the case. Declaring itself 'neither against nor in favour of a change to presumed consent legislation',[81] UK Transplant, for example, notes that '[t]he fact that Sweden has an opt-out law does not seem to influence the donation rate per million of population, which is lower than that of the UK, which does not.'[82] It is, of course, Spain rather than Sweden that is generally held up as the poster child for opting out systems. Spain has the highest rate of organ donors in Europe, but:

> In fact, while Spain is recognised as having a higher number of donors than the UK, it is acknowledged by the director of national transplant organisation in Spain himself that the increase in organ donation during the 1990s could not be attributed to a change in legislation which had remained the same since 1979. The improvements in donor rates in Spain followed the implementation of a comprehensive national procurement system.[83]

[77] Jacob, M-A, 'Another Look at the Presumed-Versus-Informed Consent Dichotomy in Postmortem Organ Procurement', *Bioethics*, 20(6), 2006: 293–300, at p 295.

[78] Ibid., at p 294.

[79] UK Organ Donation Taskforce, n 21 above, at p 9, para 4.9.

[80] Etzioni, A, 'Organ Donation: A Communitarian Approach', *Kennedy Institute of Ethics Journal*, 13(1), 2003: 1–18, at p 2.

[81] Available at http://www.uktransplant.org.uk/ukt/newsroom/statements_and_stances/statements/opt_in_or_out.jsp (accessed on 9/10/2008), transcript, p 6.

[82] Ibid., transcript, pp 4–5.

[83] Ibid., transcript, p 5.

Moreover, research has suggested that drawing a link between increased 'donor' pools and opting out systems is simplistic at one further level. Coppen, Friele, Marquet and Gevers, for example, maintain that the real impact on donation rates is not a result of the system in place, but rather about the number of deaths which are 'relevant' for transplantation purposes using World Health Organization (WHO) classifications. They note that '[c]ountries with low donation rates usually have low mortality rates relevant for organ donation, while countries with high donation rates have high relevant mortality rates.'[84] Basing their analysis on the annual reports of national transplant centres from 10 European countries, they found that 'approximately 80% of the deceased who became organ donors died of a cerebral vascular accident (CVA) or (traffic) accident. That is why these mortality categories play an important role in the effectuation of a potential organ donor and we have therefore focused on these categories.'[85] What Coppen, *et al* discovered was that:

> ... there is a strong correlation between relevant mortality rates and organ donation rates ... International comparative legal research has shown that the differences between decision systems are marginal. When the national organ donation rates are corrected for the mortality rates, the findings of the legal research are confirmed: the donor efficiency rate shows that opting-out systems do not automatically guarantee higher organ donation rates than opting-in systems.[86]

Their conclusion, then, is that 'the apparent relationship between the consent systems and organ donation rates disappears after controlling for difference in relevant mortality.'[87] Apart from those raised above, therefore, there are other more practical reasons to urge caution in moving towards a system that cannot, almost by definition, respect the autonomy of the individual. The UK Organ Donation Taskforce also concluded that 'presumed consent alone does not explain the variation in organ donation rates between ... different countries. Many other factors affect donation rates.'[88]

Recognising the need to improve the availability of organs, Etzioni argues that what is needed is that we engage in a 'full-blown moral dialogue about the fact that many people neglect to give what correctly has been called a gift of life – that is, they neglect to donate their organs when they are no longer of any use to them.'[89] Following this debate he anticipates that it will

---

[84] Coppen, R, Friele, R D, Marquet, R L, Gevers, S K M, 'Opting-out systems: no guarantee for higher donation rates', *Transplant International*, 18, 2005: 1275–79, at p 1277.

[85] Ibid., at pp 1276–77.

[86] Ibid., at p 1278.

[87] Ibid., at p 1277.

[88] UK Organ Donation Taskforce, n 21 above, at p 4, para 1.5.

[89] Etzioni, A, 'Organ Donation: A Communitarian Approach', *Kennedy Institute of Ethics Journal*, 13(1), 2003: 1–18, at p 7.

be possible to succeed in 'changing people's preferences through moral persuasion, community appreciation of good conduct, and gentle chiding of those who do not do what is considered right. The key is converting existing predispositions into active preferences.'[90] He hopes, therefore, by persuasion rather than coercion or incentivisation (financial or otherwise), to retain the altruistic nature of donation, while at the same time increasing the supply of organs primarily by reminding people of their responsibilities to others. This is an appealing idea, although of course it could be said that efforts of this sort have already been made many times, for example in educational and advertising campaigns which appear to have failed to appeal to whatever altruism may reside in those who have not registered for donation. We are left, therefore, to decide which we value more – an enhanced donor pool or respect for the wishes of the individual – or, indeed, to work out whether or not we can achieve both without losing sight of important underpinning principles such as self-determination. Our answer should be based in sound theoretical, as well as robust empirical, reflection.

Compulsion

One final possibility should be touched on briefly. Emson argues that we should regard our body as being 'on extended loan from the biomass … '.[91] Accepting that one's organs will routinely be made available for transplantation post-mortem would, under this system, be seen as a 'moral duty, rather than as a supererogatory act at the individual's discretion, as organ donation is currently perceived.'[92] This makes sense to Harris, who argues that ' … it seems clear that the benefits from cadaver transplants are so great, and the harms done in going against the wishes of those who object so comparatively small, that we should remove altogether the habit of seeking the consent of either the deceased or relatives.'[93] Spital points to the fact that the state can 'conscript people into the military, at the risk of losing their lives and devastating their families, to protect the welfare of its citizens', and asks, why it should not be permissible to 'conscript organs from cadavers, who cannot be harmed, for the same purpose?'[94] Arguably, although it is less commonly canvassed than the opting out model, this scheme would make more organs available and would avoid the problems associated with requiring people to actually do something (either opting in or opting out). It

[90] Ibid., at p 5.

[91] Emson, H E, 'It is immoral to require consent for cadaver organ donation', *J Med Ethics*, 29, 2003: 125–27, at p 126.

[92] Gerrand, N, 'The Notion of Gift-Giving and Organ Donation', *Bioethics*, 8(2), 1994: 127–50, at p 131.

[93] Harris, J, Organ procurement: dead interests, living needs', *J Med Ethics*, 29, 2003: 130–34, at p 131.

[94] Spital, A, 'Conscription of Cadaveric Organs for Transplantation: Neglected Again', *Kennedy Institute of Ethics Journal*, 13(2), 2003: 169–74, at p 173.

would, however, completely ignore the issue of autonomy and it is perhaps for this reason that it is not yet widely supported.

Conclusion

There are a number of ways in which organs may be made available for transplantation and the need for them is real and increasing. The benefits of transplantation surgery are major, and success rates – in terms of length and quality of life post-surgery – are growing apace. As we have seen, living donation is now making a significant contribution to transplantation programmes, although of course it is limited by the kind of organs that can be made available. However, at first blush it may seem that this is the form of donation that is most clearly autonomous. A competent person making a contemporaneous decision in the knowledge of risks and benefits makes a decision to donate say, a kidney, is surely the classic example of self-determination. It is also the classic example of the congruence of both individualistic and relational autonomy. While the choice may be made for self-regarding reasons – for example, to prove to ourselves what good people we are – it is also a decision made in the interests of others. This, it may seem, is the perfect combination of individual choice and contextual or relational autonomy, albeit that the voluntariness of intra-familial donations is sometimes suspect.

One critique of living donation, however, comes from an apparently unlikely angle. Kuczewski,[95] argues that pressure may not simply be intra-familial, but may also be societal saying that 'we are creating an increasingly medicalized society in which it is becoming more difficult to resist becoming involved, as a live donor or as a recipient, in this high-tech approach to organ failure.[96] Whether any such pressure is sufficient to make the case that the decision is not autonomous must, however, be moot. People who choose to donate in circumstances where their will has not been overwhelmed can still be said to be acting autonomously. In any case, little that we do is truly voluntary, and decisions that take account of others reflect the extent to which we are inter-related, while at the same time satisfying intensely individualistic motivation. Additionally, while people who accept an organ that could save their lives may indeed be faced with an overwhelming pressure to do so, we have no reason to believe that they would not choose life in any other circumstance. They act autonomously when they agree to transplantation, and indeed the recent case of Hannah Jones, a 13-year-old who refused a heart transplant,[97] suggests that not everyone will agree – people retain the

---

[95] Kuczewski, M G, 'The Gift of Life and Starfish on the Beach: The Ethics of Organ Procurement', *The American Journal of Bioethics*, 2(3), Summer 2002: 53–56.

[96] Ibid., at p 55.

[97] For discussion of this case, see McLean, S A M, 'Hannah's Choice', available at http://www.guardian. co.uk/commentisfree/2008/nov/11/health-ethics (accessed 12/1/2009); but see the case of *Re M (child: refusal of medical treatment)* (2000) 52 BMLR 124.

capacity to deliberate and decide for themselves even in the face of imminent death.

Despite the growing importance of live donation, however, there will still be incentives to improve the cadaveric donation rate as this would allow any and all transplantable organs to be made available. A number of options have been considered (although the discussion was not intended to be fully comprehensive – merely to highlight some of the major proposals).[98] The urgent need to reduce the shortfall between supply and demand and the benefits of doing so, may seem self-evident, but some urge caution in that:

> ... any attempt to increase the efficiency of organ procurement programs, without prior consideration of the wider issues of resource allocation, can be a serious social policy error. It can be deceptive to the public, if not exploitative of its goodwill, to project to it the constant message that more transplants could be performed if only more people donate their organs.[99]

Two important points are raised by this comment. First, even if we did manage to increase the number of organs available for transplantation there are significant resource issues of two sorts to be addressed. For example, they may relate to whether or not there are sufficient facilities in place to make good use of any increase in organs for transplantation. Even though it supports the opting out option, even the BMA accepts that this alone cannot solve all of the problems that beset the current system.[100] In reality, significant investment in the infrastructure would be necessary – more trained transplant surgeons and specialist nurses, more ICU facilities, and so on. This raises the second issue about resources – namely, how much of the healthcare budget are societies willing to spend on transplantation, when this is in competition with other important services?

This, of course, is not to suggest that we should not try to improve the availability of organs for transplantation. Rather, it is to urge thorough consideration of the simplistic assumption that increasing the number of available organs will inevitably equal a vastly improved service, saving infinitely more lives *ex hypothesi*.

The major apparent advantage of the opting in model is that it respects the freedom of individuals to make their own choices about what will happen to their bodies after their deaths. In this sense, it respects a form of

---

[98] For example, the possibility of elective ventilation was not canvassed. For discussion is this option, see 'Transplantation and the 'Nearly Dead': The Case of Elective Ventilation', in McLean, S A M (ed), *Contemporary Issues in Law, Medicine and Ethics*, Dartmouth, 1996, at Chapter 8.

[99] Teo, B, 'Is the Adoption of More Efficient Strategies of Organ Procurement the Answer to Persistent Organ Shortage in Transplantation?', *Bioethics*, 6(2), 1992: 113–29, at p 129.

[100] British Medical Association, 'Presumed Consent for Organ Donation', July 2008, available at http://www.bma.org.uk/ap.nsf/Content/PresumedconsentfororgandonationJuly08 (accessed on 13/10/2008).

individualistic autonomy, even though the decision to donate has significant other-regarding characteristics. It is an act of altruism to give someone the 'gift of life'. It is this that we would sacrifice by adopting the most popular alternative – the opting out system. Moreover, the evidence that changing the system alone would result in more organs and therefore more transplants is simply not there. Abandoning the importance of consent in the face of the dubious benefits of an opting out system seems unnecessary.

However, the current system also often leaves the decision to families, as only around 26% of the population (in the UK at least) register their wish to donate. Siminoff and Chillag point out that, 'the gift metaphor has not been especially effective in promoting donation.'[101] This, they say is possibly because '"gift giving" or altruism is not necessarily the primary motivation when families decide to donate.'[102] The reasonably high refusal rate of relatives also suggests that altruism is not at the forefront of their minds when asked to consent, often in the face of a sudden death or with a loved one on a ventilator still looking as if they were alive. Thus, it must be borne in mind that 'the evaluation of attitudes through the use of public opinion polls is superficial considering the emotionally charged situations in which consent decisions occur.'[103] The 'evidence' often used to claim widespread support for the opting out system is as weak as this commentary suggests. Even where a pre-mortem decision has been made by the individual him or her self, some question what are the consequences of encouraging donation, arguing, for example, that ' … under the guise of altruism we are uncritically medicalizing our lives and commodifying our bodies, especially as new means of procuring organs are advanced.'[104] The extent to which we should take this seriously in light of the genuine tragedy resulting from the shortage of organs is debatable. Indeed, while medicalisation is or can be a problem, other values may counter-balance the concerns associated with it.

If the most important goal is to provide more organs for transplantation, it would seem that the opting in system is not working. I have argued, however, that we should not treat opinion evidence as definitive of the actual numbers willing to donate, and Siminoff and Mercer agree, saying '[s]trong public support for organ donation seems at odds with current real consent rates.'[105] Of course, apathy may be the explanation for the apparent failure of people to turn their purported wishes into registered intentions, but it may

---

[101] Siminoff, L A, Chillag, K, 'The Fallacy of the "Gift of Life"', *Hastings Center Report*, 29(6), 1999: 34–41, at p 40.

[102] Ibid.

[103] Siminoff, L A, Mercer, M B, 'Public Policy, Public Opinion, and Consent for Organ Donation', *Cambridge Quarterly of Healthcare Ethics*, 10, 2001: 377–86, at p 383.

[104] Kuczewski, M G, 'The Gift of Life and Starfish on the Beach: The Ethics of Organ Procurement', *The American Journal of Bioethics*, 2(3), Summer 2002: 53–56, at p 53.

[105] Siminoff, L A, Mercer, M B, 'Public Policy, Public Opinion, and Consent for Organ Donation', *Cambridge Quarterly of Healthcare Ethics*, 10, 2001: 377–86, at p 383.

also be the case that people, when asked, are unlikely to say that they would not be prepared to be altruistic, even if that is in fact how they feel. It is difficult to be overtly selfish, especially when there would seem to be widespread awareness of the success of organ transplantation.

It is worth returning briefly to the alternative systems proposed. One of these is that incentives, financial or other, might be offered to encourage people to participate in the programme. While some have argued that – especially if the incentives are financial – this would not only negate autonomy, it would also be discriminatory or coercive of the poor and disadvantaged, these arguments have been critiqued and not found to be entirely convincing. Childress suggests that we should recognise that the motives for decisions are 'often, and perhaps usually, mixed ... ', and concludes that if we accept this then 'we can begin to consider not only how the society could remove disincentives to donation, but also how it might provide incentives ... without replacing a moral sense of altruism or moral obligation.'[106] There is, however, often an instinctive reaction against an incentive based system, which it may be difficult to overcome even in the face of reasoned argument. Making the human body – or rather parts of it – the subject of a financial transaction, or offering further incentives to encourage people to participate, offends many who believe that there is something so special about the human body even after death that it should be used only where consent is real and unquestionable.[107]

The most popular alternative by far seems to be the opting out system, which is now supported by many august medical bodies and, it would seem, senior politicians in the United Kingdom.[108] While I am not privy to the rationale behind their support for opting out, it is interesting that perhaps the most outspoken medical body to support opting out – the BMA – has been at pains to attempt to conceptualise opting out as a system which *respects* autonomy. While this may be an attempt to reconcile its current position with its previous one – which firmly declared that organ donation must be a gift and specifically disapproved of opting out – it also, as I have suggested earlier, defies logic. At least it does so, unless we are prepared to invest more authority than I have argued we should in the anecdotal 'evidence' that comes from opinion polls and the like. If anecdotal evidence is treated as just that, it becomes virtually impossible to argue that an opting out system is a general respecter of autonomy. In any case, since the BMA's 'soft' version of opting out would still see relatives playing a role – that is,

[106] Childress, J F, 'The Failure to Give: Reducing Barriers to Organ Donation', *Kennedy Institute of Ethics Journal*, 11(1), 2001: 1–16, at p 10.

[107] To a very large extent, this was the sense that underpinned the aggrieved relatives in the inquiries into organ removal and retention referred to *supra*.

[108] See, for example, the report that the UK Prime Minister had apparently endorsed the opting out system, available at http://news.bbc.co.uk/1/hi/health/7186007.stm (accessed on 17/10/2008).

they could still veto a transplant in specific circumstances – there is really no way to be sure that this system would actually increase the supply of organs. Further, we have already seen that, when properly analysed, it is not the case that opting out systems by themselves actually do have a direct effect on the number of available organs.

Realistically, therefore, opting out is a relatively ineffective system, which in my view stands in opposition at least to individual self-determination. On the other hand, even an individualistic account of autonomy is not inimical to a successful organ transplantation programme. What the individualistic model does is to emphasise the right of individuals to make their own choices; it does not require that these decisions are selfish, nor that they do not take account of the needs of others. Nonetheless, it has been suggested that we should stop thinking 'in terms of individual rights' and start considering what 'kind of society we wish to foster … '.[109] This mandates that we 'need to ask what might be the realistic goals of organ procurement and what toll such practices might exact on the values of a society.'[110] In other words, what values would we sacrifice to obtain others?

Let us assume that as a society we prioritise the needs of those dying for want of an organ, and perhaps even take into account the economic and other advantages that could arise from restoring their health. It would seem that the most effective way of achieving this would be compelling donation or 'conscripting organs'. That is, the assumption would be that no consent at all would be necessary for the removal of cadaveric organs; rather, the state could do so in the interests of those who are in need. While completely ignoring the concept of autonomy this system, it is said 'is more likely to be effective.'[111] It could be argued that in the interest of saving lives, the state should be entitled to assume quasi-property or property rights over the deceased, who are beyond being harmed; individual autonomy has no role post mortem.

This takes us back to the question of what kind of society we want to have, and the extent to which – and what kind of – autonomy is valued. For the moment, the law in some, but not all, countries seems to hold to a mixed approach. In the case of living donors, for example, laws seem *prima facie* to support individualistic autonomy, but in reality the form being respected is a hybrid. In permitting people to authorise a kind of maiming which is, for them, non-therapeutic, and might otherwise be unlawful, the law is using a relational or contextual account of autonomy. On the other hand, the law's insistence that consent is obtained reflects the individualistic

[109] Kuczewski, M G, 'The Gift of Life and Starfish on the Beach: The Ethics of Organ Procurement', *The American Journal of Bioethics*, 2(3), Summer 2002: 53–56, at p 54.

[110] Ibid.

[111] Spital, A, 'Conscription of Cadaveric Organs for Transplantation: Neglected Again', *Kennedy Institute of Ethics Journal*, 13(2), 2003: 169–74, at pp 172–73.

account. In the case of deceased donors, while it is generally said that people should be able to control what happens to their bodies after death (just as we can with our property) it appears that there is increased enthusiasm for moving from the system which *prima facie* defends individual autonomy towards one (opting out) which I would argue manifestly does not. It might, of course, be argued that opting out systems – like live donations – can render what would normally not be permitted legally acceptable because of the societal purpose it serves. And, of course, the dead person could be said to have less interest in their bodies and body parts than the living person, further vindicating the rather casual approach to autonomy inherent in the opting out system. These arguments, however, are vulnerable to the evidence that suggests that the system itself will not in fact be effective.

Sacrificing concern for individual rights on the altar of the greater or common good may sometimes be justified, but this is not always so. Nor is the greater good always obvious. For example, when Oliver Wendell Holmes justified the compulsory sterilisation of mental 'defectives' in the case of *Buck v Bell*,[112] he too appealed to the common good, or public interest, to justify trampling over individual rights. Few, if any, would now endorse his position. This, presumably, is one of the primary reasons that many proponents of the opting out system attempt to clothe their proposal in the mantle of autonomy (even if, as I have suggested, this is an essentially implausible argument). Further, it has been argued that ' … the common good is not about more organs for transplantation alone. It is not about "medical care" alone. It is about a "continuum of care" in which transplant medicine is one kind of care. Medicine should assist us without consuming us.'[113]

The final question, therefore, is this: what rights, interests or principles are we or are we not prepared to juggle or even sacrifice in order to benefit those whose lives will end prematurely because of the shortage of transplantable organs? In permitting living donation, I have already argued that a compromise has been made. While non-therapeutic surgery would otherwise be outlawed (even cosmetic surgery has some benefits for the individual) a relational approach is taken to justify permitting people to maim themselves. However, what differentiates this from opting out (or the conscription of organs) is that consent has been obtained – real, knowledgeable agreement to participation which is on all fours with the requirements of the individualistic model. If, on the other hand, we were to apply a relational account of autonomy to cadaveric organ harvesting, why would we not prefer the conscription option to the softer, and almost certainly less successful, opting out system?

[112] 274 US 200 (1927).
[113] Kuczewski, M G, 'The Gift of Life and Starfish on the Beach: The Ethics of Organ Procurement', *The American Journal of Bioethics*, 2(3), Summer 2002: 53–56, at p 56.

In law, we value consent which it has been said, 'acts as a deontological constraint on physicians by ensuring that they respect the rights, needs, and interests of patients, as determined by patients or their families.'[114] In the long run, in the case of organ transplantation, Glannon argues that '[m]ost people would support a system that increased the number of transplantable organs, but not at the expense of choice and their ability to make momentous decisions at the end of life.'[115] Arguably, the current position is to be preferred since it respects individual choice while at the same time not preventing people from acting in a manner which recognises the importance of community and the responsibilities to others that go with that. The apparently growing enthusiasm for opting out rather than opting in betrays yet another ambivalence in the state's (and perhaps ultimately the law's) position on what kind of autonomy it is there to protect. The case of organ transplantation is also a further example of the artificiality of the distinctions drawn between the two main accounts of autonomy discussed in this narrative and further highlights the law's apparent ambivalence about autonomy itself. While at present the law seems to favour the consent-based model, the pressure to move from this is mounting. Yet '[a] move way from requiring explicit consent would put organ donation out of step with prevailing practices ... '.[116] If we are to sacrifice the importance of individual consent for the greater good (assuming that this would be the result) we surely need robust theoretical and empirical evidence of benefit; evidence that is currently lacking.

---

[114] Glannon, W, 'The Case against Conscription of Cadaveric Organs for Transplantation', *Cambridge Quarterly of Healthcare Ethics*, 17, 2008: 330–36, at p 331.

[115] Ibid., at p 335.

[116] UK Organ Donation Taskforce, n 21 above, at p 9, para 4.9.

Chapter 8

Conclusion

This discussion has focused on two main issues. First, it has evaluated the claim that the law of consent is firmly based in the concept of autonomy and serves to translate it into law. Second, by analysing a number of specific areas, the way in which law interprets autonomy has been considered and critiqued. Behind each of these strands of the discussion has been the underpinning question as to what *kind* of autonomy is favoured in law. As the foundational principle on which the law of consent is said to operate, it has been instructive to clarify whether or not the claims made for the importance of autonomy in the law are borne out in reality. It has also been proposed that there should be a level of consistency in how autonomy is described and used in law and clarity about what is actually being respected. In other words, in the reasonable interest that individuals have in being able to predict against what kind of standards their behaviour will be judged, it should be possible to identify a common strand that permits some level of certainty. That is, people should be able to anticipate that the rules that will be applied are based on identifiable legal principles that are grounded in coherent, rational values and are consistently applied.

Autonomy revisited

There are many and varied accounts of autonomy, some of which are touched on only briefly in this narrative. The reasons for this are first that the author is not a philosopher and it would manifestly be absurd to pretend an in-depth knowledge of, for example, Kantian ethics. Equally, I have deliberately chosen to use two specific accounts of autonomy that are of contemporary interest, and are frequently reflected in the literature on healthcare ethics and law. In the long run, what is important is not just the models used, I would argue, but the extent to which we can detect the value of autonomy in legal decisions and policy-making; the two accounts I have selected for consideration most clearly demonstrate the occasional ambivalence of the law to respect for self-determination when it comes up against social and other concerns.

Autonomy is a status; the decisions of an autonomous person deserve respect. The autonomous individual is one who is both free and able to make his or her own decisions based on the values that inform his or her life. The general presumption that adults are autonomous is encapsulated in the legal concept of competence. It is assumed that competent adults are free to act as they choose, so long as their behaviour does not harm others. In principle, then, decisions made by such individuals are in and of themselves to be respected in law. Indeed, in a number of cases courts have made it clear that no inquiry as to the rationale(s) for the choices of competent people is necessary; just making the decision is sufficient to give it validity.

However, for some, the mere presence of decision-making capacity is an insufficient account of autonomy. For those who prefer a more relational account, truly autonomous decisions are based in, or recognise the importance of, community and inter-connectedness. This approach, closely identified with communitarianism and feminism, attempts to challenge the validity of decisions which are purely selfish or self-centred (individualistic), and to that extent it has great appeal. People function in and with communities; they do not stand entirely alone. All true, it must be agreed, but – ideological aspirations aside – I have tried to argue that the purported difference between individualistic and relational autonomy is by no means so great as at first appears. Nonetheless, if such differences as do exist are used without care, they may lead to variable outcomes some of which arguably seem somewhat perverse. For example, the importance of inter-relatedness can result in an undue focus on the interest of others and this is evident, for example, when the decisions of pregnant women are disregarded in the interests of a future child. While society might prefer women to behave in certain ways, the law's alleged respect for the autonomous decisions of competent people should have prevented many of the judgements highlighted in Chapter 5. Equally, the interests of others in the decisions we may want to make can sometimes be used to frustrate the free exercise of individual will at the end of life. While in theoretical terms the differences between the relational and the individualistic accounts of autonomy can be exaggerated, therefore, in the 'wrong' hands or for policy reasons they can be manipulated to defeat autonomous choice. In addition, as we have seen, the law seems inconsistent as to which version of autonomy it applies, which is fatal for any expectation of certainty.

While the contributions of philosophers in support of one model of autonomy or another make for an interesting debate, the law's aims are reputedly clear. Self-determination trumps other values – even those as fundamental as the sanctity of life. The business of the law is to support autonomous decision-making and ensure respect for both the decider and the decision. This it allegedly does using the doctrine of consent, and its corollary, refusal. Patients are to be protected in their right to make the choice to accept or reject medical treatment. However, on closer inspection, it became clear that the rules about consent are functionally unable to achieve this. Because of the way courts operate, and given their perceived need to take account of policy as well as personal interests, the rules developed to translate the ethical concept of autonomy into law have resulted in considerable drift. However an autonomous decision is described in theory, in practice it becomes generic rather than specific. There are a number of reasons for this. First, consent in law depends on decision-making capacity – not on the quality of the decision or its impact on others (save in certain circumstances where harm results from respecting individual choice). Second, the law places considerable weight on the notion of voluntariness, which requires that information is provided to the patient in order to enable him or her to make a decision. While autonomy and competence might seem to be on all fours, when the question of information sharing is introduced additional considerations become relevant. For example, to be able to make a truly voluntary decision, it has to be decided how much information is needed; is it feasible, for example, to demand full disclosure? Would this be a meaningless exercise given patients' capacity for understanding? Each of these questions forces courts to establish ground rules that have had the effect of building a structure that is dominated by legalism and policy, rather than autonomy-based, considerations.

While voluntariness is important to autonomy, its significance here lies in the relatively abstract concept of liberty; the freedom to make decisions that reflect personal values. In consent law, on the other hand, the central question is about the relationship between doctor and patient and how it can best be managed both to facilitate patient choice and to encourage the practice of medicine. Further, court decisions are not designed to deal with the abstract; rather they are expected to apportion responsibility or blame. Inevitably, therefore, a balancing act is needed. In consent law, this generates two major deviations from the 'pure', or abstract, notion of self-determination. First, lines are drawn that limit what needs to be disclosed for both functional and policy reasons. Second, although the individual patient may expect that his or her own interests and needs will be the primary focus of attention, in setting boundaries the law has, perhaps out of necessity, established generalised standards as to what it is reasonable and necessary to offer patients by way of information. As a result, the instant patient becomes the 'reasonable patient'; his or her own concerns are homogenised to facilitate the operation of the courts and to avoid successful challenges to medical decision-making derived from the benefit of hindsight. In light of this, consent law bears only a very limited relationship to any particular concept of autonomy. When individuals claim that they have been prevented from making a self-determining decision because they have been inadequately informed, their perception that their self-determination has been impeded is secondary to the law's focus on objective standards – reasonable doctor or reasonable patient.

So, while consent is heralded as the legal equivalent of autonomy, in fact it is close only to that part of autonomy that relates to status – to the question of competence. What it does not do is to support unequivocally the right to make an autonomous decision. Mechanistically, then, patients may take decisions that have some of the characteristics of an autonomous choice – for example, they may be free from external influences and in full possession of their faculties – but the law does not demand that what might be called the 'psychological' aspects of a truly autonomous choice are met. In building the rules around consent to treatment, courts have stopped short of ensuring that people are fully informed and therefore truly able to weigh their decisions and act in a self-determining manner.

Indeed, Laurie says that ' ... the conflation of autonomy with consent robs the former of much of its meaning and strips it of much of its ethical credibility.'[1] McGrath adds that:

> The risk is that bioethical 'talk' about autonomy may only create the illusion of providing the self-determining protection supposedly afforded to the individual by the application of this principle. By engaging in such rhetoric, bioethicists are unwittingly undermining the very value they profess to support.[2]

There are two main reasons for supporting these critiques. Practically speaking, rules about consent have grown over time with an eye very much on the consequences for healthcare, and its practitioners, of the standards developed. In fact, a number of commentators point to the significant influence that these interests have had on the law. Annas points out that the rules about consent were 'imposed' on doctors by the law,[3] but far from creating rules bound intimately with respect for autonomy, Schneider argues that those making the law instead used 'a literature to which doctors and medical ethicists contributed crucially.'[4] As a consequence, ' ... lawmakers have essentially established rules intended to hold medicine to its own standards and then mostly left the system to work unmolested.'[5] Although Jones argues that if consent rules are capable of describing 'a guide to the minimum requirements of good practice in seeking informed consent the judges will have a crucial opportunity to set the parameters for and, indeed, some of the substance of the doctor patient relationship',[6] there is evidence from decided cases that they have failed to do so to a level, or in a manner, that facilitates a genuinely autonomous decision.

---

[1] Laurie, G, *Genetic Privacy: A Challenge to Medico-Legal Norms*, Cambridge University Press, 2002, at p 184.

[2] McGrath, P, 'Autonomy, Discourse, and Power: A Postmodern Reflection on Principlism and Bioethics', *Journal of Medicine and Philosophy*, 23(5), 1998: 516–32, at p 517.

[3] Annas, G J, *American Bioethics: Crossing Human Rights and Health Law Boundaries*, Oxford University Press, 2005, at p 97.

[4] Schneider, C E, 'Void for Vagueness', *Hastings Center Report*, January–February 2007: 10–11, at p 10.

[5] Ibid., at p 10.

[6] Jones, M A, 'Informed Consent And Other Fairy Stories', *Medical Law Review*, 7, Summer 1999: 103–34, at p 109.

In any event, as I have already suggested, it is unclear that the law of consent has precisely the same goals as does the concept of autonomy. Although they are often taken to be equivalent, when reaching decisions and balancing the rights and interests of the parties concerned, courts take account of agendas which reflect a wider spectrum of interests than those directly in front of them, for example the effect on society of reaching one decision or another. While the concept of autonomy is focused on respecting the individual and his or her decisions, the law on consent is concerned to strike a balance between competing, and sometimes conflicting, claims and interests. In light of this, a 'full on' commitment to the individual is disregarded. While autonomy is theoretically valued because 'it is an instrument of promoting the patients' well-being',[7] the concept used by courts is more closely aligned to the protection of the interests of both patients *and* healthcare professionals.

Having said that, the rhetoric of the law is often very similar to the individualistic model of autonomy. Even if not able or willing to require that patients always receive the kind of information that would allow them to reflect knowingly on their decisions before taking them, the language used in judgements prioritises the importance of self-determination. The presence of competence sets in motion a process that theoretically, if not practically, leads to respect for the individual *qua* individual. In this way, the law adopts a model that tries to ensure that 'individuals can fend off unwanted intrusions from others ... ',[8] while at the same time not bringing medical practice to a standstill. It is, of course, possible that in the long run this benefits patients, not least in that it allows medical practitioners to act in their best medical interests while at the same time seeming to take account of their views. Doctors can as a consequence act 'beneficently' by controlling the flow of information in an effort to ensure patient consent, thereby attempting to balance the professional obligation to advance the patient's health with the sometimes competing one to respect autonomy. If we accept that beneficence and respect for patients' rights can be separated in the way that this implies, this has the consequence that one has sometimes to take priority over the other. For the doctor, this will often mean the prioritisation of beneficence, while the patient might well prefer that respect for autonomy should prevail. Seeing the two goals as distinct can also have the effect of shaping the doctor/patient relationship into a quasi-adversarial competition between patients' interests and those of healthcare professionals, viewed through the lens of legal policy. I have tried to propose, however, that a beneficent medical act is one that is closely aligned to respect for autonomy.

---

[7] Varelius, J, 'Voluntary Euthanasia, Physician-Assisted Suicide, and the Goals of Medicine', *Journal of Medicine and Philosophy*, 31, 2006: 121–37, at p 124.

[8] Donchin, A, 'Understanding Autonomy Relationally: Towards a Reconfiguration of Bioethics Principles', *Journal of Medicine and Philosophy*, 26(4), 2001: 365–86, at p 368.

While affirmative consent is subject to specific tests that have sought to strike a balance between the interests of individuals and those of healthcare, given the law's commitment to preventing unwarranted and unauthorised interventions on patients' bodies (or minds) it might be expected that when it comes to refusal of treatment these tests would be irrelevant. In this situation, the adoption of legal rules based firmly in self-determination should be more straightforward. After all, autonomy necessarily includes the right not to be subjected to enforced treatment. However, when we considered the law of consent (or rather refusal) in a series of specific examples, a certain ambivalence emerged that has resulted in an inconsistent application of apparently clear legal rules, and – on occasion – a perceptible drift away from respecting the individual's choices and preferences, sometimes in the alleged interests of others and on other occasions with an eye to policy implications. This has occurred despite the legal rules that are said to endorse the right to refuse even optimal medical treatment and the law on assault. At the same time as maintaining that the individual's right to make self-regarding decisions is central to consent (and specifically to refusal), in practice this commitment is variable and certainly not robust.

A brief review of the specific areas selected for special consideration should serve to highlight this. In end of life cases, for example, although the language of the law is often individualistic in tone, closer inspection suggests that this is only true in certain circumstances. Because of the law on assault, it is impermissible to force treatment on an unwilling patient – this is why consent is needed. The right of individuals to refuse treatment, then, is as much about the rules concerning assault as it is about decisional autonomy. However, when it comes to treating like cases alike, the law falters. I have argued that the rejection of life-sustaining treatment is a decision essentially on all fours with the choice to seek an assisted death (given that the arguments in opposition to legalisation of assisted dying can be defeated). If so, then it is reasonable to assume – even given that the issue of assault is not relevant in this case – that each choice for death would be dealt with in the same way. While accepting that patients cannot demand that their doctors provide certain services (such as a lethal injection, for example) this is not the important point here. What matters is that the patient's decision is freely taken and reflective of a self-determined, voluntary choice taking account of the patient's own values. At this point, however, external considerations sometimes come into play and subtly move away the law from the model of autonomy that underpins treatment refusal cases. Although Beauchamp believes that the so-called 'right to die' is 'an impressive example of the triumph of autonomy in bioethics ... ',[9] it has only been conceded in a very few jurisdictions, and sometimes in a relatively restrictive manner. In fact,

---

[9] Beauchamp, T L, 'The Right to Die as the Triumph of Autonomy', *Journal of Medicine and Philosophy*, 31, 2006: 643–54, at p 644.

the principles which shape the law on assisted dying are sometimes in direct conflict with patient autonomy. Although, for example, the sanctity of life argument is explicitly said to take second place to respect for autonomy, it apparently does so only in certain cases. The person who has life-sustaining treatment that can be rejected is free to do so assuming that they are competent; the sanctity of life principle is irrelevant. No inquiry is made into the reason for their decision and no account is taken of its likely effect on others. In that sense the law recognises the need to respect autonomy as choice or decisional capacity, and applies an individualistic model meaning that the (legal) validity of the choice is based solely on considerations that reflect the patient's own wishes. However, when the patient needs active assistance to bring about the same outcome – a chosen death – other concerns intrude, including the alleged interest of the state in preserving life.

In addition, in an effort to justify treating the two cases as completely distinct, the law also has other devices at its disposal. One of these involves giving credence to the alleged distinction between acts and omissions. Letting someone die, on this argument, is not culpable (in certain cases, of course) whereas actively helping them to die is or should be. Despite the relative ease with which this difference can be discounted, courts and legislators seem comfortable to hold to it – sometimes even justifying this by reference to the fact that *doctors* think they are different. Acts/omissions and doctors' perceptions serve to supplant autonomy. Beauchamp proposes that the question of autonomy is 'not only *a* relevant consideration in understanding the difference between killing and letting die; it is *the most* relevant consideration' (original emphasis),[10] and although self-determination is referred to in each situation, it is not, however always taken to mean the same thing. In the case of rejecting life-sustaining treatment, individualistic autonomy triumphs. In these cases, people prefer death to continued existence and, assuming them to be legally competent, doctors are prohibited in law from treating them against their will. However, should the individual prefer death to continued existence in circumstances where there is no life-sustaining treatment to refuse, their preference is scrutinised intensely and routinely rejected save where legislation permits assisted dying. The reasons for this are not in any real sense concerned with the individual's legal capacity or ability to make autonomous decisions. Rather, they concern factors external to the individual, such as those already mentioned, as well as the likely impact of their decision on third parties (whether loved ones or society as a whole). Their decisions are tested against a version of autonomy that seems more akin to a relational model. Thus, while the decisions of one group of people making end of life decisions are supported by an individualistic account of autonomy, those of others are viewed through a different prism. On reflection, I have suggested that no morally convincing reasons emerge to

---

[10] Ibid., at p 649.

justify this discrepancy. Slippery slope arguments are weak, the sanctity of life is clearly not always the highest priority and the acts and omissions doctrine amounts to a distinction without a morally relevant difference.

When caring for a patient, the doctor obviously has an interest in the best medical outcome, but s/he should also have an equal if not greater interest in ensuring that patients make their own decisions and reach their own conclusions. This obligation is owed to one individual patient with whom the physician has a relationship and most models of medical ethics are based in this as the paradigmatic characteristic of the healthcare enterprise. But what happens when the doctor believes him- or herself to have obligations to more than one patient, particularly where the decision of one could have devastating consequences for the other? This problem has arisen in the last few decades in the area of pregnancy and childbirth. In part this has resulted from advances in technology which 'have led to widespread endorsement of the notion that fetuses are independent patients, treatable apart from the women on whom their existence depends.'[11] The perception that the embryo or foetus has interests – even rights – separate from those of the pregnant woman has resulted in egregious practices that have reduced women to little more than foetal containers and elevated the interests of the state in future life over concern for the rights from which existing lives should benefit.

While adults are otherwise entitled to make their own choices, even if they result in damage or death, pregnant women have faced a unique attack on their rights, finding themselves coerced into behaviour designed to protect the embryo/foetus they are carrying, irrespective of their own preferences or interests. By imposing moral opprobrium on these women, the law takes what *ought* ideally to be done and turns it into something that *must* be done. Donchin argues that this 'representation of maternal/foetal relations discounts the foetus' actual dependence on the pregnant woman even for its biological survival, nullifies her agency, and redefines the agendas of obstetricians and researchers.'[12]

For many years, not only were women vulnerable to the second-guessing of their behaviour during pregnancy in the interests of potential persons, but their decisions at the point of birth were also over-ruled, seemingly ignoring the presumption in favour of respect for self-determination and resulting in some cases in forced interventions in pregnancy and childbirth. While it is plausible that the application of the European Convention on Human Rights might sound the death knell for such practices in those European countries covered by the Convention, no such protection exists in other countries where the purported interest in saving foetal life remains a powerful driver in

---

[11] Lyerly, A D, Mahowald, M B, 'Maternal-Fetal Surgery: The Fallacy of Abstraction and the Problem of Equipoise', *Health Care Analysis*, 9, 2001: 151–65, at p 154.

[12] Donchin, A, 'Understanding Autonomy Relationally: Towards a Reconfiguration of Bioethics Principles', *Journal of Medicine and Philosophy*, 26(4), 2001: 365–86, at p 371.

controlling women's choice. Prioritising the interests of the embryo/foetus again seems akin to a more contextual or relational model of autonomy; the individual is not permitted to vindicate her own choices, in the purported interests of others (even 'others' not yet born). As an aside, the feminist writers who so forcefully argue for a relational model of autonomy are also among the fiercest critics of state intervention in pregnancy and childbirth. Yet, if autonomous decisions are those that reflect the interests of others and should be valued for their relational qualities, it could plausibly be argued to be entirely legitimate that women should be compelled to take into account the interests of their foetus in having a life, or the interest that society could claim to have in protecting future life. The option of acting for purely self-regarding reasons would be denied in the interests of others. As we have seen, this is precisely the situation that has arisen in a number of cases, and the threat remains real in some jurisdictions.

Managing more than one patient has also become an issue in genetics. While doctors are most accustomed to dealing with one patient, the reality is that genetic information is not of exclusive interest to the instant patient but will also have potential implications for their relatives and in some cases for their partners (whether or not they are also patients of the doctor). The decision to seek genetic information may be taken by intending parents, by parents on behalf of incompetent children or by individuals themselves. In each case, the choice has ramifications. For example, what if parents wish to obtain genetic information in respect of their young children? Although this could be argued to be responsible parenting, some commentators object that it 'compromises the present and future autonomy and privacy of the tested individual.'[13] This, it is said, is because the acquisition of the information means that the child will not be able, as an adult, to opt not to know their genetic status since the information is already in the 'public' domain. Of course, parental requests for screening or testing may be designed to have direct benefits for the child. The information gained from the test may allow the family to ameliorate the impact of the condition and prepare the child for what may be to come. However, it is likely that the test results will also be designed to benefit third parties, such as the parents themselves and other family members. Although genetic information is regarded as highly sensitive, perhaps more so than other medical information, it would seem that parental decisions taken (in whole or in part) in the interests of others than the tested child will be legally respected, although evidence suggests that geneticists – perhaps because of their more sophisticated understanding of what genetic information means – are less likely than their colleagues in paediatrics to accept parental authority unquestioningly.

---

[13] Patenaude, Andre F, 'The Genetic Testing of Children for Cancer Susceptibility: Ethical, Legal, and Social Issues', *Behavioral Sciences and the Law*, 14, 1996: 393–410, at p 394.

Finally, and most importantly for this discussion, is the adult who presents for testing. Adults have an expectation of confidentiality or privacy, which leads to the assumption that healthcare information will be maintained in confidence and will not be disclosed to third parties. Of course, some individuals will readily share obtained genetic information with others likely to be affected by the information – indeed, as we have seen, some undergo tests with that precise aim in mind – but others may be reluctant or completely unwilling to do so. As Patenaude says:

> Genetic researchers face many dilemmas concerning communication of familial risk to other at-risk members of identified families. Protecting individual autonomy often involves not revealing genetic test results of particular family members.[14]

In this situation, there would appear to be a discrepancy between the medical and the legal view. The law retreats to an individualistic account of autonomy and refuses to compel the individual to share the information with those whom it may affect, although it could be argued that genetics is a prime example of an area where the value of a relational approach is at its most clear. On the other hand, doctors – while encouraged to try to persuade their patients to make disclosure – may be justified in breaching confidentiality in certain, albeit relatively limited, circumstances should the patient refuse to do so. In the latter case, the interests of third parties are prioritised over those of the individual. Finally on this subject, seeing the tested individual as part of a social (familial) network, thereby justifying disclosure, cannot always be said to be a way of avoiding harm – a primary justification for limiting the right to have autonomous choices respected. In fact, the potential harm associated with disclosure is also real. Increasingly, there is an impetus to develop a 'right not to know'. Just as genetic information may devastate those who willingly seek it out, so too it may harm those who did not search for it but who are provided with it nonetheless in their purported interests.

Finally, the issue of organ transplantation was considered. This topic was included because, while organ donation has traditionally been seen as a matter of individual choice, there is mounting pressure to achieve social goods – a successful transplantation programme with sufficient numbers of available organs – by reconsidering the role of individual decision-making in this area. Historically, the gift analogy dominated accounts of the virtue of the act of donation. People who freely chose to donate their organs were lauded for their altruism and concern for others, but the decision to give the 'gift of life' was fully theirs. Recently, however, there has been considerable enthusiasm for changing the basis on which cadaveric 'donation' rests.

[14] Ibid., at pp 404–5.

Defending the individualistic model of autonomy – thereby prioritising the freedom to donate or not – has, it is argued, created, or contributed to, a serious gap between needed and available organs. As a result, there is growing political and clinical support for changing to a system which essentially assumes that people want to donate and requires them only to make any objections clear. In other words, the theory is that the ultimate good is the rescuing of lives that would otherwise be sacrificed for want of an organ. Although proponents of this so-called opting out system still attempt to justify it as being compatible with autonomy or self-determination, I have challenged this argument. Valuing the individual and respecting his or her individualistic autonomy may well result in the death of others, and few can be satisfied with this. However, the decision to donate also has relational characteristics – it is taken in light of its effects on others, even on society as a whole. The current law in the United Kingdom, however, is concerned primarily with the individual(istic) characteristics of the choice albeit that it is an act that more clearly than many respects the inter-connectedness of people with their community. Prioritising the relational element would, however, strip people of rights which they usually value. Again, it is for society to decide, but we should not pretend that the preferred alternative to the current system – opting out – is anything other than an abandonment of the value of self-determination. As I suggest in Chapter 7, if this is acceptable it is proposed in a somewhat half-hearted manner; compulsory collection of organs would surely serve us better, but this is an option favoured by few.

What is autonomy?

It has been assumed that autonomy is an important element of what it is to be fully human; that the right to self-determination is highly prized. King and Moulton suggest that there are a number of reasons why autonomy has come to take on such significance in modern healthcare:

> 1) protecting autonomy is more easily aligned with existing legal principles and precedents; 2) promoting patient autonomy may relieve the physician of some responsibility and liability; 3) emphasizing patient autonomy coincides with and supports the recent shift towards consumerism in medicine; and 4) promoting autonomy appears less paternalistic than beneficence, but still permits physicians to control the flow of information.[15]

This commentary suggests that the goals of respecting autonomy are not all about self-determination. This, however, is the legal account; the ethical one would perhaps discount some of these reasons as irrelevant. However, if the

[15] King, J S, Moulton, B W, 'Rethinking Informed Consent: The Case for Shared Medical Decision-Making', *American Journal of Law & Medicine*, 32, 2006: 429–501, at p 436.

goal of respecting and facilitating autonomy is to allow people to make independent decisions, then the authority should surely rest with them as will the consequences of their decisions. Yet, as we have seen there are differing views on what autonomy really means and what amounts to an autonomous decision. The two accounts focused on in this discussion are often seen as being in direct conflict with each other, although I have tried to argue that the distinction between them is exaggerated. Ho says that:

> From Descartes to contemporary theorists, many philosophers consider self as individualistic, isolated and ahistorical, assuming that the criteria that determine one's moral identity over time are independent of the social context in which they are situated. One of the effects of such ancontextual notion of identity is the refutation of the inherent significance of intimate relationships, which are characterized by collectivity, particularity, nonconsensuality, sensibility and favouritism.[16]

Yet, it is virtually, if not entirely, impossible to imagine a decision that is not in some way shaped not only by our own values (which after all will have developed in a context) but also by the opinions of those about whom we care. In other words this 'acontextual' decision-maker is fun for theorists to contemplate and makes for an interesting debate, but is much more difficult to find in reality. As Gylling says:

> To properly understand the meaning and role of autonomy and its connection to social life, it is of utmost importance to realize that our moral values cannot be fully separated from empirical reality, epistemological beliefs, and our personal identity but instead reflect our hierarchy of values, our personal preferences, and our views on good life and ideal society.[17]

This is not the picture of an atomised individual but rather a description of someone embedded in the values of others, even if we are ultimately prize the freedom to decide for ourselves and prioritise our own interests. Gentzler says that ' ... life is never a solo performance, but is always carried on in elaborate and complex cooperation with others. I can achieve my ends, and help others achieve their own, only by depending on others to do things that I need to have done but cannot do for myself.'[18] Finally, on this point, Donchin, a feminist writer and defender of the relational account of

---

[16] Ho, A, 'Relational autonomy or undue pressure? Family's role in medical decision-making', *Scand J Caring Sci*, 22, 2008: 128–35, at p 129.

[17] Gylling, H A, 'Autonomy Revisited', *Cambridge Quarterly of Healthcare Ethics*, 13, 2004: 41–46, at p 41.

[18] Gentzler, J, 'What is a Death with Dignity?', *Journal of Medicine and Philosophy*, 28(4), 2003: 461–87, at p 468.

autonomy, endorses my assertion that the two forms of autonomy need not be seen as antagonistic. As she says, '[b]y valorizing a norm that is itself problematic, autonomy and interpersonal connection are set in opposition to one another as mutually exclusive ways of relating. Associations are overlooked that might show how they could ground one another.'[19]

Thus, despite the debate that was described at the beginning of this book, some congruence between the two most influential contemporary models of autonomy seems both feasible and desirable. This, however, does not answer the second main question of this discussion, which was concerned with the relationship between autonomy and consent. From our consideration of consent (and refusal) and how it has been approached in a number of different areas two conclusions can be reached. First, the law of consent bears only a limited relationship to any ethical concept of autonomy; second, where autonomy is appealed to in law the meaning given to it varies, sometimes dramatically, depending on the policy concerns which commend themselves to the judiciary and to policy makers, even when they are addressing issues which seem indistinguishable from each other. The differences between the two accounts, such as they are, are used to support social and judicial policy with no transparent explanation as to why this legal ambivalence, with its corresponding negative impact on certainty and consistency, can be justified.

Autonomy and the law

By and large the law is concerned with righting wrongs and with defending the rights of individuals. However, it also serves as a vehicle to reflect public policy (and sometimes even to shape it). Smith says that '[t]he juridical field ... enables the law, and its legally sanctioned protagonists, to define and resolve conflicts according to its own principles and rules of engagement.'[20] For that reason, it may fall short of abstract ideals. The devices used in law to resolve complex issues can mould it into positions that seem less than principled and may even be inconsistent with its purported values. In the area of healthcare, it would seem that a combination of legal niceties and external social pressure has led to a situation in which identifying what the law takes autonomy to mean can be both difficult and confusing. Certainly, it makes certainty and predictability difficult to attain.

In the standard medical interaction, seeking the consent of the patient for the proposed treatment is said to be a reflection of respect for patient autonomy. While a laudable aspiration, analysis of the rules of consent

---

[19] Donchin, A, 'Understanding Autonomy Relationally: Towards a Reconfiguration of Bioethics Principles', *Journal of Medicine and Philosophy*, 26(4), 2001: 365–86, at p 374.

[20] Smith, C, 'The sovereign state v Foucault: law and disciplinary power', *The Editorial Board of The Sociological Review*, 48, 2000: 283–306, at p 283.

seems to suggest that they are unlikely to succeed in achieving this. Of course, in those interactions between doctor and patient which do not reach a court, there is no way of knowing whether or not patient autonomy was *in fact* respected. While physicians are increasingly alert to the need to involve their patients in treatment decisions, whether or not they are fully and appropriately engaged will more often than not remain hidden. The worry, however, is that awareness of the need to eschew paternalism and respect autonomy, rather than encouraging a full and frank discussion, could in fact lead to a situation where 'so-called "rituals of trust" have emerged as substitutes for "organic trust" … '.[21] In other words, a mechanistic approach, which superficially appears to respect autonomy, supplants an actual relationship in which the parties have discrete but interconnected roles. The 'rituals' involved in seeking consent take priority over the importance of the enterprise itself and the values it espouses. Nonetheless, even if the legal rules about consent have shortcomings, they could satisfy some of the legitimate expectations of patients. These might include the right to be informed about benefits, risks and alternatives to recommended treatment options and to be assisted by this information to make their own decisions. If both physicians and patients recognise the need for genuine respect – or trust – in the relationship, it becomes meaningful not mechanical. I would suggest, however, that this is unlikely to be attainable when the legal rules remain as they are because of the limitations placed both on the amount of information required and because the patient's grievance is not dealt with directly.

In cases where patients object that they have not been adequately informed, and have therefore not been enabled to act autonomously, case law suggests that the interests of the healthcare provider (or the healthcare system itself) still carry considerable influence. Whatever patients might want to receive, the courts have traditionally and consistently distanced the issue from *that* patient's interests, whether by focusing on what doctors believe is good medical practice or what some imagined patient might have wanted. This may be inevitable given the nature of law itself, but it is scarcely satisfying for patients who want to see their right to receive information, and use it in accordance with their own values, vindicated by the courts. The ambivalence of the law as to what it is actually protecting means that patients continue to feel short changed and physicians may feel themselves to be at risk of litigation; this situation benefits neither party.

The specific examples discussed highlight further matters of concern. However inadequate consent rules are in respecting autonomy, at least they are consistently applied in cases concerning information disclosure. However, in other situations, there seems to be considerable ambivalence about what consent (and refusal) laws are designed to protect and confusion about what

[21] Tauber, A I, 'Sick Autonomy', *Perspectives in Biology and Medicine*, 46(4), (autumn) 2003: 484–95, at p 485.

interests are at stake; the individual or the community of which they are a part. On the one hand, people can refuse life-sustaining treatment while on the other they may not be permitted to reject unwanted obstetrical interventions. In the former case, an individualistic position is taken whereas in the latter the alleged interests of others (in this cases embryos or foetuses) have sometimes prevailed. In situations where knowledge about one person has a direct and possibly significant implication for others, such as is the case with genetic information, the law holds to an individualistic account by not compelling disclosure; when people could help others by providing a transplantable organ after death, the pressure is on to ensure that their consent becomes irrelevant. One way or the other, the picture is of decisions that are at the mercy of perceived, albeit not necessarily transparent or accountable, policy considerations.

Conclusion

Autonomy is probably the most highly valued ethical principle in the contemporary world, and is argued also to be foundational in law. Engelhardt says:

> Autonomy is a cardinal notion because it is at the root of morality: autonomy is the ground of accountability. Only if moral agents can choose are agents indeed agents, persons responsible for their actions. Autonomy is self-rule. Autonomy is most fully self-rule when there is a deep congeniality between the moral self and the moral rule the self imposes on itself.[22]

There is no doubt that the law has played an important – some would say a leading[23] – role in the development of modern bioethics including its emphasis on autonomy, but in real terms its record in engendering and maintaining respect for the autonomous person and his or her decisions has been less impressive. It is perhaps time to re-evaluate the claim that consent laws are intimately connected to protecting autonomy and instead reinvestigate their actual functions and limitations. Little purpose is served by maintaining the pretence that the law either does or can uphold individual autonomy when it manifestly has an agenda that is only in part concerned – in healthcare at least – with the concept (in any of its forms). The claim that consent and autonomy are brethren under the skin may have served a purpose in leading healthcare professionals away from their traditional preference for paternalism and towards closer engagement with patients' rights,

---

[22] Engelhardt, H T, Jr, 'The Many Faces of Autonomy', *Health Care Analysis*, 9, 2001: 283–97, at p 286.

[23] See, Rothman, D J, 'The Origins and Consequences of Patient Autonomy: A 25-Year Retrospective', *Health Care Analysis*, 9, 2001: 255–64.

but it has not resulted, and probably cannot result, in prioritising patients' interests. Indeed, it seems incapable of elucidating and defending the coherent concept of autonomy that theorists (and patients) would want to see. What would be the outcome of any such inquiry is unknown, but it could result in a better understanding of the values that the law will apply and might allow both patients and healthcare professionals better to identify what their rights are and when their interests will be prioritised.

Index

Lightning Source UK Ltd.
Milton Keynes UK
UKOW06f0753130116

266319UK00005B/95/P

9 780415 473408